AMAZING NORTHEAST

TRIPURA

AMAZING NORTHEAST

TRIPURA

Edited & Compiled by
Aribam Indubala Devi

Vij Books India Pvt. Ltd.
(Publishers, Dustributors & Importers)
4675-A, 21, Ansari Road, Darya Ganj,
New Delhi-110002

Published by
Vij Books India Pvt. Ltd.
(Publishers, Distributors & Importers)
4675-A, 21, Ansari Road, Darya Ganj,
New Delhi-110002
Phone: 91-11-65449971, 91-11-43596460
Fax: 91-11-47340674
E-mail: vijbooks@rediffmail.com

Copyright © Publishers

First Edition: 2010

ISBN: 978-93-80177-31-1

Contents

Preface

In India, the Northeastern region is quite charming and interesting enough, to be known about. Among the eight Northeastern States, Tripura is strategically situated between the river valleys of Myanmar and Bangladesh. Encircled almost on three sides by Bangladesh, it is linked with Assam and Mizoram, through land.

Tripura has its unique tribal culture and a fascinating folklore. The history of Tripura can be learnt from 'Rajmala' chronicles of king of Tripura and writings of historians. There are references of Tripura even in the *Mahabharata* and the *Puranas*. According to 'Rajmala', the rulers were known by the surname 'Fa' meaning 'father'. There is a reference to rulers of Bengal, helping Tripura kings in 14th century. Kings of Tripura had to face frequent Mughal invasions with varying successes. They defeated the Sultans of Bengal in several battles. Nineteenth century marked the beginning of the modern era in Tripura, when Maharaja Bir Chandra Kishore Manikya Bahadur modelled his administrative set-up on British-India pattern and brought in various reforms. His successors ruled Tripura till 15 October 1949, when the state merged with the Indian Union. Initially, a part 'C' state, it became a centrally administered territory with the re-organisation of states in 1956. In 1972, Tripura attained the status of a full-fledged state.

This small but comprehensive and compact book on this northeastern state, offers all information, within one cover. Hopefully, it would serve all those working on or interested in knowing about northeastern India, be they scholars, researchers, journalists, students or general readers. This is in fact, 'Knowledge in Nutshell'.

— *Editor*

Tripura

An Overview

Governor	:	D.Y. Patil
Chief Minister	:	Manik Sarkar
Speaker	:	Remendra Chandra Debnath
Chief Secretary	:	Sudhir Sharma
Capital	:	Agartala
High Court	:	Guwahati (Bench at Agartala)

Brief Description

Tripura, literally meaning land adjoining water, is located in the extreme southwest corner of the Northeast. This hilly landlocked State spreads over a total area of 10,492 sq km, covering approximately 0.29 per cent of the Indian landmass and 3.9 percent of the entire North-East. This land of hilly slopes, flat lands, rivers, lakes, hillocks and forests stretches between 91.09° to 92.20° East longitude and 22.56° to 24.32° North latitude. Tripura shares 856 kilometre long international boundary (84 per cent of its total border) with Bangladesh and is surrounded by that country from the north, south and west sides. Tripura is connected with

Facts and Figures

- *Area:* 10,492 sq km (4% of total area of North-East)

- *Geographical Location:* Situated between latitude 22°N to 24°N & longitude 90°E to 92°E

- *Capital:* Agartala

- *Population:* 3,191,168 (2001 Census) (8.2% of population of North-East)

- *Density of Population (per sq km):* 304 (National Figure: 324)

- *Male:* 16,36,138

- *Female:* 15,55,030

Contd...

the rest of India by only one road connecting the state with Assam's Cachar District.

Following India's independence, Tripura acceded to the Indian Union as a 'C' category state. It became a Union Territory in November 1956. Tripura attained full Statehood on 21 January 1972. Administratively it is divided into four districts, 15 subdivisions, 38 rural development blocks, 31 revenue circles, 183 teshils, 874 revenue moujas, 962 gram panchayats, 3 zila parishads, 18 notified areas, 1 municipal council.

Despite being geographically the smallest state in the region, Tripura is the 2nd most populous state in the North-East, after Assam. According to Census 2001, Tripura has a total population of 3,191,168, with a density of 304 persons per sq km. It constitutes 0.31 per cent population of India and 8.18 per cent of the North-East. Even though Tripura was initially a tribal majority state, it has lost its tribal nature largely due to large-scale migration from neighbouring Bangladesh. Tribals have been reduced to a minority status leading a social upheaval in the state.

Agriculture is the mainstay of Tripura's economy. The sector provides employment to nearly 51 per cent of the total workers in the state and contributes to about 48 per cent of the State Domestic Product (SDP). A variety of horticultural/plantation crops including pineapple, orange,

- *Population below Poverty Line:* 34.4% (National Figure: 27.5%)
- *Sex Ratio:* 948 females to 1,000 males (National figure: 933 females to 1,000 males)
- *Literacy Rate (2007):* 80.2% (National Figure: 67.6%)
- *No. of Towns (as per 2001 Census):* 23
- *No. of Villages (as per 2001 Census):* 870
- *Per Capita income (in Rs.) (2006-07):* 27,777 (National Figure: Rs. 29,901)
- *Net State Domestic Product (NSDP) (Rs. in crore) (2006-07):* 9,533 (National Figure: 33,42,347)
- *Per Capita NSDP (2006-07):* Rs. 27,777 (National Figure: Rs. 29,524)
- *Per Capita GSDP (2004-05):* Rs. 24,984 (National Figure: Rs. 25,944)
- *Birth Rate (2006):* 16.6 (National Figure: 23.1)
- *Death Rate (2006):* 6.3 (National Figure: 7.4)
- *Infant Mortality Rate (2007):* 39 (National Figure: 55)
- *State Bird:* Green Imperial Pigeon
- *State Animal:* Phayre's Langur
- *State Flower:* Nageshwar
- *No. of Districts:* (04) North Tripura, West Tripura, South Tripura, Dhalai.
- *Major Towns:* Agartala, Badharghat, Jogendranagar, Dharmanagar, Pratapgarh,Udaipur, Kailashahar, Teliamura, Indranagar, Khowai, Belonia

Contd...

cashew nut, jackfruit, coconut, tea and rubber are produced in Tripura. The industrial sector has remained undeveloped. The secondary sector contributes only about five per cent of total employment and about seven per cent of the total SDP of the state.

The per capita Gross State Domestic Product (GSDP) in 2004-05 is rupees 24,894 and the per capita Net State Domestic Product in 1999-2000 is rupees 10,213. Tripura ranks 22nd in the human resource development index and 24th in the poverty index in India. Bengali and Kokborak are the two principal languages in the state. The literacy rate of Tripura is 73.66 per cent.

- *Major Crops:* Rice, Sugar cane, Cotton, Jute, Mesta
- *Major Plantations:* Tea, Rubber, Coffee
- *Major Fruits, Vegetables & Spices:* Banana, Pineapple, Orange, Mango, Guava, Litchi, Potato, Papaya, Tomato.
- *Major Minerals:* Fire Clay, Quartz, Silica
- *Airport:* Khowai

Insurgency has remained a major bottleneck for development in the state. Principally, two tribal insurgent outfits remain active and have seriously affected the growth of infrastructure in Tripura. Divide between the Bengali and the indigenous tribal population is another continuing issue of concern, despite steps taken by the State Government to address it.

Area, Population and Headquarters of Districts

S.No.	District	Area (sq km)	Population	Headquarters
1.	North Tripura	2,820.63	5,90,913	Kailashahar
2.	South Tripura	2,151.77	7,67,440	Udaipur
3.	West Tripura	2,996.82	15,32,982	Agartala
4.	Dhalai	2,552.47	3,07,868	Ambassa

[Based on Latest Official Data Available]

Tripura

Outline Map

Geographical Map

(xiii)

Tourist Map

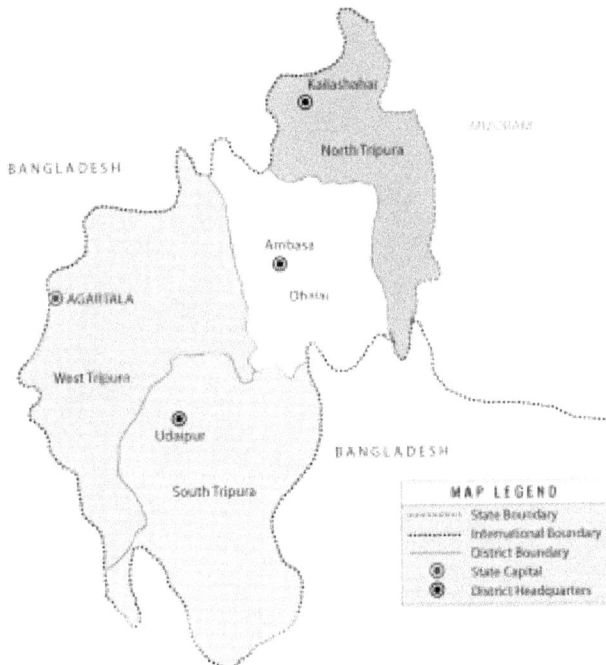

Districts of the State

$$\boxed{1}$$

Introduction

- -

Tripura is one of the eight states in the Northeastern part of India located between 22°56' and 24°32' N latitude and between 90°09' and 92°20' E longitude. It is bounded on the north, west, south and southeast by Bangladesh whereas in the east it has a common boundary with Assam and Mizoram.

There is a common belief that the name of the state has originated from *"Tripura Sundari"* — the presiding deity of the land which is famous as one of the 51 pethos of Hindu Pilgrims. Apart from this traditional view it is believed that originally the land was known as *"Tuipra"* meaning a land adjoining the water. It is fact that in days of yore the boundaries of Tripura were extended up to the Bay of Bengal when its rulers held sway from Garo Hills to Arakan.

The history of Tripura as an administrative unit dates back to the days of Maharajas when the territory was a native State. It is significant to note that although Tripura was conquered by force of arms in 1761, no Political agents was appointed in the state till 1871 — a gap of 110 years.

The former princely state of Tripura was ruled by Maharajas of Manikya Dynasty. It was an independent administrative unit under the Maharaja even during the British rule in India though this independence was qualified, being subject to the recognition of the British, as the paramount power, of each successive ruler. After independence of India, an agreement of merger of Tripura with the Indian Union was signed by the Regent Maharani on September 9, 1947 and the administration of the state was actually taken over by the Govt. of India on October 15, 1949. Tripura became a Union Territory without legislature with effect from November 1, 1956 and a popular ministry was installed on July 1, 1963. On January 21, 1972 Tripura attained statehood. It has excellent opportunity for Tourism. It has many places of interest. Folk dances of Tripura speak its rich cultural heritage.

Historical Aspects

The State of Tripura has a long history. The Kingdom of Tripura in its peak included the whole eastern region of Bengal from the Brahmaputra River in the north and west, the Bay of Bengal in the south and Burma to the east during the 14th and 15th centuries AD.

The last King of Tripura was Kirit Bikram Kishore Manikya Bahadur who reigned from Agartala (1947-49), after whom the kingdom was merged with India in 1949. He passed away on November 27, 2006 and the new head of the royal house of Tripura is Maharaja Pradyot Kishore Manikya Deb Burman.

Tripura finds mention in the Mahabharata, the Puranas and pillar inscriptions of Emperor Ashoka. Tripura has a long historic past, its unique tribal culture and a fascinating folklore. In the distant past Tripura was known as Kirat Desh. There are references of Tripura in the Mahabharata and the Puranas. Tripura, the descendent of King Druya and Bhabru, contemporary of Yudhishtira, was the ruler on whose name Tripura is named. One more explanation says that the territory is named after the temple of Tripuri Sundari, located at Radhakrishnapur.

Tripura was a princely state before its merger with the Indian Union. The Tripuri Kings (*Habugra*) held the title of Manikya and ruled Tripura for 3,000 years until its merger. Udaipur, in South Tripura District, was the capital of the Kingdom. The capital was shifted to Old Agartala by King Krishna Manikya in the eighteenth century, and then to the present Agartala in the 19th century. The 19th century marked the beginning of Tripura's modern era, when King Bir Chandra Manikya Bahadur Deb Burman modelled his administration on the pattern of British India and enacted various reforms.

The *Ganamukti Parishad* movement led to the integration of the kingdom with India in 1949. Tripura was heavily affected by the partition of India and the majority of the population now comprises Hindu Bengalis, many of whom came as refugees from East Pakistan after independence in 1947. Tripura became a centrally administered Union Territory on July 1, 1963 and attained the status of a full-fledged state on January 21, 1972.

Armed conflict in Tripura has been a problem since the end of the 1970s as an aftermath of 1971 Indo-Pak war. Mass migration of Bengalis from Bangladesh during this time has resulted in wide-spread insurgency and militancy in the state with groups such as the Tripura National Volunteers, the National Liberation Front of Tripura and the All Tripura Tiger Force aiming to drive away the Bengali people.

Mythological Period

The origins of the kingdom is shrouded in the myths written in Rajmala, the chronicle of the Kings of Tripura, which meanders from Hindu mythologies and Tripuri folklores.

Every aspect of the history of Tripura is extremely intriguing and there are a number of controversies regarding Tripura — origin of name. There are a number of historians who debate the origin of the name of Tripura and they put forward a number of theories regarding Tripura — origin of name. A major problem in tracing Tripura — origin of name is the lack of authentic documents on the history of the region. Rajmala is probably the only written document on the region which sheds light on its history.

The Rajmala, which is the court chronicle of Tripura, points out that the region had an ancient King named Tripur. It is believed that Tripur was a tyrant King and many historians argue that it was after him that the region was named. However, this theory about Tripura — origin of name has been challenged by historians who argue that Tripur is an historical and imaginary character.

The etymological origin of the word Tripura explains its origin to a large extent. The compound word of Tripura when broken gives two separate words, 'Tui' (water) + 'Pra' (near). The geographical location of the region thoroughly justifies its name.

It is also argued that Tripura is a distortion of the word Twi-bupra, which means confluence of waters and many of the Tripuri villages are named after the confluence of different rivers.

Another very strong probability of Tripura — origin of name is the Temple of Tripureshwari. This Temple in Udaipur is a major pilgrimage spot in the region and is one of the Shakti Peeths.

Ancient Period

The ancient period can be said from around 7th century when the Tripuri Kings ruled from Kailashahar in North Tripura and they used "Fa" as their title, "pha" in Kokborok means "Father" or "Head".

The history of Tripura points out at its regal past and the Tripura Kings are an integral part of this royal past. An in-depth study of the past of Tripura reveals the long dynamic history of the Tripura Kings. Long back in the 7th century the Tripura Kings adopted the title of 'pha' and ruled the region from the then capital city of Kailashahar in North Tripura.

It was in the 14th century that the most important dynasty of Tripura ascended the throne. The Tripura Kings of the Manikya Dynasty ruled the region for more than 3,000 years and shifted their capital to Udaipur and finally to Agartala. The prestige and power of Tripura reached its apex under the Tripura Kings of the Manikya Dynasty.

Tripura Manikya Dynasty

The very first historical evidences about Tripura appears in the Rajmala, the royal chronicle of the Tripura Manikya Dynasty. The Tripura Manikya Dynasty originated in the 1280 AD when the King of Tripura Ratna Fa assumed the title of Manikya. Indo-Mongolian in origin, the Tripura Manikya Dynasty ruled over the region for hundreds of years.

It was under the regime of the Tripura Manikya Dynasty that the Kingdom of Tripura reached the apex of its heydays. Under their rule a number of military victory earned Tripura the suzerainty over Myanmar, Bengal and Assam. The prosperity of the Tripura Manikya Dynasty was all round as their fame and power was even acknowledged by the Mughals who were their contemporaries in North India.

It was only in the 17th century that the Mughals extended their imperialistic hands towards Tripura but even then the Tripura Manikya Dynasty maintained some of their authorities. Even when the colonial British rule captured most parts of Eastern and Northern India, the administrative power of Tripura was left to the Tripura Manikya Dynasty.

After India earned independence the Regent Maharani of the Tripura Manikya Dynasty signed an agreement that approved the merger of Tripura with the Indian Union. The last ruling King of the Tripura Manikya Dynasty was Bir Bikram Manikya who was succeeded by Maharaja Kirit Bikram Kishore Manikya. The current head of the Tripura Manikya Dynasty is Maharaja Kirit Pradyot Deb Burman Manikya Bahadur who is the son of late Maharaja Kirit Bikram Kishore Manikya.

Modern Period

The modern period starts after the domination of the Kingdom by the Mughals and the further tribute to the British India after the British defeated the Mughals. During this period, the capital of the kingdom was shifted to Agartala, in West Tripura, the present state capital in the early part of 19th century AD.

Tripura Tiger Force: The Tripura Tiger Force is one of the major militant groups that operates in the city of Tripura. The group drifted apart from the Tripura National Volunteers under the leadership of Ranjit Deb Burman. The faction of the group was called the All Tripura Tribal Force that was formed on 11th July, 1990. The group later renamed itself as the All Tripura Tiger Force in the year 1992.

The small faction of extremists worked in the remote areas of the districts of Tripura. Gathering force by inculcating the tribal youth of the region, the group grew to become an influential militant association that has been correlated with other groups like the Tripura Tribal Youth Force, Tripura Lion Force, Tripura Liberation Organisation and the Tripura National Army.

Although strictly administered, the All Tripura Tiger Force had faced disappointment when a group of 1,600 cadres laid down their arms in the year 1994. The remaining members of the extremist group continued to function and were declared as banned in the year 1997 according to the Unlawful Activities (Prevention) Act of 1967. The organisation works to retrieve the rightful land of the tribal people by eviction of the Bengali immigrants who settled in the state of Tripura. The insurgencies continue to achieve the objective of the group.

The organisational head of the group is Ranjit Deb Burman who leads as the president of the All Tripura Tiger Force. The political faction of the group, Tripura Peoples' Democratic Front, is believed to run a parallel government in the fringes of the state. The organisational headquarters is at Tarabon in Bangladesh where the president has taken refuge.

Geographical Aspects

The geography of Tripura reveals the physical features of the state and the laden topographical characteristics. The state is situated between the geographical coordinates of 22°56' N and 24°32' N latitude and 90°09' E and 92°20' E longitude. It shares its borders with the country of Bangladesh and the states of Assam and Mizoram.

The state of Tripura is marked by distinct geographical features. The south Tripura District has three hill ranges that rises to high altitudes. The Deotamura stretches across 85 kilometres. The two other hill ranges are the South Baramura and a part of Atharamura hill range.

The state is watered by several rivers and their tributaries. The chief river of the region is the Gumti that passes through various districts of the state. The River Muhuri also originates in the hills in Tripura. The River Feni separates the country of Bangladesh from the state of Tripura.

The demographic study of Tripura shows that it is populated by 3,199,203 people who reside in the four districts of the state. The population density of the region is 305 people per square kilometres. The state has a sex ratio that scores above the national average. The sex ratio of Tripura is 948 females per thousand males.

The region falls under the subtropical and the temperate climatic zones. The region is dominated by the monsoon season.

Soil

Tripura soil is marked by characteristic features that vary with the topographical changes in the state. The other factors that influence the prevalence of the different types of soils in the state are the climatic changes, prevalent rock material and the vegetation. Soil erosion caused by chemical weathering of the soil in the state has led to the bed rock of the region being revealed.

The soil can be classified into five distinct categories. 43.07 per cent of the total land area of the state is occupied by the red loamy soil and the sandy soil. The soil taxonomic units of this category are the Typic/Ultic Hapludalfs, Typic Ustochrepts, Ultic Haplustalfs, Udic Ustochrepts, Typic Paleudalfs and the Typic Ustochrepts. The soil covers a total area of 4,514 square kilometres. The reddish yellow brown sandy soil of the region covers a total area of 3,468 square kilometres. The soil type is the second most dominant type in the region covering 33.06 per cent of the land area. The three other types of soil that prevail in the region are the lateritic soil, younger alluvial soil and the older alluvial soil.

The soil of Tripura is faced with the problem of rapid soil erosion. This occurs due to chemical weathering with the high annual rainfall. Another factor that is responsible for the rapid erosion of soil is the withdrawal of vegetation in the state which has caused the high velocity of the wind to remove the soil cover.

Minerals

Tripura houses a lot of mineral resources. The most important minerals are glass sand, lignite, clay, limestone, and building material. The most important of all the minerals that are associated with the state is natural gas and oil.

There used to be a number of sources of natural gas and oil in the state including a place close to the Ampi Bazar and the stream of Chara.

Clay is one of the major minerals of Tripura. White-coloured plastic clay is available in many regions of the state close to Dharmanagar, Agartala and Bisramganj. It is also found at the Ampi Bazar-Teliamura road crossing and also close to Jogindernagar and Khowai.

Glass sand is one of the most important minerals. There are good sources of white sand on the bank of the water body called *Bijainadi* close to the place called old Agartala. Some other reserves are found in the western and eastern parts of Champamura.

Limestone mineral deposits are found in the Jampui and the Sakhan mountain ranges. Lignite is one of the main minerals. Small deposits of lignite are obtained in the rocky regions of the Unkoti Kolangshi Hill, towards the north of Kumarghat, in Sabrum and Betaga. The deposits of shale at the Atharamura mountain range can be used as building material. Another important building material, grey sandstone, can be obtained from Gagrachara.

Rivers

There are quite a few rivers, which help to drain the entire state. The main rivers are Gumti, Manu, Khowai and Haora.

These rivers are often classified into two broad groups; a few rivers of the sate follow the north direction and the rest of the rivers follow the west direction.

The main rivers that flow towards the north are Khowai, Manu, Doloi, Langai and Juri. The rivers that flow towards the west are Gumti, Feni and Muhuri.

The Gumti is the biggest river of the state. It is considered very sacred by the people who live in this region. This river has originated in the Tirthamukh. The sacred Dumbur falls is located at this region.

River Manu is one of the major rivers. It has its origin in the mountains of Tripura. It finally enters the district of Maulvibazar in the neighbouring country of Bangladesh.

The Khowai River has its origin in the eastern area of the Atharamura Hills. The river enters the Bangladesh through Balla. It finally pours into River Meghna River. The Haora River has its origin in a hilly locality of Tripura in the central area. The name of the hills is the Boromura Hills. The river finally unites with Padma River, which is one of the main rivers of Bangladesh. All the above rivers form a significant part of the geography of the state and have a lot of importance to the people of the region.

Flora and Fauna

The state is located in the biogeographic zone of 9B-North-East Hills and possesses an extremely rich biodiversity, the local flora and faunal components of Indo-Malayan and Indo-Chinese subregions. There are 379 species of trees, 320 shrubs, 581 herbs, 165 climbers, 16-climbing shrubs, 35 ferns, and 45 epiphytes.

Wildlife sanctuaries of the state include Sipahijola Wildlife Sanctuary, Gumti Wildlife sanctuary, Roa Wildlife Sanctuary, and Trishna Wildlife Sanctuary. National parks of the state include Clouded Leopard National Park, Sepahijola, and Rajbari National Park, Trishna.

Climate

The climate of Tripura is influenced by its location in the Northeastern part of India. The climate displays characteristics that are typical of the hilly and mountainous region. The change in the topographical features of the region also causes a change in the climatic conditions. The seasonal rhythm lays a mesmerising charm on the visitors. Tripura records a low average temperature of 10°C in the winter season which rises to a maximum average of 35°C in the summer. The altitude of the state also influences the climatic conditions.

The state influences a monsoonal climate with the well-demarcated subtropical and temperate zones. The climate along with the other factors of the terrain and the soil are suitable conditions for horticulture. The horticultural sector is dependent on the seasonal rainfall that dominates the seasons.

The state witnesses four distinguishable seasons. The winter prevails from the month of December to February. The months of March and April witness the premonsoon season. The longest season of the state is the monsoon season that continues between the months of May to September. Tripura receives maximum rainfall in the month of June. The state records an average annual rainfall of 2,100 mm. Kamalpur receives the maximum amount of rainfall of 2,855 mm while Sonamura receives the lowest average of 1,811 mm.

Social Aspects

Tripura Society and Culture represents a fine blend of traditional and contemporary aspects. The society primarily comprises a number of tribal groups. Manipuri and

Bengali communities are the other human groups that are inhabiting the land of Tripura from a very long time.

Tripura was one of the exclusive independent units of India even in the days of British rule. Previously, it was under the dominion of the famous Manikya Empire. In fact the rulers of Manikya Dynasty governed Tripura for a considerable period of time. It was only in the year 1972 that it had been recognised as one of the Indian states.

The social structure shows a harmonious coexistence of various tribal communities and other general human groups. There are various marriage customs and property inheritance system that showcases the inherent traits of the society. Bengali speaking people are known to constitute a major portion of the total population. There are Manipuri communities too that are living in the land from ancient ages.

The cultural domain of Tripura is rich with a wide gamut of various multidimensional features. Festivals, folk dance and music are the prime elements of the culture. Being one of the oldest places of India, surrounded by hilly terrains, Tripura boasts of a number of folk dances. Each and every tribe has its own line of dance and music tradition.

The festivals like Kharchi Puja, Garja Puja, Durga Puja and Ker Puja are celebrated in the state with much fanfare. All the tribal communities, along with the Bengalis and Tripuris, join in the festivals that take place at different time of the year. Tripura Society and Culture is a manifestation of the ancient and enriching customs and beliefs of the state.

People

A diverse ethnic element among the people of Tripura is that — there are two major racial elements, namely, the Indo-Aryans represented by the Bengalis and the Indo-Mongoloids represented by a few communities like the Tripuris, the Reangs, the Jamatis, the Noatias, the Kukis, the Halams, the Chakma, the Mogh and the Lushai. Besides these nine major tribes, there are ten more tribes. All the nineteen tribes are classified as 'Scheduled Tribes'.

The Tripuris also called *Tripuras* or *Tipras* are the original inhabitants of the state. They constitute about a little over 16 per cent of the total and 57 per cent of the tribal population of the state. The formal rulers of the land is believed to be the descendants of the Kshatriyas. In course of time, a section of this community came into close contact with the Bengali settlers, and was much influenced by their language, culture and custom. Then a new community, now known as Natun Tripuris, a sort of breakaway group of the original (Puram) Tripuris.

A few among the Tripuris who were close to the royal family (known as Thakur) settled in and around Agartala. They are quite advanced in education and general enlightenment. High public officials, writers, musicians, engineers and doctors are found among them.

The other group who live on the hill-slopes are not much improved regarding economic status or nature of occupation. They practice *jhooming* (or shifting cultivation), fetch wood from the forests, sell vegetables and bamboos. The women help men in jhooming, weave cloth on their traditional loin looms and take care of pigs, fowl, etc. Their houses made of bamboo, are built five to six feet above the ground to avoid hazards from wild animals.

The Reangs, the tribal group, constitute about 14 per cent of the tribal and 4 per cent of the total population of the state. They are broadly divided into two groups. Meksha or Mechka and Marchai or Malchai. The former is again subdivided into Masha, Raichak and some other subgroups, while the principal subgroups among the latter are Apet and Champung. The community is governed by a well-defined hierarchical institution; the chief enjoys the title Rai.

The Reangs are considered as one of the strongest pillars of the states military forces. The Reangs are Hindus and generally believers in the Sakti cult. Like other tribals they also believe in animism.

Another section of the Tripura community is known as Jamatia — the term seems to have originated from jamayet, which means a gathering or mobilisation. Like the Reangs, the Jamatias also constituted the fighting force during the time of Tripura King. Their system of worship comprises both Hindu practices and animistic rites. Having many social institutions in common with the Bengalis, the Jamatias are taking to plough cultivation in preference to jhoom and are now settling down in the plain areas of the state.

Tripura Bengalis

Tripura Bengalis are populating the state from many past decades. The influence of the Bengali culture in the society of Tripura proves the dominance of this particular community in the state. Bengali speaking people are found in almost all the corners of Tripura. From the festivals to the beliefs Bengalis have a major contribution towards the formation of today's Tripura state.

Rabindranath Tagore was known to be acknowledged for his poetry in the Royal Court of Tripura for the first time. Ever after this event the local people of Tripura became ardent followers of the art style of Rabindranath. Till date, the artists of Tripura are known to be immensely inspired by the artistic mastery of the Bengali Nobel Laurette, Rabindranath Tagore. In fact, the Bengalis of state feel proud to associate themselves with this great art personality.

Durga Puja is one of the biggest festivals which is celebrated by the Bengalis. Between the month of September and October Durga Puja is followed by the Bengali community for four or five whole days. Dedicated to goddess Durga, the divine power, this festivals attracts the attention of all the other communities inhabiting the land. During the days of celebration, the Bengalis encourage all the tribal communities and other groups to participate in various cultural events.

Although the social customs of Bengalis are quite different from the Manipuri communities or tribal groups, yet they have merged well with people of other faiths. This shows that local Bengalis had the perseverance to cope up with the existing communities.

It is believed that the Bengalis are one of those communities that have existed in the state peacefully along with many other groups from several past centuries.

Tripura Tribes

Tripura Tribes represent a range of human communities that are living in the state from quite a long time. The Tripuri Tribe of the state constitutes a large percentage of the total tribal population. The Lebang Boomani and Garia are the two prominent folk dance forms of Tripuri tribe. Reang tribe although has a large population, yet it lacks sufficient educational and economic independence. It is believed that this community is inhabiting the land from as early as 15th century.

Chakma tribal group belongs to the Buddhist faith. There are various sections in which the Chakma tribe is divided in Tripura. The Mog tribes have come to inhabit the land in 957 AD. People of Mog community follow the ritual customs of Buddhism. Halam tribe is yet another ancient clan which has many subsections. Being the followers of Saka faith, the Halam community has Malsum as one of its groups. Murasing community has derived its name from the fact that the ancient people of this tribe used to hang horns of animals in their homes.

There are a total of 19 tribes in Tripura. All these tribal groups have their own festivals, rituals and customs. Living on the here from a long a time, the various tribes of the state are known for their peaceful existence. Agriculture is the main source of livelihood of all the major tribes. Inhabiting the different parts of the hilly terrains the tribes of the state contribute significantly towards the cultural and economical richness of the place.

Ethnicity

Tripura ethnicity is one of the most important aspects about the state. There are quite a few different tribal groups who have their individual characters. A variety of crafts, dance forms and music contribute to the rich cultural life of the state.

The tribal people who shape up the ethnic character belong to as many as 19 different groups. The names of the major ethnic groups of Tripura are Reang, Halam, Chakma, Usai, Mog, Tripuri, Chakma, Reang, Lusai, Halam, Darlong and Garo. The tribal people live in houses constructed at a height of about 3 to 4 metres above the level of the ground. One has to climb up a ladder to enter such a house.

The various music and dance forms are also worth mention. Some of the most significant dance forms of the place are the Bizu dance of the Chakmas, the Garia dance of the Reangs and the Hai Hak dance of the Halams.

The art and crafts constitute one of the most significant parts of the ethnic life. One of the most popular crafts is bamboo and cane products. A variety of handicrafts are made by the people of the state with very easily available ingredients like cane, yarn, palm leaves and bamboo.

Some most demanded products are lamp stands, bamboo screens, sitalpati and tablemats. They are also very deft at woodcarving. The silver ornaments created by them are great works of art. The different festivals and fairs form an integral part of the ethnic life. Some of the most popular festivals of this part of India are Ker, Bisu and Sena, Kharchi, Hojagiri, Ama, Hangrai and Maikwtal and Mamta.

Demographics

Tripura is the second most populous state in North-East India, after Assam. According to the census of 2001, Tripura has a total population of 3,191,168 with a density of 305 persons per square kilometre, and ranks 22nd among Indian states. It constitutes 0.31 per cent population of India and 8.18 per cent of the North-East. In the 2001 census of India, Bengalis represent almost 70 per cent of Tripura's population and the native tribal populations represent 30 per cent. The tribal population comprises several different tribes and ethnic groups with diverse languages and cultures with the largest tribal group being the Kokborok-speaking tribes of the Tripuri (16 per cent of the state's population), the Jamatia, the Reang, and the Noatia tribal communities. There is some tension between these native tribal populations and Bengali settlers in tribal areas. Tripura ranks 22nd in the human resource development index and 24th in the poverty index in India according to 1991 sources. The literacy rate of Tripura is 80.2 per cent, higher than the national rate of 67.6 per cent.

Hinduism is the majority religion in the state, with 85.6 per cent of the population following the religion. Muslims make up 8.0 per cent of the population, Christians 3.2 per cent, and Buddhists 3.1 per cent.

Communities in Tripura

Community	*Language*	*Language Family*
Bengali	Bengali	Indo-European
Tipra/Tripuri	Tripuri	Sino-Tibetan
Bishnupriya Manipuri	Bishnupriya Manipuri	Indo-European
Manipuri	Meitei	Sino-Tibetan
Chakma	Changma Vaj	Indo-European
Kuki	Kuki	Sino-Tibetan
Lushai	Mizo	Sino-Tibetan
Mogh	Mogh	Sino-Tibetan

This represents a major change in the religious composition of the state over time. In 1941, the population was 70 per cent Hindu, 23 per cent Muslim and 6 per cent followers of tribal religions. It should be noted that in 1951 Tripura had 649,930 inhabitants, and the number was even less in 1941 because the Hindu exodus had not begun from East Bengal, although that would not really become a factor in the state's population until the 1970s.

Today most of the Hindus in Tripura, both those who are Bengali and the Tripuri and numerous tribes, are adherents of an animist — Shaktism hybrid of Hinduism, which was the state religion under the Tripuri Kings. Brahmin priests (called *chantais*) are regarded as custodians of *dharma* and occupy an exalted position in Tripura society. Important gods are Shiva and Tripureshwari (patron goddess of Tripura and an aspect of Shakti). Several fertility gods are also worshipped, such as Lam-Pra (the twin deities of sky and sea), Mailu-ma (goddess of corn, identified with Lakshmi), Khulu-ma (goddess of the cotton plant), and Burha-cha (god of healing). Durga Puja, Navaratri, Vijayadashami, and the worship of the *Chaturdasha* deities are important festivals.

Traditional Dress

Tripuris have their own traditional dresses. This dress is similar in style to that of other North-East Indian peoples. It is, however, totally different in terms of the pattern and design. The clothing for the lower half of the body is called *rignai* in Tripuri and for the upper half of the body the clothing has two parts *risa* and *rikutu*.

The risa covers the chest area and the rikutu covers the whole of the upper half of the body. Formerly, these garments were woven by ladies using home-spun cotton thread. Nowadays, the threads are bought from the market and the risa is not worn; instead a blouse is worn by most Tripuri women. Girls are wearing rignai with tops also.

Each Tripuri clan has its own rignai pattern and design. The patterns of the rignai are so distinct that the clan of a Tripuri woman can be identified by the pattern of the rignai she is wearing. However, there is intermingling of the rignai, different clans are wearing rignai of other clans freely and new designs are being woven differently. The rikutu is plain cloth of a different colour and shade than the other items of clothing. Today, the rikutu is woven by the Tripuri ladies.

The different fashion types that are woven in the rignai borok by the Tripuri women are as follows:

- Anji,
- Banarosi,
- Chamthwibar,
- Jirabi,
- Khamjang,

- Khumbar,
- Kuaiphang,
- Kuaichu,
- Kuaichu bokobom,
- Kuaichu ulta,
- Malibar,
- Miyong,
- Muikhunchok,
- Monaisora,
- Muisili,
- Natupalia,
- Phantokbar,
- Sada,
- Salu,
- Similik yapai,
- Takhumtei,
- Temanlia,
- Thaimaikrang,
- Thaiphlokbar,
- Tokbakbar,
- Tokha,
- Toksa,
- Toiling,
- Toprengsakhitung,
- Rignaichamwthwi,
- Rignai mereng,
- Metereng trang,
- Rignai khamchwi,
- Kwsakwpra,
- Rignaibru,

- Rignaikosong,
- Kwsapra,
- Songkai,
- Sorbangi and many more.

It is said that at the time of Subrai Raja, the most famous and legendary King of Tripura, through his 250 wives he had invented two hundred fifty designs of rignai. He married those women who invented a new design. But all these designs have been lost over time and only a few remain. An effort to rediscover the lost designs is in process.

The male counterpart for the loin area is *rikutu* and for the upper part of the body is the *kamchwlwi borok*. Today, however, very few men are wearing this style of dress except in rural Tripura and by the working class. Males have adopted the modern dress of adopted internationally.

Heritage and Culture

Tripura has several diverse ethno-linguistic groups, which has given rise to a composite culture. The dominant culture is Bengali, while minority cultures are those of the Tripuris, Jamatia, Reang, Noatia, Koloi, Murasing, Chakma, Halam, Garo, Kuki, Lushai, Mogh, Munda, Oraon, Santhal, and Uchoi.

Tripura has a rich cultural heritage of music, fine arts, handicrafts and dance. Music is an integral part of the tribal people. Some of their indigenous instruments are the *sarinda, chongpreng,* and *sumui* (a kind of flute). Songs are sung during religious occasions, marriages, and other festivals. Agricultural festivals are integral to the culture of the state.

Dance is important to the tribal way of life. Dances are performed during Goria Puja. Hojagiri dance is performed by standing on a pitcher and is performed by the Reang clans. The Bihu dance is performed by the Chakmas during Chaitra Sankranti (the last day of the month of *Chaitra*).

Festivals

The Tripura Festivals comprise both religious and cultural festivals. The cosmopolitan culture has resulted in the celebration of numerous festivals in the state. Since the major part of the population is Hindus, the festivals that are celebrated here are the common festivals celebrated all over India. Apart from this there are many festivals that are unique to the state.

Throughout the year, there are a number of festivals celebrated in Tripura with great pomp and gaeity. Some of the popular religious festivals that are rejoiced by the people are Ashokastami Festival Unakoti in the month of April, Kharchi Festival in July, Manasa

Mangal in August, Diwali Festival in November, Pous Sankranti Mela in January, Rasha Festival in November, Durga Puja in October and many more.

While among the cultural festivals Rabindra and Nazrul Jayanti in May, Orange and Tourism Festival at Jampui Hill Range in November, Book Fair at Agartala in January are few of the names. These festivals attract large number of pilgrims and tourists from all over India.

- Durga Puja in Tripura;
- Ganga Puja;
- Kharchi Puja;
- Garia Puja;
- Tripura Tourism Festival.

Capital of the State: Agartala

Agartala is the capital of the Indian state of Tripura. It lies on the Haora River and is located 2 km from Bangladesh. It has several temples and palaces. The population of Agartala was 367,822 in 2004 after the municipal expansion (189,327 in the 2001 census).

History

Foundation: The ancient Capital of the then Princely State 'Swadhin Tripura' was at Rangamati (Udaipur, South Tripura) by the bank of the River Gumati and in 1760 AD, it was shifted by the Maharaja Krishna Kishore Manikya (r. 1829-1849) of Manikya Dynasty to present old Agartala by the bank of the River Haora and was named 'Haveli'.

Due to frequent invasion of the Kuki's and also to keep easy communication with the British Bengal, the Maharaja Krishna Kishore Manikya started the process of shifting the Capital from Old Haveli to New Haveli (present Agartala) in the year 1849 AD. During British Raj, Agartala was the capital of the erstwhile 'Hill Tippera' state, it became a municipality in 1874-75, and in 1901 had the population of 9,513.

Agartala Municipality: The Agartala Municipality was established during the reign of Maharaja Chandra Manikya (1862-96) within an area of 3 sq mi having a population of only 875 by a royal proclamation in the last part of 1871 AD. Mr. A. W. S. Power, the 1st British Political Agent for Tipperah was also appointed as the Chairman of the Agartala Municipality in the year 1872 AD who held office from 1872-73 AD.

Planned City: Maharaja Bir Bikram Manikya Bahadur is called the founder of the planned city of Agartala. During the period of the early-forties, the entire town area was reorganised infrastructurally in a planned manner with strong roads and a market building.

Contemporary History: On October 1, 2008 a series of 5 bomb blasts rocked the city.

Geography and Climate

Agartala is located at 23°50' N 91°17' E. It has an average elevation of 16 metres (52 ft). The city is situated in a plain along the Haora River, though the city also extends to the low lying hills on its northern parts. Agartala has extreme climate all through the year.

- Summer : (March to June) — Hot.
- Monsoon: (July to September) — Humid and lots of rainfall.
- Winter : (October to February) — Cold.

Demographics

As of 2001 India census, Agartala had a population of 189,327. Males constitute 50 per cent of the population and females 50 per cent. Agartala has an average literacy rate of 85 per cent, higher than the national average of 64.84 per cent; with 52 per cent of the males and 48 per cent of females literate.

Area, Population and Headquarters of Districts

S. No.	District	Area (sq km)	Population	Headquarters
1.	North Tripura	2,820.63	5,90,913	Kailasahar
2.	South Tripura	2,151.77	7,67,440	Udaipur
3.	West Tripura	2,996.82	15,32,982	Agartala
4.	Dhalai	2,552.47	3,07,868	Ambassa

2

Salient Features

- -

Tripura is mainly a hilly territory with altitudes varying from 50 to 3080 ft above sea level, though the major population of the state lives in the plains. The state is located in the Bio-geographic zone of 9B-Northeast Hills and possesses an extremely rich biodiversity.

The local flora and faunal components of Indo-Malayan and Indo-Chinese subregions. There are 379 species of trees, 320 shrubs, 581 herbs, 165 climbers, 16 climbing shrubs, 35 fernsa and 45 epiphytes.

The State of Tripura lies approximately between the latitudes 22 degrees 56 minutes, and 24 degrees 32 minutes North and between longitudes 91 degrees 0 minutes and 92 degrees 22 minutes East. South Tripura District is situated approximately between East longitude 91 degrees 18 minutes and 91 degrees 59 minutes and between North latitude 22 degrees 56 minutes and 23 degrees 45 minutes.

The South Tripura District is bounded on the North by Dhalai District and West Tripura District, while on the other sides by international border with Bangladesh.

The climate of the District is mostly warm and is characterised by a humid summer and a dry cool winter with plenty of rains during July to October. Rainfall is received from the Southwest Monsoon, which normally breaks in the month of May. Hailstorm generally occurs during the month of April and May, occasionally causing damage to the field crops.

Autumn and Spring are of very short duration. Average annual rainfall in the district is about 2,000 mm and the temperature varies between a maximum of 35.23° and a minimum of 7.43° Celsius. The variation in temperature is much lower during the rains than during any other season.

Tripura is the second smallest state in India. It was formally declared as Union Territory on November 1st, 1957 and was elevated to the status of a full-fledged state on January 21, 1972. It is bordered by Bangladesh on the west, south and north, by Assam on the northeast and by Mizoram on the east.

The state is covered by picturesque hills and dales, deep and green valleys, which have added beauty to its landscape. The state is connected with the rest of India by only one road, which runs through the hills to the border of Cachar district in Assam. The state has four districts with ten subdivisions. The four districts are West Tripura with Agartala as its headquarter (which is also the state capital), North Tripura with Kailashahar as its headquarter, South Tripura and Dhalai with Udaipur and Ambassa, respectively as district headquarters.

From the east the principal hill ranges are the Jampoi, Sakham Tiang, Langtarai, Athara Mura and Bara Mura. The highest peak of the state is Be-talang-Shiv (3,200 ft.) in the Jampoi hill range. A number of broad and elongated valleys — Agartala, Udaipur, Sabrum, Khowai, Teliamura, Amarpur, Silachari, etc. are located between the north-south trending, parallel to subparallel high ranges (topographic highs) such as the Baramura-Deotamura ranges, Atharamura ranges, Langtari ranges, Sakham ranges and the Jampui hill ranges.

The soil in the valley is fertile with rich alluvial deposits and therefore suitable for the cultivation of paddy, jute, oilseeds, pulses, fruits and vegetables. About 54.5 per cent of the land is under forest. Only about 24.3 per cent area is available for agricultural use.

The West Tripura District lies approximately between latitude 23 degrees 16' to 24 degrees 14' north and longitude 91 degrees 09' east to 91 degrees 47' east. The West Tripura District is bounded by Bangladesh in the north and west by North Tripura in the east and by South Tripura in the south.

General Features

Tripura encloses a rich cultural heritage of music, fine arts, performing arts, and handicrafts. Being dominated by the Bengalis, the state's prevalent culture is Bengali. As it has numerous diverse ethno-linguistic groups, such as, Tripuris, Jamatia, Reang, Noatia, Koloi, Murasing, Chakma, Halam, Garo, Kuki, Lushai, Mogh, Munda, Oraon, Santhal, and Uchoi, a composite culture has emerged on the whole.

The Inhabitants

A diverse ethnic element among the people of Tripura is that — there are two major racial elements, namely, the Indo-Aryans represented by the Bengalese and the Indo-Mongoloids represented by a few communities like the Tripuris, the Reangs, the Jamatis, the Noatias, the Kukis, the Halams, the Chakma, the Mogh and the Lushai. Besides these nine major tribes, there are ten more tribes. All the nineteen tribes are classified as 'Scheduled Tribes'.

The Tripuris also called Tripuras or Tipras are the original inhabitants of the state. They constitute about a little over 16 per cent of the total and 57 per cent of the tribal population of the state. The formal rulers of the land is believed to be the descendants of the Kshatriyas.

In course of time, a section of this community came into close contact with the Bengali settlers, and was much influenced by their language, culture and custom. Then a new community, now known as Natun Tripuris, a sort of breakaway group of the original (Puram) Tripuris.

A few among the Tripuris who were close to the royal family (known as Thakur) settled in and around Agartala. They are quite advanced in education and general enlightenment. High public officials, writers, musicians, engineers and doctors are found among them.

The other group who live on the hill-slopes are not much improved regarding economic status or nature of occupation. They practice jhooming (or shifting cultivation), fetch wood from the forests, sell vegetables and bamboos. The women help men in jhooming, weave cloth on their traditional loin looms and take care of pigs, fowl, etc. Their houses made of bamboo, are built five to six feet above the ground to avoid hazards from wild animals.

The Reangs tribal group constitute about 14 per cent of the tribal and 4 per cent of the total population of the state. They are broadly divided into two groups. Meksha or Mechka and Marchai or Malchai. The former is again subdivided into Masha, Raichak and some other subgroups, while the principal subgroups among the latter are Apet and Champung. The community is governed by a well-defined hierarchical institution; the chief enjoys the title Rai.

The Reangs are considered as one of the strongest pillars of the states military forces. The Reangs are Hindus and generally believers in the Sakti cult. Like other tribal they also believe in animism.

Another section of the Tripura community is known as Jamatia — the term seems to have originated from jamayet, which means a gathering or mobilisation. Like the Reangs, the Jamatias also constituted the fighting force during the time of Tripura King. Their system of worship comprises both Hindu practices and animistic rites. Having many social institutions in common with the Bengalese, the Jamatias are taking to plough cultivation in preference to jhoom and are now settling down in the plain areas of the state.

Historical and Geographical Features

Tripura has its unique tribal culture and a fascinating folklore. The history of Tripura can be learnt from *'Rajmala'* chronicles of King Tripura and Writings of historians. There are references of Tripura even in the *Mahabharata* and the *Puranas*. According to *'Rajmala'*, the rulers were known by the surname *'Fa'* meaning *'father'*. There is a reference to rulers of Bengal helping Tripura Kings in the 14th century.

Kings of Tripura had to race frequent Mughal invasions with varying successes. They defeated the Sultans of Bengal in several battles. Nineteenth century marked the beginning of the modern era in Tripura when King Maharaja Bir Chandra Kishore Manikya Bahadur modelled his administrative set-up on the British India pattern and brought in various reforms. His successors ruled Tripura till 5 October 1949 when the state merged with the Indian Union. Initially, a Part 'C state, it became a centrally-administered territory with the reorganisation of states in 1956. In 1972, Tripura attained the status of a full-fledged state.

Tripura is strategically situated between the river valleys of Myanmar and Bangladesh. Encircled almost on three sides by Bangladesh, it is linked with Assam and Mizoram in the northeast.

Geographical Features

Tripura was known as 'Hill Tipperah' and the very much nomenclature is suggestive of its hilly nature of undulating surface made uneven by inter-sparced low hills. A series of hill ranges running north and south divide the territory into broad parallel valleys, consisting of undulating tillas (hillocks) covered with jungle with *tortuous streane*. There are six principal hill ranges in the state increasing in height as one moves west to east (from the summit of the ranges one has a striking view of the surroundings, a heaving monetary of evergreen landscape). Out of the six principal ranges, Baramura and Deotamura ranges and Atharamura ranges partly fall within West Tripura.

Baramura and Deotomura Ranges: The portion of the above ranges lying in West Tripura District is the Baramura range, which is almost 47 km having the highest peak Saisum Sib (249 metres).

Atharamura Range: This range starts from Amarpur Subdivision of South Tripura District and then enters into the Khowai Subdivision of West Tripura and runs along the border of West Tripura and North Tripura District. Its highest peak in the West Tripura District is Niungnanwra (481 metres).

It is true that the state as a whole was, in the bygone days, far richer in forest wealth but with the increasing pressure on land through population increase has rendered this rich forest susceptible to decay, through the process of reckless falling of the trees for different reasons like settlement of land-use and jhumes in some cases and for also augmenting the revenue of the erstwhile princely State even since the past great wars.

With the increase in population, the pressure on land was intensive and the tall tress of the forest had to give way to the increasing need to settling the refugees who came in exodus to this tiny state as well as for maintaining jhum cycle for the considerable percentage of Tribal who still continues to practise jhum cultivation. Without being scholarly to discuss the extent of ecological imbalances created by such indiscriminate exploitation of forest for immediate reasons, it is very much clear that the state has suffered quite heavily in the forest wealth during the past decade.

The experimentation for introduction of rubber plantation, which was found suitable for the soil and climatic condition of the state has also proved to be successful and thus brightened the prospect of this sector which might go a long way in the total economic development of the state as a whole. The total area under rubber plantation has been increased to 3,320.77 hectares from the experimental minimum of 5.80 hectares in 1963. The Tripura Forest Development and Plantation Corporation Limited, a public sector enterprise under the State Government have also taken intensive programme of development of rubber plantation in the whole state as well as West Tripura District.

Coffee plantation is another addition in the sector, which has attained a coverage of 10,183 hectares in 1981 from 2.40 hectares in 1975. Tripura, being a land locked State is having constraint in importing coal for domestic use. The extent of firewood supplied from forests is about 1,77,000 cu ms. The supply of firewood from the forest is also a main source of livelihood for the population residing in the interior forest area.

The quantity of timber produced from the forest as in 1980-81 is about 37,204 cu ms As stated earlier, the details for the district in particular are lacking but the overall picture of the state will reflect the position as obtained in the West Tripura District.

Irrigation and Power

Geographical area of Tripura is 10,49,169 hectare. It is assessed that about 2,80,000 hectares of land is cultivable. As on 31 March 2004, an area of 77,722 hectares of land has been brought under assured irrigation by providing lift irrigation, deep tube-well, diversion, medium irrigation shallow tube-wells and pump sets. This is about 27.75 per cent of the cultivable land in the state. 1,178 L.I. Schemes, 160 deep tube-wells, 25 diversion schemes have been completed and 3 medium irrigation schemes namely, (i) Gumti, (ii) Khowai, and (iii) Manu are providing irrigation water to the part portion of the command areas as canal system has not been completed.

The Gas Based Combined Cycle Thermal Project at Monarchak under Sonamura Subdivision, West Tripura District was initially planned for 500 MW capacity by NEEPCO Ltd. Subsequently, the project has been downsized to 280 MW due to revision in gas availability from ONGCL.

However, the capacity will be enhanced to 500 MW on receipt of gas availability of require quantum. At present, the own generation of the state is 70 MW against an installed capacity of 105 MW.

The present peak demand of the state is 163 MW. Government of Tripura has committed to purchase 70-80 MW from the 280 MW of Monarchak Project of NEEPCO. Sanction towards installation of 1×21 MW GT project at Rokhia, West Tripura for Rs. 80.94 crore has been obtained from Government of India and order placed to M/s BHEL for supply and erection of the same.

Another scheme of 2×21 MW GT Project at Baramura, West Tripura was submitted in June 2002. The Planning Commission agreed for inclusion of 1×21 MW GT set at Baramura, West Tripura in Tenth Plan of NEC. As on 31 March 2004, 57,450 families below poverty line category are connected with electricity under *kutir jyoti* scheme.

Geological Features

The study of rocks of Tripura dates back to 1908 when H. C. Dasgupta first classified the folded sedimentary rocks into 'coal measures' and ' Tripura Groups'. The rocks encountered in Tripura state range in age from lower Tertiary (40 million years old) to Recent (less than 1 million years old). The sedimentary rocks of Tripura can be divided into 'Formations', 'sub-Groups' and 'Group' on the basis of their litho logical composition, depositional characteristic and structural features.

Major Rivers

The Khowati, the Manu, the Haorah, the Muhuri and the Gomati are some important rivers of Tripura. Gomati is the largest river. Like the Ganges in North India, the Gomati is considered to be the most sacred of all the rivers in Tripura.

The source of the river is taken to be Tirthamukh where lies the beautiful Dumbar falls — one of the most important holy places. The rivers Khowai, Doloi, Manu, Juri and Langai are flowing towards the north and those flowing towards west are the Gomati, Muhuri and Feni. The following rivers flow within the West Tripura districts:

Gomati: The Gomati which is the principal river is formed by the confluence of two rivulets; Raima and Sarma. The Raima originates from the Longtharai range and the Sarma from the Atharamura range and the two meet near 'Dhuchaibari' in the South Eastern boundary of the South Tripura district and then assuming the name of Gomati Nadi running through gorges up to the Dumbur fall in the Amarpur subdivision. Gomati with length of 133 km (a bi river) and runs across the Amarpur and Udaipur subdivisions of south Tripura District and Sonamura subdivision in West Tripura district and then flows towards Bangladesh by the side of Sonamura Town of West Tripura District.

The tributaries of the Gumti river on the right bank are Labachhara, Datakchhara, Sarbongchhara, Saugang, Patav-gang and Noachhara and on the left bank are Rambhadhachhara, Ekchhari, Chelagang, Kurmachhara, Maharanichhara and Ranigan.

Khowai: Source of the river is the Longtharai range. It is 166 km in length and it taken its way almost towards Northwestern direction up to Teliamura of West Tripura District and then towards north till it enters into Bangladesh. Its tributaries on the right bank are Baluchhara, Jeulchhaara, Chamalachhara, Alladiachhara, Baskarach-hara, Maharanichhara, Tuirupachhara, Samruchhara and Lalchhara and on the left bank are Gulechhara, Nunachhara, Kakrachhara, Brahmachhara, Sarduchhara, Trishnachhara, Gangraichhara and Solaichhara.

Howrah: It rises from the Baramura range and its tributaries are Dowaigang, Ghoramara and Debda on the right bank and Charupanadi, Dhobatilachhara and Bangeswargang on the left bank. The length of Howrah River is 53 km and it flows towards west and enters into Bangladesh by side of Agartala town, the capital of the state.

Burigang: It rises from Baramura and flows towards west and ultimately enters into Bangladesh. There are long river valleys extending over a vast area in different subdivisions formed mostly of deep alluvial deposits with rich fertility excellently suited for the cultivation of paddy jute, oil seeds, spices, fruits and vegetables would be evident from the aforementioned position.

The sources of all rivers are in Tripura itself. Due to the indiscriminate felling of trees the ecology of Tripura is being affected to a great extent, Human beings and trees belong to the category of living species. There is a gap of feeling, which might be attributed to the factors of immediate benefit as the very question of subsistence is involved particularly when the majority of the people in Tripura are below poverty line. Exploitation and not extinction should be the way of life.

If that were the case the forest resources, which are national wealth, should be preserved in such a way that they are exploited and not extinct. Else danger is inherent in expressing their displeasure.

The signs of danger are apparent when we see erosion of soils due to indiscriminate felling of trees. There is uneven rainfall. Water flows merry-go-round. It carries sands, which turns into deposits causing heavy damage to fertile lands, which are going to be scarce particularly when the population is increasing in geometrical progression.

Political Features

Tripura is governed through a parliamentary system of representative democracy, a feature the state shares with other Indian states. Universal suffrage is granted to residents. There are three branches of government. The legislature, the Tripura Legislative Assembly, consists of elected members and special office bearers such as the Speaker and Deputy

Speaker, that are elected by the members. Assembly meetings are presided over by the Speaker or the Deputy Speaker in the Speaker's absence. The judiciary is composed of the Guwahati High Court (Agartala Bench) and a system of lower courts.

Executive authority is vested in the Council of Ministers headed by the Chief Minister, although the titular head of government is the Governor. The Governor is the head of state appointed by the President of India. The leader of the party or coalition with a majority in the Legislative Assembly is appointed as the Chief Minister by the Governor, and the Council of Ministers are appointed by the Governor on the advice of the Chief Minister. The Council of Ministers reports to the Legislative Assembly.

The Assembly is unicameral with 60 Members of the Legislative Assembly, or MLAs. Terms of office run for 5 years, unless the Assembly is dissolved prior to the completion of the term. Tripura sends 2 representatives to the Lok Sabha and 1 representative to the Rajya Sabha. Auxiliary authorities known as *panchayats*, for which local body elections are regularly held, govern local affairs. Tripura also has an autonomous tribal council, the Tripura Tribal Areas Autonomous District Council which has its headquarters in Khumulwng.

The main political parties are the Left Front and the National Socialist Party of Tripura. The state is currently governed by Left Front, with Manik Sarkar as Chief Minister. Until 1977 the state was governed by the Indian National Congress. The left front governed from 1978 to 1988, and then returned in power in 1993. During 1988-93, the state was governed by a coalition of the Congress and Tripura Upajati Juba Samiti. In the last elections (2008) the Left Front gained 49 out of 60 seats in the Legislative Assembly, 46 of which went to the CPI(M).

Language

Bengali is spoken and understood by more than 50 per cent of the state's population. However, Kokborok (also called *Tripuri*) as well as Bengali are the official languages of Tripura. The other major language spoken in the state is Manipuri. The tribal communities have their own dialects for communication. English is liberally used for official and administrative purposes.

Religion

Hinduism is the most practiced religion in Tripura. Both Bengalis and Tripuris follow Hinduism with ardent fervour. Islam, Buddhism and Christianity are also followed by people in minority. However, most of the tribals are adherents of animist-Shaktism. Brahmin priests, known as Chantais, are believed to be the custodians of religion (dharma). The main gods worshipped by the people are Lord Shiva and Goddess Tripureshwari. Besides, many fertility gods are also worshipped.

Fairs and Festivals

Since Tripura is mainly subjugated by the Hindus, the festivals common in rest of the country are mostly celebrated here. For example, festivals like Durga Puja, Navaratri, Vijayadashami, Dol Jatra (Holi), Pous Sankranti, Ashokashtmi, and Diwali are the most celebrated festivals. Besides, there are many other festivals that are unique to Tripura. Some of the important tribal festivals are Garia, Ker Ganga and Gajan. Other state festivals are Rabindra/Nazrul Festival (May), Boat Festival (August), and the Orange and Tourism festival (November).

Seat of Higher Learning

Tripura University, Agartala, Pin: 799 004.

Art and Architecture

Tripura Arts and Crafts have a rich and historical tradition. The handicrafts are famous all over India. Rich variety of handicraft items are made by the local people all over the state. The items are mostly made up of bamboo and cane.

Like any other state in India, Tripura also nurtures some special types of art and craft items that are inseparable parts of the state's tradition. Arts and Crafts is well known in the country, especially the traditional bamboo craft and cane craft items.

Arts and Crafts are integral parts of the lifestyle of the people. This rich tradition of handicraft not only enriches the culture of the state but also contributes to its economy. Tripura Arts and Crafts also adds to the tourist interest of the state. The artifacts and handicrafts of the area depicts an honest picture of the Tripura Society and Culture.

The state is well known for the Rock Cut Carving, Bamboo and Cane Work, Jewellery, Sculpture and Paintings. These arts and crafts products are an excellent way to decorate the interiors of one's home.

The main arts and crafts items that the is famous for are:

- Bamboo roots;
- Floor mats;
- Folk Painting;
- Bamboo Dining tablemats.

Music

Tripura Music is an essential part of the life of the people of the state. Music also forms an important part Arts and Crafts. Like any other tribes, music and dance are rooted deep into the lifestyle of the tribal people.

Music and Dance come in rich variety and styles. For the welfare and prosperity of their people, the Garia dance is practised in Tripura. This dance form is popular among the Reang community. The Chakma tribes have their Bizu dance and the Halam tribes have dances like Hai Hak and Cheraw. The Basanta Raas is performed by the Hindu Manipuris.

The music colleges provide music courses that follow syllabuses with a lot of emphasis on traditional Tripura music. The state feels proud of its unique and traditional musical instruments like the Sumui, Sarinda, Dundoo, etc.

Musical Instruments

The Musical Instruments of Tripura reflect the rich musical heritage of the state. Unlike some other regions of the country, Tripura has not forgotten its musical roots. The traditional Tripuri musical instruments are made with typical materials like bamboo, animal hide, animal horns and wood.

Some of the old but widely used musical instruments are:

- *Uakhrap:* It is a combination instrument. Uakhrap has a base of skin with attached strings. The semi-circular shaped instrument is made of trunk of different trees like Garjan, Gamai and Koroi.

- *Chongpreng:* One of the popular musical instruments, the Chongpreng, is another stringed instrument. The bamboo made lute instrument has a fretted neck.

- *Lebang-Lebangti:* A typical Tripuri instrument, Lebang-Lebangti is entirely made of bamboo.

- *Sarinda:* The Sarinda looks much like the mandolin. The instrument has a hollow wooden chamber that resonates the sound. This string instrument is one of the popular musical instruments.

- *Kham:* The Kham is a barrel shaped traditional drum with skin surfaces on both the sides.

- *Sumui:* One of the oldest instruments of the region, Sumui is an enchanting bamboo made flute.

- *Dangdoo:* Made of iron tongs, the Dangdoo is a harp like instrument.

Dances

The dances of Tripura are elegant and rhythmic. Music and dance forms an inseparable part of the culture of the state. The state has a rich cultural heritage. The cosmopolitan culture has been continuously enriching it. It is inhabited by 19 tribal communities, Manipuris, Bengalis and people belonging to many other communities. All the communities have their own distinct dance forms. Most of the folk dances are performed during festivals or on festive occasions.

The dances are performed by both men and women. They generally wear traditional dresses while performing the dance. The dances are accompanied by a number of the musical instruments like bamboo cymbal, Khamb, Flute made of bamboo, Khenggarang, Dhukuk, etc. The traditional essence of these dances are maintained even today. The main dances are as follows:

- Hozagiri Dance,
- Hai-Hak Dance,
- Lebang Boomani Dance,
- Wangala Dance,
- Bizu Dance,
- Garia Dance,
- Cheraw Dance.

Architecture

Tripura is the second smallest state of India. The architecture of the temple of Lord Jagannath is interesting and worth studying. It rises from an octagonal base. The Ujjayant Palace, dating back to Bir Bikram, is equally interesting with its Indo-Saracenic architecture. Old buildings and ruins worth exploring are in plenty like the lake palace called *Neer Mahal* on Rudrasagar Lake in Udaipur, the ancient capital. Sipahijala is an interesting area to spend the day. There is a comfortable guesthouse in the complex surrounded by forests and overlooking a large lake where one can go boating.

Economic Features

Agriculture forms a primary sector of the economy of Tripura. More than 75 per cent of the state's total workforce is dependent on agriculture for their subsistence. In fact, about 24.3 per cent of the state's net area is reserved for agricultural purposes of which, about 2.5 lakh hectares fall under the net cultivated area. Paddy is the principal crop that is reaped in Tripura. Besides paddy, jute, sugarcane, wheat, oilseeds, coconut and turmeric are also grown in plenitude in the North-East Indian state. The state takes elaborate measures to spruce up the agricultural infrastructure. New technologies, fertilizers, improved seeds and protective chemicals have been implemented to keep the state's agriculture in top shape.

The remote location, lack of power facilities as well as a well-developed transport and communication network hindered the growth and development until the year 1950. However, today several small-scale industries have mushroomed in the state that deal with the manufacture and production of handicrafts and handloom products, jute and tea. Natural gas and fruit processing units have also sprung up in the state.

Industries

The remote location, lack of a well-developed transport and communication network as well as the poor power facilities had hindered the growth of industries in Tripura, till about the 1950s. Currently, however, several small and medium-scale industries have mushroomed in the state.

Tripura Handloom and Handicraft Development Corporation Ltd. is employing a whole array of novel marketing schemes to market the local handicraft items. The All India Handicraft Board has also established an outlet in Agartala which specialises in the improvement of quality of the products. In fact, more than 5,000 people are now employed in the handloom and handicraft industry, a burgeoning sector of the Tripura economy. The state is also a repository of glass sand, clay, lignite and building material.

Silk industry and sericulture used to be another core sector of the state's economy. However, today the flourishing industry has dwindled to a solitary village in Agartala. Currently, 500 hectares of land are reserved for mulberry cultivation and the estimated production is said to be 5,000 kg per year. A jute mill has also been established at Agartala whose production capacity is 20 tonnes of jute products per day with a net workforce of 2,000 people.

The latent hydroelectric potential of the state is also being exploited to further the state's industrial development. 5 industrial estates have also boomed in Dharmanagar, Kumarghat, Arundhutinagar, Dhwajanagar and Dhukli while three industrial centres have come up in Agartala, Udaipur and Kailashahar.

For further information on Tripura Industries, navigate to any of the following:

- Tripura Natural Gas Industry;
- Tripura Fruit Processing Industry;
- Tripura Rubber Industry;
- Tripura Tea Industry;
- Tripura Handicraft Industry;
- Tripura Handloom Industry;
- Tripura Tourism Industry.

Fisheries

Fisheries in Tripura form an integral part of the state economy. With the increase in the demand of fish in Tripura, the State Government has taken adequate steps to increase the production of prawn seed, table fish and fish seed. More emphasis is laid towards creating more cultivable water areas, so the production of fish can be increased.

Besides, the Government of Tripura is also working towards increasing the productivity of the existing water areas. 3,160.70 hectares of water area has been created by the Farmer Development Agencies since 1977-78. 4,364.54 hectares of water areas is brought by the Farmer Development Agencies under the Scientific Fish Culture. Moreover, it is noteworthy that Government of India has ratified a FFDA, during 1997-98, for the Dhalai District.

The first Cooperative Movement in Fisheries was initiated in 1951 by Rudrasagar Udbastu Fishermen Cooperative Society at Melagarh (Sonamura Subdivision). The number of Fishermen Cooperative Society reached 129 till 2000. The Cooperative societies are supported by the Department of Fisheries for their proper growth.

The Cooperative Societies are covered under 'Fishermen Accident Insurance'. Through the aforesaid insurance, the Cooperative Societies can avail of the benefits extended to the Cooperative Societies. Fishermen Accident Insurance also provides housing and drinking water facilities to the fishermen and their families. 520 houses have been constructed till 2000.

Agriculture

Agriculture of Tripura mainly comprises horticulture products. Blessed with a salubrious climate and an average rainfall of 2,500 mm, Tripura produces several delicious fruits that add to the economic strength of the state. The warm and humid climatic condition of state is perfect for producing plenty of fruits, spices and vegetables. Rubber and tea are also produced in some parts.

Agriculture is the backbone of the economy. Most of the indigenous local inhabitants of state are engaged in the traditional occupation of cultivating fruits, and vegetables. Some of the important agricultural productions of the state are:

- Jackfruit,
- Orange,
- Pineapple,
- Banana,
- Mango,
- Litchi,
- Lemon,
- Kharif Vegetables,
- Potato,
- Rabi Vegetables,

- Cashewnut,
- Coconut,
- Areca-nut,
- Turmeric,
- Ginger,
- Chilly.

The farmers of the state practise organic cultivation of fruits, vegetables and spices. Most of the cultivators follow traditional methods of producing crops. The State Government has taken special steps to improve the agricultural growth of the region.

The well-maintained network of markets helps in the easy marketing of the agricultural products. The juicy and delicious fruits are exported to other countries that enable the state to earn revenues and hence build a strong economic base.

Tripura has several small fruit processing centres that produce numerous products from the fruits of the state. Agriculture is one of the main sources of earning income for the rural inhabitants.

Transportation and Communication

Tripura is connected with the rest of the country through Assam by metre gauge railway line extending to Lumding and Silchar. The main railways stations are in the northern towns of Dharmanagar and Kumarghat. National Highway 44 connects it to Assam and the rest of India.

Agartala Airport, which has flights to Kolkata, Guwahati, Bangalore, Chennai, Delhi, and Silchar, is the main airport of the state.

Most of the major Telecommunications companies of India are present in the state, with the state capital and regions of the state being served by Airtel, Aircel, Reliance and BSNL landline, mobile, and broadband networks.

Transportation

Roads: The total length of roads in Tripura is 15,227 km of which major district roads constitute 454 km and other district roads are for 1,538 km.

Railways: The total length of lines within the state is 64 km. It has been extended up to Manughat. Work of extension of railway line up to Agartala is in progress.

Aviation: The main airport at Agartala is connected with Kolkata Guwahati. There are airports at Kailashahar and Kamalpur though they are not functioning at present.

Environment

The climate of the state is generally hot and humid. The average maximum temperature is 35°C in May-June and the average minimum temperature is 10.5°C in December-January. The monsoon starts generally in April and continues up to September. Summer starts in March and continues up to May and is followed by rainy season extending over about three-four months (May-August). The pleasant season lasts only for about two months (September and October). Then follows winter, which continues up to February.

Characterised by moderate temperatures and highly humid atmosphere, Tripura is best visited after the Southwest monsoons in October. 10°C to 35°C; Average Annual Rain Fall 2,100 mm; Highest Rain Fall 2,855 mm (Kamalpur); Lowest rainfall 1,811 mm (Sonamura).

Sport Features

Football and cricket are the most popular sports in the state. The state capital Agartala has its own club which organises football championships every year where many local clubs compete in a league and knockout format.

Tripura participates as an Eastern state team in the Ranji Trophy, the Indian domestic Cricket competition. The state also is a regular participant of the Indian National Games and the Northeastern Games.

Tripuri Games and Sports

Like many parts of the world, the Tripuri community has its own traditional sports. It is common in almost all the clans of Tripuri. It is called *Thwngmung* in Tripuri language (Kokborok). Tripuris are by nature very sporting people. They love to play these game and enjoy their free time by playing various game and sports. In recent years, these traditional sports are being gradually abandoned as more people become attracted to modern games and sports. But some of the sports are still played today and preferred in rural Tripura. Out of many traditional Tripuri games and sports some are listed below:

Achugwi Phan Sohlaimung: It is type of wrestling. It is played between two young men to test their strength. Two young men sit on the ground facing each other spreading their legs. A thin bamboo pole or tree is placed between them for staking their legs. The two contenders hold horizontally a peace of bamboo, two and half cubits of length approximately which remain high above the ground between them. When pulling begins each contender tries to pull it towards his own side. Who could pull the bamboo his side wins the game.

Bumanikotor: This is basically a hide and seek game. Played in groups one party hides, other group finds out the hiding party.

Dwkhwi Sotonmung: It is basically tug of war. Played between two groups of children or men.

Phan Sohlaimung: This is a pole wrestling played between two individuals. A bamboo pole is used to play the game. The players stand at a specific distance from each other. A mark is put in the middle. The two ends of the bamboo pole are placed under the right armpit and each participant grasps it firmly with both hands. Both the players then try to cross over the marking between them by pushing each other back.

Kaldong or Kadong: A small foot step is tied on two pieces of bamboo about two feet above the ground level. The player walks on this foot step which make the riding person tall, there is competition like who could run faster and remain on the kaldong longer without falling from it.

Longoi Chokmung: This is a swinging game played by the Tripuri children. Two long ropes or strong creepers are tied to the branch of a tree, and a wooden platform is tied in the lower end to make a seat. Turn by turn the children swing while other push him/her. They also sing beautiful melodious song while swinging.

Muphuk Sagwnang: This game is played to test the strength of a young man. A child clings to the chest of a man chose waist is tied with one end of rope. Another man holding the other end of rope firmly stands back. As the game begins the man with the child on his chest force to move forward child the other who stands back try to draw back his opponent.

Musta Seklaio: This game is played between two young individuals. A bamboo is cut within the joint to make it cylindrical one. One person holds it firmly down on the surface, the other one grips just above the grip of first one and then tries to snatch it by rotating it. It is to test the grip strength of a young man.

Sohlaimung: Tripuri *"sohlaimung"* literally it means wrestling. This is a free hand wrestling which is common in most of the world is also very popular among Tripuri children. There are rules and regulation playing the sports. Generally one of the senior spectators become the referee.

Tourism

- West-south Tripura Tourism Circuit: (i) Agartala (ii) Kamalsagar (iii) Sepahijala (iv) Neermahal (v) Udaipur (vi) Pilak (vii) Mahamuni
- West-North Tripura Tourism Circuit: (i) Agartala (ii) Dumboor Lake (iii) Unokuti (iv) Jampuri Hill

3

History

The history of Tripura dates back to primeval era of the great Indian epics, such as, the Mahabharata, the Puranas; and pillar inscriptions of Emperor Ashoka. Tripura has a long story of its origin, its distinctive tribal culture and a captivating folklore. It was called *Kirat Desh* in the earliest times. According to the mythological legends, Tripura, who was the successor of King Druya and Bhabru, was the prodigy on whose name the state was named. Another fable affirms that the state was named after the Goddess Tripuri Sundari (whose temple is situated at Radhakrishnapur).

In the 14th century the history of Tripura witnessed a change with the sifting of the capital from Kailashahar to Udaipur. It was around the same time that the Tripuri Kings adopted the title of Manikya and the Manikya dynasty which had a Indo-Mongolian origin ruled Tripura for around 3,000 years. This was probably the most glorious episode of the history of Tripura and the dominance of the Manikyas was also acknowledged by the Mughals who were the central rulers.

The 17th century is a major watershed in the history of Tripura when the administration of the region passed on the hands of the Mughals with some restrained powers of the Manikyas. With the coming of the colonial era the Britishers extended their control over Tripura but granted some independence to the Manikya Kings.

The Royal history of Tripura ended in the year 1947 when monarchy in the state was completely terminated. Bir Bikram Kishore Manikya was the last ruling Manikya King of Tripura and it was after his death that Tripura was acceded to the Union of India. In the year 1949 Tripura became an Union Territory of India and remained so until 1972 when it was made a constituent state of the Indian Nation.

Origin and Early History

Earlier the name of Tripura was Kiratbhumi, it's capital was in Tribeg. It means land of Kirat, the Tripuris used to be called previously. Some where three thousand years back its name was changed to Tripura, the reason for such is not yet settled beyond controversy.

- In One school of thought, the word 'Tripura' originated from the King Tripur who happens to rule the state. According to the legend Tripur was the 39th descendent of Druhya, who was descendent of Yayati, one of the lunar race Kings. He was so mighty that he ordered his subjects not to worship any god other than him, had no faith in god. He started torturing the subjects who defies his order. People fled in a body escape from his tyranny to near by state of Hiramba (Cachar).

There are also other plenty of example in Tripura where different Kings of Tripura named the city, towns, capitals, etc. according to their name. For example Udaipur, Amarpur, Kalyanpur, Dharmanagar in Tripura, Ratanpur, Bijay Nagar, etc. in Present Bangladesh. There are also examples of naming different lakes, Ponds, River, etc. in their mane, for example Dharma Sagar, Govinda Sagar, Kalyan Sagar, Bijay river, etc. Even the name of many Tripuri villages, area, etc. are named after the head or chieftain of the village like Chintaram Sarder Para, Ramkumar Kwpra para, etc. From this facts it was all probable that the mightiest King of Tripuri people Tripur might had changed the name of the state after his name.

There are ample of examples of many states named after the rulers name, Bharata from Bharat, Bangla from Banga, Gandhar, etc. in the history. Apart from this many countries of the world were also named after the King or individual discoverer like, Egypt, Libya, Jordan, America, Columbia, etc. So there is every reason to prove that King Tripur also named his state after his name.

- According to another belief Tripura is a corrupt form of Twi-pra. The meaning of Twi is water and that of pra is confluence not the near. Like lampra is meeting point of two roads, bupra is bifurcation point of tree branch. As such the Tripuri call their state as Tipra not as Tripura which has been corrupted in Sanskrit and its derivative sister languages to Tripura. This is the most accepted opinion among Tripuris. In fact what is more to be noted is that most of the villages, places in Tripura are named after various rivers, tributaries, etc. like Twikormo, Twirisa, Twisarangchak, Twimudul and so forth.

- In another theory, it is said that there was a totem in Tripuri mythology called Tipra, a Tortoise, which is a sort of god for Tripuri people. According to Tripuri belief whenever this tipra tortoise makes it burrow near any Tripuri home or 'jhum' (huk) a traditional agricultural hillock the family is bound to have a bad luck or omen in that year. The burrow is called *Tiprakhor*, burrow of Tipra Tortoise.

Such tortoise is prohibited from human consumption. The Tipra tortoise is offered sacrifices so that he does not shower any bad effect to that family, like offering to the god. Whenever such Tiprakhor arise any where near any Tripuri family's habitation, the family has to worship and satisfy that Tipra tortoise to avoid the any bad effect of that god. The origin of this Tipra word is Twi (water) + Bupra (shake of) = Tipra. According to this theory it is said that the Tipra (Tripura) name of our state derived from this Tipra tortoise, the totem of Tripuri people.

- In one more theory, Tripura name derived from three district with which it was formed previously, namely, Chattagram, Kumilla, Noakhali. These districts were earlier parts of Tripura, (Tri = Three, Pura = city).

- According to another school of thought, the name Tripura was probably given to the state in honour of the temple at Udaipur, Tripureshwari, the wife of lord Shiva. But this may not be correct as the temple was built in around 1501 AD by King Dhanya Manikya during the period of his reign between AD 1490-1515, where as the name of the state was in existence long before 1501. Instead it looks more probable that the deity took the name of the state rather than the state named after the deity.

- According to Kailash Chandra Singh, a prominent historian, the word Tripura is a derivative from two different Kokborok word 'twi-pra'. Twi means water, pra means near in the Tripuri language of the inhabitant of Tripura. It is likely that the state bears the name Tripura from this fact that in ancient time the boundaries of Tripura extended up to the Bay of Bengal when its ruler held sway from Garo Hill to Arakan.

Ancient Times

As far as the ancient chronicle of the region is concerned, the literary, archaeological and historical narrations do not even hint the existence of a separate political entity named as Tripura in the ancient period. Nonetheless, there is, adequate academic support to the view that many parts now constituting southern and western sections of Tripura State were attached to the ancient Kingdom of Vanga. Nalini Ranjan Roychaudhary has rightly remarked that the archaeological evidences found in the region prove the fact that a large portion of this region, particularly south western part of the present State of Tripura, was politically attached to the Kingdoms of Eastern Bengal known as Samatata Vanga and Harikela.

The northeastern part of the region was dominated by tribal communities who did not recognise any one as their ruler excepting their tribal hierarchy. Among these tribes also it was the Tipperah tribe which with the passage of time became politically awakened and active. All other tribal communities continued to be ignorant politically for a pretty long time. No doubt, before the advent of Tipperahs, some scattered evidences have come to light but they are so insufficient and insignificant that a continuous chronological account of the religion related to that period can not be weaved.

During the heyday of the Imperial Guptas over the political scenario of the country, their appointed administrators, mostly hailing for the Gupta dynasty itself, had a complete sway over Samatata Vanga and Harikela. To begin with, the incumbents functioned as Governors of the Guptas ruling the Centre and always waited for directions before taking any likely action.

However, with the passage of time, the ambition of the appointed Governors started asserting itself and took full advantage of the long distances that divided the peripheral kingdoms from the Centre. In this region Vinay Gupta who was sent as Governor to Samatata Vanga in 507 BC, he was an over ambitious man who soon started throwing the yokes of the Imperial Guptas. In these days, there were very slender, less efficient and poor means of transport and communications and Vinay Gupta took full advantage of this situation. He soon became an independent ruler of Samatata Vanga, Vinay Gupta was succeeded by Gopa Chandra, Dharmaditya and Samachandradeva. These rulers are believed to have had their administrative headquarters somewhere in eastern Dhaka or northern Tipperah.

For obvious reasons the territory around Tipperah and Dhaka became the core of the kingdom. The famous Chinese scholar-traveller Hiuen Tsang has mentioned in his travelogue that during his extensive travels in India during the seventh century, the Samatata Vanga was a powerful kingdom independent of the central rule. From his narration, one finds, on a deeper probe, that the district of Tipperah as a part of the Samatata Vanga Kingdom included a part of Central Bengal also.

The Tipperah copper plate carries an account related to Samanta Lokanatha who is believed to have founded a house of feudal chiefs that ruled eastern Bengal around mid seventh century. He was one of the three feudal chiefs who ruled the different parts of Vanga under the supreme command of paramesvara.

Others were Jayanturgavarsha and Jivadharna. Among them it was Lokanatha who was ambitious, tactful and crafty. He not only succeeded in overthrowing the suzerainty of Paramesvara but also defeated the other feudal chiefs and ultimately became the virtual ruler of the region.

It is said that Lokanatha traced his lineage from the Rishi Bharadwaj. Srinath is supposed to have followed the Rishi who was himself followed by Bhavanatha and Lokanatha succeeded Bhavanatha. In a way, there was Nath rule in the region.

The Nath rule came to be succeeded by the Rata rule. This fact has been obtained from a copper plate found at Kailam. The Village of Kailam is located towards the Southwest of Comilla town now falling in Bangladesh.

The plate also carries a reference that the Rata rulers had their administrative headquarters at a place named Devaparta. This place, as indicated on the plate was located within a meander of a stream named Khira. This stream is now a dried up rivulet. In one of its major meanders, a hillock named Main mati carrying some ruins has been found.

It is conjectured, that although for easy supply of water, it was essential that the capital town be built on the bank of a stream, yet a low altitude hillock surrounded by the river course was selected so that the capital town could be saved from the wrath of floods during rainy period. The Rata dynasty was succeeded by the Deva dynasty as the ruling house and this ruling family also ruled from Devaparta.

It is also inferred by some scholars that the latter ruling house also derived it dynastic nomenclature from the capital town of Devaparta. The Natha were Vaishnavites but the Devas were Buddhists. The Buddhist ruling house was followed by another Buddhist ruling family, Khargas.

As per Chinese sources the Khargas came from the adjoining mountainous areas and with their prowess succeeded in routing the Devas and ultimately came to occupy the vast region consisting eastern Bengal, southern Bengal and Tipperah by the concluding years of the seventh century.

Kharagoyama was the founder of this rule and after his name the entire ruling house came to be known as Kharaga dynasty and some rulers also used "Kharaga" as a prefix with their names. Jatakharaga, Devakharaga and Rajarajbhatta have been identified as later rulers of this dynasty.

The Chandra dynasty held its sway over eastern Bengal and Tipperah between 875 AD to 1035 AD. According to some scholars the Chandras originally came from the Larnai Hills of Comilla now falling in Bangladesh.

However, a Chandra ruling dynasty was also found to had been ruling the Arakan region in Burma. Some historians opine that the Chandras were a tribe of quite an ambitious people living near Comilla. But they were no match for the Kharagas and earlier Devas.

Thus in their adventure they crossed over to Burma where finding the situation fluid, they succeeded in thrusting themselves as rulers. At a later stage when the conditions in eastern Bengal also became unstable, a powerful section of the Chandras came back and over threw the Devas to assume rulership. Nonetheless, the later Chandras had to bear the brunt of outside invasions quite often.

For soiree time the peripheral territory kept on Changing hands. The last Chandra ruler, Govinda Chandra failed to resist the foreign invasion and yielded to Karna, the General of the Rajendra Chola. The Cholas instead installed Burmans (may be they originally hailed from Burma and thus carried the suffix of Burmans) in place of Chandras in East Bengal. Five Burman Kings ruled the territory one after the other. The last Burman ruler, Bhoja Burman was defeated by Vijayasena who came to establish Sena dynasty.

During the pre-medieval period when Naths, Ratas, Kharagas, Devas and Chandra ruled over eastern Bengal and Tipperah hill tract it was a Deva Chief who succeeded in founding a principality within the Kingdom. He was Madhumanthandeva. He tactfully, accepting the supremacy of the Kingdom, slowly and gradually but sneakingly moved towards an independent principality. Though his succeeding soil could not move in the direction, yet one of his grandsons, Damodradeva rose to the occasion by dint of his prowess and intelligence.

Whereas, the earlier principality had been created by his grandfather in a limited pocket on the bank of the Meghana river, he extended the frontiers of this principality over the districts of Tipperah, Noakllali and Chittagong. His son and successor Dasarathadeva equally rose to the occasion to further the tradition of his forefathers. Fle captured Vikrampur and annexed it to his kingdom.

During his time, Tughril Khan the appointee of Gyasuddin Balban in this region, revolted against the Delhi Sultanate rule. Dasarathadeva extended a helping hand to the Delhi Sultan in quelling Tughril Khan's revolt and thus earned the gratitude of the Slave ruler. Dasarathadeva had his capital at Sonargaon near Dhaka. Nonetheless, after Balian the other rulers in their ambition to extend their jurisdiction started interfering with the affairs of the Deva dynasty in this region.

Small wonder ultimately the Muslims who were equipped with better armaments and resources succeeded in uprooting the Deva rule form this area.

Medieval Times

During this period it was the Manikya dynasty which ruled over Tripura. Thus it shall be pertinent as well as interesting to trace briefly the origin of this dynasty. Rajmala is that treatise which deals with the history of this region though written in Bangala.

Earlier part of this reference manual is said to have been composed by a Tripuri priest named Durlabhendra with the assistance of two Brahman scholars, viz. Baneshwar and Sukheswar. As per narration given in Rajmala Yajati was the supreme ruler of the Universe. One of his sons, Durjho is believed to have built a city Tribeg somewhere in North Eastern India on the bank of the Brahmaputra river. Durjho after ruling this city and its surroundings for sometime renounced the world handing over the reins of his rule to his son Tripur.

It is the same King, after whose name, it is believed the region got its name Tripura is narrated as a very cruel and oppressive rulers who did not hesitate to get the eyes of criminals gouged or getting them trampled by elephants. Nevertheless, his rule soon came to an end with this sudden death and his son Trilochan succeeded him. Trilochan was simply a contrast to his father and exhibited utmost love, sympathy and considerateness to his subjects.

It is believed that he held the brutalities perpetrated by his father on the people solely responsible for the sudden death of his father. Thus, he decided to be a merciful and kind. In the Durjho lineage there came a ninety seventh successor Chhengthung Fa who founded the Manikya dynasty.

When Chhengthung Fa was the Tripperah Chief, the Muslim rule had established itself at Delhi. The Muslims were note contented by capturing only Delhi and its surroundings. They were ambitious to the extent of overpowering the entire Indian subcontinent.

On the other hand at that time the Tipperah tribal community was the largest and strongest tribal group in North Eastern India. With the passage of tune they also became ambitious, restless and expansionists who did not feel contended by limiting their field of activity to Tipperah hills alone. They whished to expand the frontiers of their domain to the adjoining plain areas also. This naturally brought them in confrontation with the Muslims. Since the Tipperahs were in an advantageous position in their gorilla tactics in view of the mountainous and forested territory with which they were fully conversant, in the ensuing collision the Tipperahs succeeded and did not permit the Muslims to have their hold here. Resultantly the Tipperahs succeeded in carving a larger kingdom for them. Which according to some scholars came to be known as Tipperah (and ultimately Tripura) after the tribe name.

On the other hand while nursing their hurt pride the Muslims always waited for an opportunity which could help them in wreaking vengeance over the Tipperahs. Ultimately the Muslim Gour (Bengal) ruler got one such pretext. A Hindu merchant with wealthy and costly gifts for the Gour Sultan was plundered of all the riches lie was carrying *en route* to the Kingdom of Gour.

The merchant reported to the Gour Sultan that his was looted by the men of Chhengthung Fa on his way to Gour. This had very outrageous reactions in the Muslim camp and the Muslim soldiers started seething with rage and waited only for orders to march up to Tipperah Hills to teach a lesson to the erring tribals.

On the other side Chhengthung Fa became alarmed as well as panicky and desired to surrender, apologise for the misconduct of some of his men and sue for peace. The Sultan of Gour was making elaborate preparations for a show down and had entrust the task of subduing the Tipperahs to one of his very trusted, capable and strong Governor, Hiravat Khan.

Chhengthung Fa's wife Tripuri Sundari did not like the week kneed policy of her husband. She strongly protested against the cowardice of her husband and she herself gave a call to all Tipperahs to unite for a common cause and pounce upon the foe in a battle to fight to the finish and instead teach a lesson to the Muslim invaders who had intruded into their domain. When the Tipperaha Hill folk found that a courageous and brave lady had come out with an unsheathed sword in her hands, they had to fight to the finish to save their clan's name and Tripuri Sundari's name from being tarnished.

Countless Tipperah hill folk with swords, spears and other weapons gathered together to defend their land. Before the armed men were ordered to march to the battlefield, the Chief's wife threw a lavish feast of meat and brew to her soldiers. Finding the Chief's wife leading them with a sword in hand the Tipperah folks fought with a rare courage and bravery. Even the reluctant chief joined his army and he too fought tooth and nail to wipe off the stigma which got, attached to him sometime ago.

It is believed that the awesome way and terror with which the Tipperahs fought was unprecedented in their annals. The Tipperahs became not only victorious but they created such an awe and terror among Muslims that they could not dare ever to have retaliatory step against the Tipperahs. At this juncture the tribal community dropped its suffix "Fa" and took over a new suffix "Manikya" meaning a jewel. Thus in this way the Manikya dynasty came into existence.

Some scholars are however, of the opinion that Manikya dynasty was an offshoot of the Chandra Vanshi Kashatriyas. Still others believe the Manikya to be either Kirats or Mongolians or Indomongoloids. They, nevertheless, speak Bodo group of dialects.

In the opinion of some scholars it is probable that the Bodos who were the natives of Tibet, migrated to Brahmaputra basin after a devastating famine in their homeland, and slowly and gradually thereafter moved to other parts of North Eastern India. After reaching Nowgong as Garo-Khasi-Jaintia, hills they entered Cechar and Sylhet where from they ultimately arrived in Tipperah Hills. However, it has become well nigh impossible to ascertain as to when did they emigrate from Tibet and also whether they had established themselves in Tipperah Hills before the Muslims came to have their hold in North Eastern India.

The above narrated view is not acceptable to a majority of related scholars in whose opinion there is now sufficient historical evidence to believe that the founder of Manikya dynasty was none else then Chhenghung Fa who later on ruled under the name of Maha Manikya. He is said to have either died or left the reins of administration around 1431 AD since his successor and son Dharma Manikya (Dangar Fa) ruled Tripura from 1431 to 1462.

Dharma Manikya was a staunch Hindu ruler and a great lover of art, literature and learning. He is credited to have built a number of temples and the Dharmasagar tank at Comilla. It was also he who commissioned Durlabhendra, Sukheshwar and Bhaneshwar to compose the history of the Manikya ruling family.

Dharma Manikya had eighteen sons. Instead of following the ages old practice of primogeniture, he decided to parcel out his kingdom into seventeen divisions for each of his seventeen sons and send the eldest son as a permanent ambassador to the Muslim rule in Gour.

The Gour ruler who had been jealous of the progress made by the Manikyas was nonetheless impressed by the personality, physical charm, pleasing manners and intelligence of Ratna Manikya who had joined the Gour rule as an ambassador of the Tripura ruler.

The defeat suffered by the Muslims at the hands of Tipperahs was still fresh in the mind of the Gour ruler. Thus the Gour Sultan planned to punish the tribals at the hands of their own kith and kin. He instigated Ratna Manikya against his brothers on the pretext that the territories held by there legitimately belonged to him only and none else. He convinced him that the real heir to the throne had been diplomatically exiled while the one who did not deserve were enjoying the fruits of the kingdom. He further promised hire full support in regaining the lost kingdom provided he was prepared to head the invading army.

Ratna Manikya fell into the laid trap and pledged to stand in arms against his all the younger brothers. With the help of the Gour forces he defeated the combined armies of his seventeen brothers and become the ruler of Tripura. In gratitude he presented elephants and riches to the Gour Sultan. Rama Manikya was also a great patron of learning and art. He invited many learned scholars, artists, men of letters, men of medicine (Vaidyas) and merchants and other functionaries (Kayasthas) from Assam to settle down in Tripura.

Ratna Manikya also reorganised and remodelled the administration on the lines of Gour administration. At a later stage in a family feud, he helped Ruknuddin Barbak Shah to snatch the reins of administration from the aged Sultan of Gour. Rama Manikya after his demise was succeeded be his son Pratap Manikya who was a very weak and indecisive ruler who soon become unpopular with his people. When the army forces also got fed tip with his pranks, an army general lost no tune in getting him eliminated.

Mukut Manikya, a younger brother of Pratap Manikya succeeded the latter. He however, ruled for a very short time. He issued a coin in his name in 1489 AD while a coin issued in 1490 AD bears the naive of Dhanya Manikya who had followed Mukut Manikya. Dhanya Manikya sternly dealt with the revolting tribes and also annexed the territories of the adjacent kingdoms who had been directly and indirectly helping and instigating some tribes to revolt against the Manikya rule.

Besides crushing the over ambitious and revolting feudal chiefs, he suppressed the Kukis with an iron hand and forced them to honour his writ. Finding the time quite opportune in view of the prolonged family feud continuing in the ruling house in Gour, he captured many parts of Gour and annexed them to his kingdom. These annexed areas included Chittagong, Meherkul, Khandal, Pattikara and Gangamandal.

Thus Dhanya Manikya is regarded the greatest ruler of Tripura during the medieval period. To commemorate his victory over Chittagong he issued a coin in his name describing himself in the inscription as "conqueror of Chittagong" in 1503. Earlier lie had issued another coin in 1500 celebrating his other victories. The inscription on the coin Vijayendra described him as "King among conquerors."

Sultan Hussain Shah the then Gour ruler (1493 to 1519 AD) made persistently strenuous efforts to regain control over the areas captured from his kingdom but so long as Dhanya Manikya was alive all his efforts fell flat on the ground. Dhanya Manikya was not only a fearless, chivalrous and dauntless warrior and an efficiently capable administrator but also extended a benevolent patronage to artists, literatures and scholars. He is credited to have got constructed the Tripuri Sundari temple at Udaipur which is held in very high esteems till today in the region particularly by the natives.

At Kasba he got built a huge tank mined Kamala Sagar, after his Queen Kamala. He is also credited to have taken effective and persuasive steps to propagate the learning of Bangala language and literature among the natives. He opined that by having a deep dive in the Bangala literature the natives were to become culturally more rich and socially more awakened. Till that time the custom of nara ball, i.e. human sacrifice was widely prevalent in this region and people were often sacrificed even on a slight pretext. Dhanya Manikya through a state decree limited the custom to only three occasions in year and that too if suitable prisoners of war were available. No wonder the human sacrifice in due course of time, gave way to animal sacrifice.

Dhanya Manikya died issueless in 1515 and was succeeded by his younger brother Dhwaja Manikya who ruled for only half a decade, i.e. till 1520. His period appears to have passed peacefully without any eventful occurrence. When he died in 1520 AD, he too was succeeded by his brother Deva Manikya. He was also an ambitious King and had all designs to expand the frontiers of his domain. He annexed Noakhali to his kingdom in 1520 itself.

Thereafter he led an adventurous expedition to Sonargaon and soon captured it be annexed to his kingdom. He was a Shakta King who made full use of his Shakh strength in subjugating some areas but his son Indra Manikya, who had come of age had become over ambitious and had no patience to wait for the natural demise of his father. He hatched a conspiracy and got father killed to usurp the reins of power.

But his younger brother Vijay Manikya had not taken kindly to the bloody *coup detat*. He only waited for an opportunity to pay his elder brother in the same coin. Vijay Manikya lost no time in creating a lobby to oppose Indra Manikya. Just after four months with the help of this powerful lobby, Vijay Manikya led an armed revolt against his brother and overthrew him to become the ruler himself.

Vijay Manikya ruled for thirty years and during these three decades lie proved to be a ruler of great acumen and calibre who similar to his father Deva Manikya has left an indelible imprint on the history of Tripura in the form of a great conqueror and efficient administrator. At that time, the Afghans had become a power to reckon with.

It was the dine when Afghans and Mughals (Sher Shah Suri, his successors and Humayun) were fighting each other to gain supremacy over Delhi and other parts of the country. Bengal could be no exception to the general trend. For some time the Afghans gained control over Delhi.

The clever and shrewed King in Manikya thought it prudent to have a meaningful report with the Afghans. He recruited some Afghan officers in his army to impart training to his troops in new war strategy and were fare. Moreover he wanted to cash upon the situation created by the Afghan Mughal struggle. After some time when the tables turned at Delhi. Vijay Manikya also changed his strategy. He not only dispensed with the services of the Afghan officers but annexed Syllet and Chittagong from the Afghan.

By that time Sonargaon had changed hands and thus provoked Vijya Manikya to regain control over it. Though in his initial attempt he could not regain control but lie succeeded in plundering and burning it. Ever Ain-e-Akbari carries a reference to Vijay Manikya, meaning thereby that at least for some time he was Akbar's contemporary.

The reference narrates that when Afghan Officers we kicked out of the state force and some Afghan territories annexed by Vijay Manikya, the Afghan soldiers in his army revolted. They were nearby one thousand in number who marched towards Chittagong fully armed and riding horses. They were, however, captured and slain on the altar of fourteen deities.

The Gour Afghan Sultan was highly enraged by this gruesome act and he lost no time in invading Tripura. The battle continued for eight months and Vijay Manikya once again defeated the Afghans establishing his supremacy in this part of India. During this battle an Afghan General was taken as a captive and he too was sacrificed at the altar of a god.

After the death of Vijay Manikya in 1563 AD his successor and son Ananta Manikya being weak, inefficient, indolent and a puppet in the hands of his over bearing, over dominating over bossing and over ambitious father-in-law Gopi Prashad could not manage the affairs of the state. Gopi Prashad was a very crafty and cunning person who had risen from the status of a cook and goruashta in the palace to the highest office of General-in-chief in the army of Vijay Manikya. Instead of serving his son-in-law as Commander-in-chief he desired to be a ruler. To being with he became a *de jure* ruler but this position failed to satiate his hunger for power. He wanted to be a *de facto* King and for it he was prepared to do anything.

In the year 1567 AD, he himself aliened his son-in-law and himself occupied the throne under the name of Udai Manikya. He changed the name the capital town of rangamati to Udaipur. The Chandra Gopinath temple and Chandra Sagar in the capital town were also got built by him. Udai Manikya's own son on the other hand also desired to be ruler and he too was impatient to wait till the death of his father. In 1572 AD, he poisoned his father to death and became the Tripura ruler under the name of Joy Manikya.

The members of the original Manikya house were naturally upset in the fast moving developments. For obvious reasons they did not want the aliens to rule a kingdom so laboriously created and nursed by their forefathers. Their sneaking efforts continued to uproot the usurpers and regain the control over the throne. In 1577, Amar Manikya a brother of Vijay Manikya achieved the goal by ousting Joy Manikya. So as to leave an impression on his subjects of being a real ruler Amar Manikya paid due attention towards territorial aggrandisement and administration.

In a fast sweep he captured the areas of Tirap, Sylhet and Bhulua and to commemorate his victory, he issued a coin in his name in 1581. He also got a palatial royal palace in Udaipur and named it as Amar palace. The Amar Sagar in Udaipur was also got built by him. A part of the Rajmala was also got composed by him.

So long as Amar Manikya limited his annexation operations within Bengal, he always emerged victorious but the moment he crossed over to other areas he ran into difficulties. With the help of some Portuguese adventurers he attacked Arakan region then ruled by Muhammad Shah. The latter not only repulsed the attack but charged a counter attack.

In this move Muhammad Shah annexed Chittagong and entered the capital of Udaipur where he unleashed a terror of massacre loot and arson. In fact, Muhammad Shah played a tact to deceitfully annex Chittagong area. Because of its physical environment the Tripura region and particularly its forests are known as haven for elephants. The Mughal rulers had a weakness for elephants and they needed a region that could continuously supply them elephants for pomp and show and for exhibiting their grandeur.

It was with this vested interest that the Mughal forces attacked Tripura. On the plea that the season of Durga Pooja had dawned, the Mughal forces withdrew with an understanding that they won't attack Tripura till the Durga Pooja festivities were over. But the Mughal forces re-attacked at a time when the entire Tripura was in the midst of annual rejoicings. Notwithstanding, the betrayal of the enemy the Tripura valiant warriors came out to defend their land and initially they had an upper hand but as the destiny had otherwise willed right at the moment when final victory was round the corner the Commander-in-Chief of the Tripura forces was trampled to death by an elephant who had gone amuck. As history repeats itself, at the sudden and unexpected removal of the general the forces ran helter and skelter. Amidst this panic and confusion the enemy forces managed to over power the situation. Finding his forces defeated in the battle field Amar Manikya retreated to a forest.

In the forest hide out the Kukis to settle their outstanding score with the Tripura ruling started harassing the King and his forces. Amar Manikya was not prepared for such a humiliation and he felt utterly helpless. No wonder he consumed some poisonous herb and thus committed suicide on the bank of the Manu river.

Amar Manikya was succeeded by his son Rajdhar Manikya in 1586. Rajdhar Manikya was a deeply religious man who was least interested in worldly affairs. Finding him as a weak ruler the Mughs (Molts) started ransacking the capital town. Rajdhar Manikya instead of putting an end to the nuisance shifted his administrative headquarters from Udaipur to some safe place. He devoted much more time to meditation than to the affairs of the state. When the Muslim ruler of Gour got an air about it, he thought it a fit moment to capture the Tripura territory. Thus with this objective in mind Adin Tughril the Muslim Gour ruler attacked Tripura but the Tripuri soldiers fought so valiantly that Tughril was defeated and he took to heels. Rajdhar Manikya to offer thanks to the Almighty for this timely help distributed some land among the Brahmans and also got a Vishnu temple built.

Somewhere towards the concluding years of the Sixteenth century. While Rajdhar Manikya was picking up an idol of Vishnu floating in the Guinti steam, he himself was washed away by the swift current and this way came the end of Rajdhar Manikya. He was followed by his son Ishwar Manikya whose rein is believed to have been very short. There are no historical records available pertaining to his rule. Nonetheless, coins issued in 1600 AD carry the name of Yashodhar Manikya who was Ishwar Manikya's son. Thus it is surmised that former's rule might limited to some months only.

When Yashodhar Manikya became the ruler, Delhi had Alamgir Nasiruddin Muhammad Jahangir at the Mughal Throne. Khan Abrahim Fatehjung was Jahangir's Subedar in Bengal. He wanted to expand the frontiers of the Mughal Empire by annexing the Arakan region to it. For this purpose he had to widen his base in Bengal itself.

Resultantly a large army consisting of infantry, cavalry, naval fleet and a herd of elephants were sent by the Bengal Governor to annex Tripura so as to broaden the base of the Bengal Kingdom. Yashodhar's resources in men and material were a poor match to the imperial army. Small wonder Yashodhar Manikya along with his harem fled to forests but the imperial forces gave a hot chase and took them as captive. They were detained it.

Dhaka as prisoners and Yashodhar died in the Mughal detention itself in 1623 AD. On the other hand at about the same time a devastating drought and accompanying epidemics forced the Mughal forces to flee from Tripura.

After the Mughal forces fled from Tripura the people of the region decided to put Kalyan Manikya on the throne. The historical records are, however, silent about Kalyan Manikya's antecedents. He not only revamped the administration but completely restored law and order, reorganised his forces and brought some of the lost territory under his control. With a view to bring about socio-economic uplift of his subjects lie sincerely desired peace with the Mughals so that they did not interfere with the affairs of Tripura. Hence, for attaining this objective he sent his second son Nakshatra Roy as an Ambassador to the Mughal Court. The temple of Kali at Kasba and the construction of Kalyan Sagar were also his creations.

But the Mughals were not happy with these welfare measures which they could not provide to their own subjects. Hence, on a very slight pretext the Mughals felt defied as well as offended an doddered the Nawab of Murshidabad to teach a lesson to the Tripura ruler. Nonetheless, the first attempt of the Mughals was defeated. To average this humiliation the Mughal forces sent a large army under Prince Shah Shujah to suppress the Tripura rebel ruler.

The valiant soldiers of Tripura undoubtedly gave a dogged fight but could not stand the much superior and large forces. In this way Tripura was added to the "rent roll" of the Mughals, *i.e.* the state had to regularly pay rents to the Mughal Empire annually and obey its orders.

Kalyan Manikya died a heart broken King in 1660 AD and as per the law of primogeniture his eldest son Govinda Manikya came to the throne. Nakshatra Roy no doubt was a hostage in the Mughal Court but with his pleasing manners he had created a soft corner for himself in the heart of the King.

Moreover, the pomp and show of the court had made him ambitious and he wished to be the ruler of Tripura. For achieving his goal he wished to use the services of the Mughal Empire. He persuaded the Governor of Bengal to lend him a helping hand.

The governor sent his forces with Nakshatra Roy who in the very first invasion uprooted Govinda Manikya and occupied the capital town of Udaipur. Govinda was exiled out of Tripura territory. Nakshatra Roy came to the throne of Tripura as ruler under the name of Chhatra Manikya in 1661 AD. Govinda Manikya after being ousted had taken refuge in the Arakan rule. He also planned to pay a tit for tat to his usurper brother with the tacit help of the Arakan Kingdom.

In 1667, with the help of Arakan forces Govinda Manikya defeated his brother Chhatra Manikya at Bhuyan where the latter was killed also. In this way Govinda Manikya regained his lost kingdom but so as to keep his continuous hold he had to appease and please the Mughals who had earlier helped Chhatra Manikya to capture the Tripura throne.

Thus Govinda Manikya bought peace with the Mughals and pledged to gift five elephants annually to the Mughals as yearly tributed. Besides being a strategian, shrewd ruler and diplomat administrator, Govinda Manikya was a great patron of art, scholarship, learning and knowledge. One section of the Rajmala was also got composed at his instance. He also got the Brihannarada Purna translated into Bangala. Nobel Laureate, intellectual giant and a great humanist Gurudev Rabindranath Thakur (Tagore) has immortalised the qualities of head and heart of Govinda Manikya in his treatises Visarjan and Rajrishi. He breathed his last in 1676 AD after presiding over the destiny of Tripura for about two decades in terms. He was succeeded by his son Ramdeb Manikya. He ruled till 1685 AD.

The Tripuri Sundari temple had been very badly damaged by lightning and it was Ramdeb Manikya who got it completely repaired in 1681 AD.

Ramdeb Manikya left a minor son, five year old Ratna Manikya II as heir apparent. He was made a titular ruler and the Regent was a *de facto* King. However, his court became a hot bed of intrigues, conspiracies and counter conspiracies. He had a step brother Ghanshyam younger to him. When he also came of age the intrigues and conspiracies started thickening. The courtiers came to be divided into two rival groups.

The exchange of diplomats between Tripura and Assam was the most Significant event of his times since it helped in creating a united Hindu front against the Mughals. It was the Ahom (Assam) King who desired to have a United Confederation of Hindu rulers in Eastern India against the nefarious designs of the Mughals. Thus he sent Ahom diplomats to all the nearby Hindu kingdoms.

The Ahom ruler Rudra Singh sent Ratna Kandali and Arjundas Vairagi as ambassadors to the Tripura court. The objective was to have friendly relations and assess the help and support the Tripura ruler could extend to the Ahom ruler in ousting the Mughals from Eastern India.

As a reciprocal gesture Ratna Manikya II sent Rameshwar Bhattacharya Nayalankar and Udayanarayan Biswas as the Tripura ambassadors in the Ahom Court. The diplomats on both the sides were heartily welcomed and treated as esteemed guests of honour on all occasions of festivities and ceremonies.

Ghanshyam Barthakur, the step brother of Ratna Manikya II had become hand in glove with the Mughals and his sole aim was to oust Ratna Manikya II so that he himself could become the ruler of Tripura.

The Mughal Court of Bengal commissioned the talks of extending support and help to Ghanshyam Barthakur, to its two most trusted generals Murad Beg and Mahmud Sapi. Thus on 10 May, 1712 Ratna Manikya II was overthrown and Gharishyam Barthakur became the new Tripura ruler under the name of Mahendra Manikya.

The new ruler ruled barely for one year and two months. During this period lie tried to establish friendly relations with the Ahom King. He treated the Ahom — envoys already stationed in the Court with courtesy acid honour. He also sent Aribhim Narayan as his envoy to the King of Assam.

Mahendra Manikya expired in July 1713 and was replaced as a King by his son Durjoy Singh — who took the name of Dharma Manikya II. Whereas, Dharma Manikya I brought about glory to Tripura as an effectively powerful ruler and a great patron of art and learning, Dharma Manikya II brought the downfall of Tripura. Being an imprudent ruler and also knowing fully well that his resources of men and material were no match to the mighty Mughal Empire he all of a sudden stopped paying the annual tribute to the Mughal Court.

Obviously the Nawab of Bengal felt insulted and he decided upon to punish the erring King who had stopped the payment of yearly tribute without any reason. Fortunately the Tripura Kingdom at that time had a very valiant and sacrificing Tripura Kingdom at that time had a very valiant and sacrificing Commander-in-chief in the person of Ranabhim Narayan who defended the territory for eight months against very heavy odds.

On the other side Jagatram, a direct descendent of Chhatra Manikya was aspiring to be the King of Tripura. To gain his objective he entered into a conspiracy with Aqsa Sadiq, a Muslim landlord of Patpashe Pargana of Bengal. Aqsa Sadiq had very close links with Mir Habib, an influential courtier with the Dhaka Durbar. Aqsa encouraged Habib to make full use of an advantageous situation.

The Tripura ruler had a very poor intelligence and lie could not know about the march of the Mughal forces against him even when the forces had crossed the Brahmaputra and arrived in the close vicinity of the Tripura capital. Totally unprepared for such an eventuality the Manikya ruler fled to a hide-out which was however unfortunately located by the enemy forces and thus the whole of the Tripura Kingdom fell into the hands of Habib.

Jagatram was elevated as ruler of Tripura by the Mughals on a condition that he shall continue to pay the yearly tributes to Mughals Court at Dhaka. This way the Mughal Empire got a very substantial part of the annual revenue of Tripura. Aqsa Sadiq the man behind the entire show was posted a faujdar in the Tripura Court by the Nawab of Bengal.

Though the apparent cause for this appointment was the protection of Jagatram (Jagat Manikya) against the evil designs of the rival group yet in reality the Nawab of Bengal intended to keep the Tripura ruler under his Light grip. Nawab Shujauddin the then Mughal Nawab of Bengal was very happy with Mir Habib who had annexed Tripura to the Bengal court. In recognition of the services rendered by Habib to the Mughal Court at Dhaka, the Nawab conferred upon Habib the title of Khan and the territory of Tripura was renamed as Roshanabad, i.e. the land of light. A large number of troops were stationed in the capital town of the state of Tripura.

Dharma Manikya II on the other hand made a fervent appeal to the Nawab to restore to him the territory of Tripura on terms favourable to the Mughal Empire. Finding the subjects of Tripura preferring Dharma Manikya II to Jagat Manikya, the Nawab read the writings on the wall and restored Tripura to Dharma Manikya II and thus avoided the bloodshed which would have otherwise surely followed. Nevertheless, the Mughal Nawab of Bengal extended his own terms and conditions. He granted the Zamindari right to Dharma Manikya II on the lands of Tripura on an annual rent of rupees five thousand.

Since then the ruler of Tripura had simply been a Zamindar and not a King. Dharma Manikya II expired in 1729 AD and was succeeded by his brother Chandramoni as Mukunda Manikya. The latter was later on imprisoned by the Mughals for the non-payment of an annual tribute in the form of five elephants every year. Being chained and humiliated. Chandramoni out of sheer depression and disgust committed suicide.

Rudramoni, a brother of Govinda Manikya, who was a man of rare intelligence, prowess and courage awakened the people of Tripura against the impending danger to their motherland. He organised a militia of the Tripuris and with its help one fine morning in a swooping raid occupied the town of Udaipur. His lightning action pleased the people of Tripura beyond description and they decided to have hire as their ruler in preference to the direct descendants of Mukunda Manikya. Rudramoni assumed the title of joy Manikya in 1739 AD. Indra, the son of Mukunda Manikya entered into an alliance with the Mughals to regain control over Tripura.

With the help of Mughal forces Indra captured the throne of Tripura in 1744 AD. Indra Manikya had a very difficult time because the dethroned ruler Joy Manikya ran a parallel government from a hide-out in the Moti Hills. However, he was always kept away from Udaipur by the Mughal forces and Indira Manikya rare a puppet government. Joy Manikya on the other hand was extended support by some influential Zamindars.

Coincidentally Joy Manikya and Indra Manikya died almost around the same time. Now it was Joy Manikya's brother Vijay Manikya who occupied the throne. Vijay Manikya refused to pay the annual tribute to the Mughals. Under the pretext of non-payment of annual tribute the Mughals took Vijay Manikya as prisoner to Dhaka where he died under very mysterious circumstances.

Consequently Tripura was turned as a province of the Mughal Empire and Shamsher Ghazi, a notorious plunderer was appointed as the first Mughal Governor. He made a son of Dharma Manikya as a puppet ruler. But when this step failed to pacify the natives he unleashed a rein of terror.

After Indra Manikya died at Dhaka, his brother Krishnamoni made an effort to recapture Udaipur. On the other hand the unscrupulous Shamsher Ghazi also had an ambition to become the ruler of Tripura. With his vested interest he convincingly conspired with Lakshman a grandson of Dharma Manikya.

This led to a strife between Shamsher Ghazi and Krishnamoni. In the ensuing battle Krishnamoni lost the game and retreated to the forests. There he roamed about in a vain hope of mustering enough force and strength to oust Shamsher Ghazi. Shamsher Ghazi appointed Lakshman Manikya as a puppet ruler and after some time the himself usurped all powers and became a ruler. To win the hearts of the people he planned some welfare measures. He constructed some tanks and allotted rent free land to some people.

Basically being a dacoit and plunderer he continued his nefarious activities secretly. He posed threat even to the Nawab of Bengal. He unleashed a reign of terror to the extent of utmost repression. Thus the Nawab of Bengal got him chained and also got him shot at the mouths of canons after his 12 years' rule of terror in Tripura. Krishnamoni finding the time opportune lost no time in becoming the Tripura ruler. The Nawab of Bengal who was fed up with the nefarious activities of Ghazi heaved a sigh of relief by recognising Krishnamony as new ruler of Tripura.

Modern Times

In the second half of the eighteenth century AD, when British interference started permeating to Tripura, modern period of its history began. Krishnamoni became the ruler of Tripura in 1760 under the name of Krishna Manikya. He shifted his headquarters from Udaipur to Agartala (old). At about the same time, some people of Murshidabad revolted against the Nawab of Bengal.

The situation so full of confusion and chaos in Murshidabad appeared to be advantageous to Krishna Manikya and he intended to make full use of the same. As a first step, so as to assess the reaction of the Nawab, he forthwith stopped the revenue payment to Nawab. Nawab's Foujdar Reza Khan first sent his Dewan for the collection of revenue but with no results. Later on he himself went to Tripura but he also returned empty handed.

The East India Company which had its coveted eye on Tripura, started interfering in the matter although neither its mediation nor interference was warranted from any angle. Vanisttart, the then Governor of the Company directed the managers of the Islamabad Factory to take a stern action against the erring ruler. Verlset, the President of the Factory despatched on armed force headed by Lieutenant Matthews the February 25, 1761 to take action against the Tripura ruler.

The ruler found it an impossible task to confront two forces, *i.e.* the Nawab and the British and thus he surrendered to Lieutenant Matthews.

On March 15, 1761 Marriot an officer of the company was sent to collect the revenue. But the Tripura ruler had nothing to pay since the troops of the Bengal Nawab had plundered and ransacked his territory.

Under such circumstances Marriot thought it best to get agreements signed by the ruler. Vide one of the agreements, as narrated in Abdul Majid Khan's The Transition in Bengal, the Tripura ruler pledged to pay the revenue of one lakh one rupees and according to another agreement, he promised to pay a *nazarana* or *salami*, i.e. tribute to the company amounting the Rs. 1,11,191, annas 6 and pie 3. He further pledged to clear all the payments in thirteen monthly instalments. To execute the agreements and to have a strict vigilance over the movements of the ruler Ralph Leak was sent as the first British Resident to Agartala. In this fashion an independent state turned into a princely state under the British supremacy:

On the other side Balram Manikya a descendant of Jagat Manikya gained control over Roshanabad and declared himself as ruler. The Nawab of Bengal accorded recognition to Balram Manikya. The British who had entered into a treaty with Krishnamoni, helped him to capture Roshanabad from Balram Manikya. Abdul Razzaq, who was as administrator of Roshanabad during Shamsher Ghazi's time also started sneaking raids to gain control over Roshanabad. He took up cudgels even with the Nawab of Bengal and in encounter with the Nawab's forces he lost his life.

Khuchung Chang a Kuki Chief instigated his tribal brethren to rise in revolt against Krishna Manikya who after a prolonged and difficult campaign suppressed the Kuki revolt. At about the same time even the British claimed their right over Roshanabad. The action was not limited to the staking of the claim but Leak in a surprising move occupied Roshanabad. Krishan Manikya had no resources to fight the British and thus ate the humble pie silently and forgot about Roshanabad.

Nonetheless, his calmness and no reaction on the issue brought him Roshanabad back after a decade. Krishna Manikya was also a King interested in cultural affairs. The Seventeen jewel temple, i.e. satero Ratna Mandir at Jagannathpur was his creation. Besides granting land plots to some poor Brahmans he is also said to have performed many sacrificial feats. He expired on July 11, 1781. After him there ensued a dispute over his succession. The main dispute was between Durgamoni a son of Lakshmana Manikya and Rajdhar Manikya a nephew of Krishna Manikya.

The deceased had died issueless. The widow of the deceased, so as to avoid a civil war, thought it wise to become ruler herself. Thus Jahnavi Devi herself took the reins of administration in her hands. She ruled for about a couple of years and her time witnessed one of the worst faminer in the history of Tripura.

The East India Company that had her vested interest in the region desired to have a King of their choice. No wonder Warren Hastings, the then Governor General of the Company, raked up the succession dispute and forced the Queen to quit. Warren Hastings resolved the dispute in 1785 by making Rajdhar Manikya as the King and Durgamoni Manikya as the Yuvaraj, i.e. Prince, who had to be paid an honorarium from the state treasury.

In 1804, the King died and there again ensued a succession dispute between Durgamoni Manikya and Ramganga Manikya a son of the deceased. Even the courtiers were divided into two camps. Durgamoni Manikya sought British intervention.

In 1808, the British accorded recognition to Durgamoni and made him the ruler under the name of Durga Manikya. He ascended the throne in 1809 but died just after 4 years in 1813 again giving rise to a cold war of succession. The British, however, accorded recognition to Ramganga Manikya who became ruler for the second time in 1813 for 13 years.

After his death the same story got repeated. The brothers of the deceased King, viz. Kashi Chandra and Shambhu Chandra were the main contestants. The former bribed the latter by way of granting him a monthly pension of Rs. 500 and became ruler in 1826 under the name of Kashi Manikya. He, however, died in 1829.

After Kashi's death ramganga Manikya's son Krishna Kishore Manikya succeeded to the throne in 1829. He shifted the capital from Agartala (old) to Natun Haveli: The displeased, annoyed and unhappy relatives of the new ruler secretly started inciting the Kuki's to rise in revolt in the peripheral villages. Their aim was to attract the attention of the British towards the deteriorating conditions.

The Kukis created disturbances and when the ruler failed to quell the disturbances, he came in direct confrontation with the British who desired peace at all costs. The ruler otherwise was more involved in merry making, hunting excursions, sports and such cultural activities and paid no attention towards the state administration or public welfare. His recreating activities other wise started impoverishing the state treasury.

The King died of a lightning shock in 1849 and at that time the state exchequer was totally bankrupt. Ishar Chandra Manikya, a son of Krishna Kishore Manikya had an easy access to the throne and he was coroneted in February, 1850. His period has been very eventful in the annals of Tripura. Some of the unhappy events resulted from the domineering and over enthusiastic behaviour of his Dewan Balram Hazari.

The latter in an attempt to prove more loyal than the King, became a very strict collector of revenue and other taxes from the public. In an area where natural calamities often prey upon the crops, people some times become utterly helpless. The Dewan, however, should no leniency in this regard. His sole object was to collect taxes and when people could not pay he used very cruel, barbaric and torturous methods to extract taxes. The mute and helpless people have also a limit of toleration. Amidst such worst confounded circumstances Kirti and Parikshit emerged two very strong public leaders who incited the masses to rise in arms against the Dewan and the ruler. They masterminded the 1850 revolt popularly known as Tipra Revolt.

The ruler had a very tough time and it was with a great difficulty that the King succeeded in suppressing the revolt. The First War of Indian Independence, earlier known as Sepoy Mutiny, had its echoes even in this farthest corner of Tripura. The 34 Native Infantry Battalion was stationed at Chittagong in 1857.

Some of its soldiers, on hearing the news of revolt in other parts of India revolted and deserted the battalion. They thought it safer to enter a princely State where they hoped to get shelter. The Tripura ruler like many other native princes sided with the British and instead of offering shelter to the revolting soldiers he got all such persons arrested and sent them to the British army authorities at Chittagong and thereby earned the gratitude of the British overlords.

The Kukis, as already narrated, were a highly dissatisfied lot and at times revolted against the Tripura ruler. Apart from being unhappy with the Tripura King the Kukis were unhappy with the British also. They did not entertain the entry of any alien within their jurisdiction. They wanted to live in their own way with no interference from any one. In 1860, they started raiding and plundering settlements falling not only within Tripura but also in the British controlled parts.

Since the Kukis were the residents of Tripura their such activities displeased the British towards Tripura King also. The British authorities thought of taking a direct action against the Tripura ruler but latter's services rendered in 1857 always came to his rescue. Instead of taking punitive actions against the ruler the British started discussing the issue with the ruler to find ways and means to put an end to the recurrence of Kuki nuisance.

The King, on the advice of the British agreed to create five frontier posts manned by 25 soldiers each. A 150 armed personnel stockade was also created to keep regular vigilance on the Feni stream which was often used as a course by the Kukis to trespass into the British territory. The Prince also agreed to appoint five British drill sergeants in his army so that his soldiers could receive training in the modern warfare, strategy and manipulation.

Finally the King promised to provide all facilities to the British Survey team so that every inch of the Tripura territory could be surveyed and mapped on topographical sheets.

Ishar Chandra Manikya breathe his last in 1862 and after him his younger brother Bir Chandra Manikya occupied the throne. He was a progressive and forward looking man. Fortunately he had in the person of Babu Nilmoni Das a very farsighted, foresighted as well as efficient Advisor who always used to think ahead of his times.

The ages long custom of *sati* (self-immolation of a widow on the pyre of her deceased husband) widely prevalent among the Hindu populace was legally abolished in this State. Taking cue from the British, the Tripura ruler on the advice of his Dewan reorganised, remodelled and revamped his armed forces as well as civil administration. The Sate also adopted a proper budget system.

The collection of revenue was streamlined which besides effecting timely collection also enhanced the revenue receipts. Judiciary too was also reformed and steps were taken to impart justice speedily. Babu Nilmoni Dass was behind all these welfare measures which brought happiness to the subject and peace to the ruler. In recognition of his services, Babu Nilmoni Dass was elevates as Dewan (Prime Minister) in 1873.

During Bir chandra's period, Parikshat once again raised the banner of revolt against the ruler but he had to face a crushing defeat. On the advice of his Dewan, the King this time persuaded the Kuki Nagas to put an end to the revolt. Since the Kuki's were very happy with the welfare measures adopted by the King, they whole-heartedly obeyed the orders of their ruler and ruthlessly crushed the uprising.

However, a sad event for Tripura also took place during this time. By this time the British hunger for territorial aggradisement had grown multifold and they had coveted eye on each and every inch of the Indian territory. They just hunted this or that pretext to lay their hands upon a territory. As usual in this mountainous areas, one or the other tribe is in revolt.

This time the Lushais inhabiting the belt lying between Longai and Dhaleshwari streams revolted. This revolt, howsoever insignificant it might had been politically, came handy to the British who annexed an area measuring about 850 square miles of the Tripura territory. British wrote to the King that he was unable to contain the revolting Lushais and such a situation was detrimental to the British interests.

Thus apart from annexing the aforesaid territory, the British also stationed a British Agent at Agartala to safeguard the British interests. However, this position was abolished after seven years.

Bira Chandra Manikya period was the golden period of the Tripura History.

The King besides being a good administrator was also a great patron of music, fine art, literature and learning. He himself was a fairly good poet who is credited to have composed hundreds of lyrics.

It was he who discovered and appreciated the budding genius in Young Rabindranath Thakur after reading his collection of verses entitled Bhagan Hridaya, i.e. the Broken Heart. Whereas, some chosen poets, scholars, musicians and other artists adorned his court, he extended help and financial support to many other artists living in different parts of Tripura.

Radha Kishore Manikya the son of Bir Chandra Manikya succeeded to the throne after latter's demise. Radha Kishore Manikya who had closely watched his father working in the interest of public welfare and promoting cultural activities among the masses on becoming a ruler meticulously extended his father's policies as far as the welfare of the subjects and recognition of artists and literary personnel was concerned. He had all the good intentions to further, the causes espoused by his father as also to effect changes where his father could not do anything for want of time. He reorganised the departments of police, public health, education and agriculture on western lines.

Land reforms, with a view to help small landholders, petty peasants and landless agricultural labourers, were introduced and the collection of revenue was streamlined to collect it properly so that the money thus pouring in regularly could be spent upon public welfare activities. The Victoria Memorial Hospital got built by him stands till today as a testimony of his welfare activities.

The museum, a school and the Jagannath temple are yet other instances of his benevolently philanthropic nature aimed towards the welfare of his subjects. Jagdish Chandra Bose, who later on rose to occupy a place of pride among the galaxy of world scientists of international repute and renown received financial help and generous grants from the Tripura ruler to pursue his research studies in his youth which provided him the anchor sheet for his future research projects.

The first noble laureate of this country, Guru Rabindra Nath Tagore received generous financial assistance from Radha Kishore Manikya for the establishment of Shantiniketan which today is one of the proud institutions of the country in the form of Vishwa Bharati, a Central University. The Jadavpur University Calcutta today sprawls over the campus of once the Bengal Technical Institute for the establishment and development of which Radha Kishore Manikya had extended liberal donations.

The famous blind Bangla poet Hem Chandra Bandhopadhyaya received financial assistance and patronage from this Tripura ruler. Radha Kishore Manikya also initiated the publication of the Tripura Gazetteer, the back issues of which are a reference manual to historians, sociologists, economists, geographers, bio-scientists, other academicians and researchers. However, such an enlightened, philanthropic capable ruler died in a fatal motor accident in Varanasi in 1909 in the prime of his age.

After the sad demise of Radha Kishore Manikya, which led to gloom not only in Tripura but also in the cultural capital of India, i.e. Calcutta, his son Birender Kishore Manikya succeeded as Tripura ruler. He also had the intention and will of furthering the public welfare policies of his illustrious father.

Apart from that he also thought of bringing in diversifications which could help his subjects. He too got built another school since like his father he believed that only literate and skilled subjects could be meaningfully constructive resource for the state. With a view to raise extra revenue as also to provide employment opportunities to more and more people he introduced plantations at suitable places in Tripura. Himself being an excellent painter he extended full patronage to painters, poets, scholars, musicians, dancers and other artists. But to the misfortune of Tripura he too died in the prime of his youth in 1923.

Birendra Kishore Manikya was succeeded by an equally enlightened young man, his son Bir Bikram, who had not yet attained adulthood. Thus from 1923 to 1927 when Bir Bikram came of age, he ruled as a minor King with the help of a regent. The Bir Bikram's investiture ceremony was held in 1927. Bir Bikram taking pride in his ancestral history preferred to be called Maharaja, *i.e.* King of Kings than Manikya. He asserted that the title of Maharaja had been conferred upon one of his illustrious forefather by no less than the sage Kapil Rishi and thus he should be addressed as Maharaja.

Maharaja Bir Bikram was an awakened ruler who could read the writings on the wall particularly in view of the then very vigorously pursued freedom struggle in different part of the country. The movement after having engulfed the entire Indian territory then directly under the control of the British had also started sneaking into the princely states. As a first step to appease his subjects he decentralised the state administration and also introduced certain economic reforms.

For such steps he first visited some countries of Far East, Europe and Anglo-America to gain first hand knowledge about the latest trends in public administration. First of all he constituted three bodies to decentralise his administration. These were Mantrana Sabha (Advisory Council), Mantri Prishad (Executive Council) and Byabasthapak Sabha (Legislative Council). He devised some definitely concrete plans, projects and schemes to develop the agricultural sector so as to raise the total production as well as per acre yields of different crops. He also called upon the tribal communities to give up slash-and-burn cultivation and take to settled terraced farming. The aerodrome at Singerbed near Agartala owes its existence to the foresight and far-sight of Maharaja Bir Bikram who could at that time evaluate the economic and political importance of linking Tripura by air with other parts of the country. His farsightedness can be gauged from one of his unaccomplished tasks also.

For developing the countryside he was planning to set up a Rural University (similar to the farm universities of today) in Tripura but such an idea occurred to him quite late and his death did not permit to translate his dream into reality.

On the social scenario he had visualised a great threat to Hinduism by the increasing net of Christian Missionaries in the tribal dominated areas of North Eastern India. He knew that after providing educational and medical services to these hitherto neglected people living in isolation the Christians shall slowly and steadily start their conversion to their own faith.

On the other hand he was also fully aware of the fact that Hinduism has no provision for conversion and it shall never open its doors for those who are non-Hindus by birth. Thus similar to the Harijan leader Dr. Bhimrao Baba Saheb Ambedkar, he thought of encouraging Buddhism in his state so that these people could be attracted towards this faith, an offshoot of Hinduism.

Benuban Vihar, the Buddhist monastery in Agartala was got built by him shortly before his demise. It was also in Tripura of this period that Gurudev Rabindra Nath Tagore was conferred with the title of Bharat Bhaskar, i.e. the Sun of India, in a specially convened durbar, on his birthday.

The most important event during the rule of Maharaja Bikram Singh was the extension of India's Freedom Struggle in the then relatively quiet region of India. Thus it is worthwhile and interesting as well to recall the evolution of Freedom struggle in Tripura.

Similar to all other princely ruled States of India, in Tripura also the freedom movement had two faces. A section of people lent a wholehearted support to the national level movement and wished that it must include the freedom of princely states from the autocratic, authoritarian and outmoded rule of the native princes.

On the other hand the native rulers as well as their stooges wanted that native princes should continue as such with certain concessions to the subjects in the form of their involvement in the management of local self government institutions. Nonetheless, Bengal was that part of the country at that time where activities of the terrorists and extremists were at their climax. Tripura being an adjoining territory it too started feeling the echoes and experiencing repercussions of all these activities.

The wanted leaders of the Anusilan as well as Jugantar parties of Bengal started sneaking into Tripura where like minded people gave them shelter and saved them from the British wrath. During such sojourns the leaders used to impress upon the Tripuris to overthrow the ages old bossing princely rules. As a result of it the youth of Tripura were first to be influenced.

Hence in the Year 1927, the very year when Maharaja Bir Bikram was formally enthroned the Chhatra Sangh, i.e. Students Union came into being in Tripura. It was the Anusilan Samiti of Bengal that incited and helped students to form a forum where they could very often meet and chalk out their programmes to overthrow the native rule and install a democratic set up. Some mature age group people also got inspiration from the Chhatra Sangha and formed the Bhratri Sangha, i.e. Brother's Union. To being with it was floated as a cultural organisation but soon it turned into a political body.

Slowly and gradually some other bodies of revolutionary groups started appearing in different parts of Tripura. The Matri Sangha and the Milan Sangha were such two important bodies.

Among all the afore mentioned political organisations, it was Bhratri Sangha which became active and started dominating the political scene of the region. The Bhratri Sangha celebrated 26th of January, 1930 as independence day and issued a call to the students to observe strike.

With the conniving support of the Anusilan Samiti a daring dacoity was committed on the soil of Tripura. The British authorities in neighbouring Bengal got concerned about the deteriorating law and order situation in Tripura. It was felt that either the native police was incompetent or was hand in glove with the extremists in such a manner that culprits could not be apprehended.

Thus the British coerced the King to sign axe agreement with them vide which the British police could apprehend the terrorists even within the jurisdiction of the Tripura rule. As a result of this agreement the British succeeded in arresting many members of the Bhratri Sangh who were released in 1938.

The same year the Sangha decided to recast its aims, objectives, plans, proposal and activities on the lines of the Indian National Congress. As a result of it the Organisation was given a new nomenclature also, i.e. Tripura Rajya Gana Parishad. Among the prominent pioneers of the new Organisation were Sachindra Lal Singh, Sukhomoni Sengupta, Hariganga Basak and Umesh Lal Singh. The new policies and orientations aroused the interest of the masses in its activities. The party leaders took up extensive tours of the country and listened to the grievances and problems of the poor ruralities.

The Parishad pressed for land reforms, since without that it did not see the salvation of the poor peasants. Even in those days. On the socio-economic front rural development was the thrust area of the Parishad. The Maharaja was obviously up set on the new developments. Small wonder he instigated his stooges to float a parallel party. Thus Janamangal Samiti (Public Welfare Organisation) came into existence which demanded a responsible government under the aegies of the Maharaja itself.

During the World War of 1939-45, Maharaja Bir Bikram, like an overriding number of princely rulers, lent a support to the British with men and material. Two battalions of the Tripura forces, viz., the First Tripura Rifles and the Mahabir Legion were mentioned in dispatches by the British Government for their bravery and courage exhibited during the was on the Arakan and Burma fronts.

The services rendered by the Tripura ruler were highly appreciated and the British promised to extend any help needed by the ruler at any time. At the same time the revolutionaries within Tripura accelerated their activities. Many of the hard core revolutionaries of Tripura and the die hard Bengali extremists hiding, themselves in Tripura were traced and expelled from Tripura. Notwithstanding such repressive measures taken by the Tripura ruler, the revolutionaries continued to sneak into the peripheral villages and guided as well as assisted the local people to rise in arms against the native ruler.

The British on the other hand searched for these Tripura revolutionaries in British territory, caught hold of them and handed them over to the Tripura ruler to treat them as he liked. In fact the British were repaying the native ruler for his meritorious services rendered to them during the World War. All activities of the revolutionaries as those of political activists were declared illegal during the war period. Thus all such persons were detained in the Agartala goal without any trial and were released only in 1945 after the Second World War came to its end.

The Tripura Rajya Jana Samiti, i.e. the Tripura State Public Education Society was set up in 1945. The objective of the sponsors was that once masses were educated they shall themselves start caring for their social, political and economic rights. This body helped in the opening up and management of some educational institutions for about a year. Later on as a result of dissensions created by the British, the ruler and their stooges among the rank and file of this body and those of the Janamangal Samiti came to be divided on basic issues.

Nevertheless, parallel to the Praja Mandal movement in many of the princely states, the Tripura Rajya Praja Mandal came into being in 1946. A majority of the members of the earlier two organisations joined this body while some persons with leftist leanings also joined it. The principal demand of this newly formed organisation was the formation of a responsible government elected by the people.

Similar to the national scene the Muslim subjects of the state were also divided in two diversely opposed groups. One group like the national Muslims in the Indian National Congress had joined Praja Mandal and worked for ethnic unity and did not want to be swayed by those who wanted a separate Islamic state.

The Anjumane Islamia nevertheless had different designs. This party was floated by Abdul Bari Khan popularly known as Oedu Mian. Parallel to the Muslim League some Muslims of this region also wanted a separate State but the nationalist carried the day with them. Even the Tripura Rajya Muslim Praja Majlis floated by Arman Ali and Farid Mian worked for a united Tripura. In 1946, the Tripura State Congress was also set up. It was established as a subsidiary group of the Indian National Congress and to begin with was floated as a district unit of the Bengal Provincial Congress.

The Tripura Rajya Gana Parishad was also merged in it. All these organisations with national leanings wanted the native rule to go. Maharaja Bir Bikram was otherwise an intelligent man who got convinced by the revolutionary as well as political activities going on within and outside Tripura that ultimately the native princely rules shall have no place in India. Thus credit goes to his prudence that before he breathed his last on May 17, 1947 he decided to accede Tripura to the proposed independent India.

Maharaja Bir Bikram died before the British could hand over the administration of India to its people leaving behind a minor heir apparent. The minor ruler Kirti Bikram started ruling the state with the help a Regency Council. Minor ruler's mother Maharani Kanchan Prabha Devi assumed the Presidentship of the Regency Council. Oedu Mian's Anjuman Islamia was secretly hand in glove with those who wanted Tripura to be integrated with the then proposed East Pakistan.

Oedu Mian had even made an inroad into the palace itself, so that his agents working there could deliver him the goods as and when desored by him. Nevertheless, their ill designs were intercepted and the Maharani saved the situation from going out of her hands. On the advice of the newly formed Union Government of India and particularly the then Union Home Minister and the First Deputy Prime Minister of India, Sardar Vallabh Bhai Patel, the Regency Council was dissolved and the Maharani was permitted to carry on as the sole regent for the minor King.

Thereafter, negotiations between the Maharani and the Union Government, related to the merger of Tripura with India, as per wishes of the late King, were started. The agreement was arrived at and signed by both the parties on September 9, 1949.

On October 15, 1951 the state was merged with India and accorded the status of a Part C State. A Chief Commissioner, as head of the state was appointed by the Government of India. An advisory Council with three advisers was set up to advise the head of the state. Two of the advisers were top Congress leaders from Tripura while the third was a retired civil servant. They were appointed through a Presidential Order on April 14, 1953.

The States Reorganisation Commission Recommended a Union Territory Status for Tripura. Hence on November 1, 1956 Tripura was accorded the recommended status. A 32 member Territorial Council was also provided for Tripura.

Out of them, two had to be nominated by the President of India while the rest had to be elected by the state electorate. The Council came into functional operation on August 15, 1957, exactly a decade after India won freedom. The Council had nine State subjects and one concurrent subject within its jurisdiction.

The chairperson of the Council was the political Chief while the Chief Executive Officer as head of the Union Territory Bureaucracy. The designation of the Chief Commissioner was changed as Administrator. He as Head of the state appointed the Chief Executive Officer, while the chairman of the council was elected by the council members.

In the year 1963, the Indian Parliament amended the country's Constitution to provide a Legislature and a Council of Ministers for Tripura. The number of legislators was limited to 33 out of which three had to be nominated by the President of India. Earlier to it a bill passed by the Territorial Council needed prior approval of the Parliament before being submitted to the President for his assent. But now, the bill passed by the legislature could directly go to the President for his consent.

The Council of Ministers was an advisory body to the Administrator. In case there arose any controversy between the Council of Ministers and the Administrator the verdict of the President of India had to be final. Nonetheless, keeping in view the sensitive nature and strategic location of the state, notwithstanding the provision of a popular and responsible government, the authority of the President was kept Supreme and final over the state administration.

In the year 1971, the state was provided with a Lieutenant Governor in place of the Administrator as head of the state. Finally on December 30, 1971 the Indian Parliament passed the North eastern Area Reorganisation Act. Under this act the existing arrangement terminated on January 21, 1972 and Tripura became a full fledged state of the Indian Union with a Governor as head of the state.

Post-independence Era

On 1 July 1963, Tripura was declared as the Union Territory of India. It developed into a full-fledged state on 21 Jan. 1972. After the Indo-Pak of 1971, Tripura is facing the problem of armed conflicts. The Tripura National Volunteers, the National Liberation Front of Tripura and the All Tripura Tiger Force emerged as groups during this time to chase off the Bengalis, who migrated in masses from Bangladesh.

4

Geography

- -

Geomorphology and Geology

Geomorphology

Geomorphologically, the state of Tripura represents the western fringe of typical "ridge and valley" province of the late Tertiary fold mountain belt, commonly known as Indo-Burman ranges (Purbanchal range). The general elevation varies between 780 m in the north eastern part to 15 m in the western part above mean sea level. Five prominent roughly north south trending anticlinal strike ridges traverse the state from east to west; these are Jampui, Sakhantlang, Longtarai, Athramura and Baramura. This strike ridges form the watershed of the Meghna basin of Bangladesh fed by Khowai, Haora, Juri, Manu, Dhalai, Deo, Longai, Muhuri, Feni and Gomoti rivers. Ten physiographic units have been identified by the Geological Survey of India (1999) in the state of Tripura which are given below:

Physiographic Unit of Tripura:

- Steeping slopping and slightly dissected high relief structural hills and ridges exemplified by areas like Kailashahar, Panisagar, Baramura, Teliamura, etc.

- Moderately slopping with moderately dissected medium relief parallel ridges present in north and north eastern part of Tripura.

- Moderately slopping and highly dissected, low relief structural hills and ridges found in the northwest and southern part of the state.

- Moderately to gently slopping and moderately dissected flat topped denuded hill occurring in western, central and southern part of Tripura.

- Low lying residual hill with valley represented by Gonda charra area of south eastern part of Tripura.

- Undulatory plain with low mounds and gently slopping valley situated mostly in the western and southern part of Tripura.

- Moderately to gently slopping inter-hill valley with upland mostly occurring on the northern- eastern and southern part of the state.

- Moderately to gently slopping inter-hill valleys with alluvial upland plains, represented by Kumarghat-Chailengta area as alluvial deposit of river Manu.

- Rolling upland common in some pockets of the west and northwestern part of Tripura.

- Flood plain constitute important area rornled by rivers of Tripura. Studied area Krishnakishore nagar and Jampuri fall under this group.

Geology: The state of Tripura exhibit an wide array of sedimentary rocks characteristics of marine-mixed-fluvia type origin ranging age from upper most Oligocene (38 million years from present time) to Recent period. These sediments, according to GSI, have been laid down in the Surma basin during Tertiary age (which lasted for 65 million years) in an wide range of environmental conditions governed by local tectonic movement. Tectonically, the region now comprises a series of subparallel arquate, elongated, doubly plunging folds arrange in north south direction. These folds for anticlines separated by wide flat sinclines. The group of sediments during different geological age are shown in table on litho-stratigraphy.

Table: Stratigraphy of Tripura

Age	Group	Formation
Holocene		Khowai Formation Ghilatoli Formation Teliamura Formation Kalyanpur Formation
Quaternary	Dupitila	Dupitila Formation
Upper Pliocene to Pleistocene Pliocene	Tipam	Upper Tipam FormationLower Tipam Formation
Micocene- Lr. Pliocene	Surma	Bokabil Formation
Upper most Oligocene		Upper Bhuban Formation Middle Bhuban Formation Lower Bhuban Formation (Not exposed in Tripura)

Seismic surveys in the region reveal the presence of subsurface flatus. The part of Surma basin in Tripura Mizoram area lies in close proximity to the Shillong plateau in the north and Aracan Yoma belt to the east. Tripura is therefore located in seismically active zone; because of inherent character of sediments of these areas even the minor shock during earthquake may cause devastating particularly landslides.

Natural Resources

The mineral resources of any state provide an avenue for economic development but the process of mining may have extensive impact on land, soil and water resources. The mining projects have as a consequence become a part of development sector requiring environmental clearance under Environmental Protection Act, 1986, EIA Notification 1994

In Tripura, the mineral resources are mainly glass sands, limestone, plastic clay and hard rock; all of these material are being used to a variable degree. However, the single most important resource in the state is oil and natural gas. ONGC or Oil and Natural Gas Commission has initiated massive exploration programme in the state, details of which are dealt later. As for the other minerals, following table provides an account of locations, deposit, current uses, etc. Details of clay deposit in Tripura has been dealt in the state of Environment Report for Tripura (1989). The impact of mining and quarrying of mineral resources in Tripura has so far been insignificant.

Table: Mineral Resource of Tripura

Mineral	Location	Uses
Hard Rock	Jampui Hills Longatari Hill	Road metals
Limestone	Sakhan & Jampui Range Manpui area (9,90,000t reserve)	Not suitable Cement Suitable for inferior quality of Lime Puzzolana mix.
Clay	All over the State generally in river bank deposit Good clay deposit in West and South region. Total 1.73 million ton deposit in four zone out of six zones *[* Mohanpur-Bamutia-Kamalghat; Bisramganj-Bagma; Champamura-Baldakhal-Jogendranagar; Khowai-Teliamura-Ampi; Shantirbazar-Udaipur; Kumarghat and Baidyathakurpara-Anadanagar- Maheshkhola-Dukli-Sonamura area]	Sanitary ware Stone wares Sewerage pipes Electric insulator Refractory grade
Glass Sand	Bishramganj (1,60,000t) Old Agartala (16,000t) Jogendranagar (3,627t) Sekerkota (80,000t) Dasharambari (5,330t) Mohanpur (97,875t) Baidyathakurpara- Anadanagar Maheshkhola and Dukli (NA) Total Reserve 3,62,832 tonnes	Many uses

Of the total geographical area of Tripura, 76 per cent can be marked as of "Tertiary" origin and 24 per cent belong to Quaternary period; none of these contain any major mineral resource. A GSI Report of 1982 provide a list of Non-metallic and metallic mineral vis-a-vis their location or otherwise in Tripura indicating the poor profile.

Table: Mineral Resource potential in Tripura

Sl. No.	Mineral	Status
A. Non-metallic		
1.	Lime stone	Commodity not located or absent
2.	Dolomite	Commodity not located or absent
3.	Coal	Commodity not located or absent
4.	Clay	Commodity not located or absent
5.	Refractories	Commodity not located or absent
6.	Glass sand	Good reserve, low grade
7.	Graphite	Commodity not located or absent
8.	Fertilizer	Commodity not located or absent
9.	Gravel sand silt	Good reserve, low grade
10.	Building stone	Commodity not located or absent
B. Metallic		
11.	Ferrous	Commodity not located or absent
12.	Non-ferrous	Commodity not located or absent
13.	Noble metals	Commodity not located or absent

The current production of natural gas in estimated at one million cubic metres per day. The available figure for 1990-91 to 1997-98 shows a fast increasing rate of production from 70 million tonnes per year in 1990-91 to 2.7 in 8 years reaching 196 million tonnes in 1997-98.

Natural Gas

Availability: Tripura has vast reserves of natural gas in non-associate form. The gas is of high quality, with high methane content of up to 97 per cent. ONGC has been actively engaged in exploration activities in the state since 1972. Based on the exploration work so far, ONGC has estimated the total Gas Reserves as under:

- Prognosticated Reserves: 400 BCM.
- In Place (GIIP) Reserves: 44.84 BCM.
- Balance Recoverable Reserves: 23.73 BCM.
- Present Production Potential: 4.03 MMSCMD.

The Exploration activities are being stepped up by ONGC. Not only that, one Bid Block of Tripura has also been included in third round of bidding under NELP of the Ministry of Petroleum and Natural Gas. With these ongoing efforts, the availability of natural gas in Tripura is expected to significantly go up in near future.

Utilisation

Presently, natural gas is being utilised mainly for the Power Projects of the State Government/NEEPCO (a Central Government Undertaking). The present utilisation of natural gas is about 1.20 MMSCMD. A small quantity of gas is also being used for gas supply to domestic/ commercial/small industrial consumers. Thus, the balance about 2.80 MMSCMD gas is presently available for setting up industrial projects, using natural gas as feedstock.

Gas Pricing

One major advantage in setting up a gas-based project in Tripura is the concessional pricing of natural gas for Northeastern Region. The current consumer price at landfall point is about Rs. 1,700 per 1,000 SCM for North-East, as against general price of Rs. 2,850 per 1000 SCM. Further discount of up to Rs. 300/MCM is possible in the North East, on case-to-case basis. Thus, the natural gas is available in the North East at almost half the price as compared to other parts of the country.

Prospects

The availability of superior quality natural gas, at concessional price, offers a great opportunity to prospective investors, to set up gas-based industrial units, using natural gas as Feedstock, like urea, methanol, PVC and other projects. Besides this, Natural gas can also be utilised as a cheaper source of energy for various energy-intensive industrial projects.

Tripura Natural Gas Industry

Tripura Natural Gas Industry is one of the major industries that has sprung up in the Northeastern State of India. The state is repository of natural gases that are in non-associate form. The gases are high in quality and have more than 97 per cent methane content. However, H2S, sulphur and other noxious elements are almost entirely absent from these natural gases.

The Oil and Natural Gas Corporation (ONGC), the nation's premier natural gas reserve has undertaken extensive exploration activities and research work to estimate the nation's gas reserves as follows:

- Established Gas Reserves: 30.65 BCM.
- Present Production Potential: 2.03 MMSCMD.

- Prognosticated Reserves: 400 BCM.
- Net Recoverable Reserves: 16.91 BCM.

In fact, the Government of India is on the verge of entering into a contract with M/S Oklands International of USA that will take up extensive research activities to determine the natural gas production and utilisation capacity in Tripura.

The natural gas reserves of Tripura primarily cater to the State Government and Central Government projects and statistics reveal that the current utilisation of natural gas is 0.80 MMSCMD and is expected to escalate to 1.25 MMSCMD within a very short span of time. Although, Tripura is located in the remote reaches of the northeast, the subsidised gas prices attract droves of investors, industrialists and nationwide agencies. The government is hopeful that this will augment the state's industrial growth.

The natural gas industry in Tripura credited to be one of the premier industries in Tripura that is destined to revolutionise the industrial growth and development and eventually emerge as a forerunner of the nation's business and commerce.

Land

Tripura, the ancient home of the Bodos, is situated between 20°56′ N and 24°32′ N and 91°10′ E and 92°21′ E. It is almost completely surrounded by Bangladesh on three sides, having a tenuous link with the rest of the country through the Cachar district of Assam. It has an international frontier of 1,000 kilometres towards the west, south, and northeast. Towards the north and east are the districts of Cachar and Mizo Hills in Assam. Its only access to the rest of the country is through a narrow strip of 30 kilometres into the Cachar district of Assam, the rest of the 160 kilometres frontier to Assam being through the high hill ranges of Mizo Hills.

The whole region from Assam to the Arakans, including Tripura, is traversed by a series of folds running approximately north to south which give rise to parallel hill ranges separated by broad synclinal valleys. Topographically the entire territory can be broadly classified into hill ranges, plain lands including valleys, and river basins. The hill ranges broadly run north to south losing altitude till they merge into the plains of Bangladesh. They gradually increase in height from west to east. They send out lateral ranges or offshoots which closely approach others sent out from the successive main ranges.

These divide the territory into broad parallel valleys, the area of which consists of low undulating *tilas*. The floors of the valleys also rise in succession from west to east, co-respective of the drainage of the country. Tortuous streams with innumerable small tributaries flow from these ranges through these valleys into the plains of Bangladesh where they mingle and merge with the waters of the Padma and the Ganges.

The six principal hill ranges in Tripura are the Jampui, Sakhan, the Longtharai Atharamura, the Sardang, the Baramura-Devtamura and Atharamura ranges.

The Jampui range is situated in Dharamnagar subdivision and is 74 kilometres in length. One of its peaks, the Betling Sib (1,000 m), is the highest altitude found in Tripura. This range is mainly inhabited by the Lushais and the Reangs, the Lushais having their villages on the top of the ridge and the Reangs on both the slopes.

The top villages have now been connected by a jeepable road which will connect with Damcherra Phuldungsei. These villages in their turn are connected with Reang villages on the slopes and in the valleys by narrow tracts constructed by the local people themselves with the help of the government. The Sakhan range forms the boundary of the Dharamnagar and Kailashahar subdivision and its northern part is known as the Unakuti. The length of this range is 58 kilometres and that of Unakuti 20 kilometres. Its highest peak is the Sakhan (840 m) on which the Lushais have made a delightful village.

This range like others is also solely occupied by the tribals amongst whom are the Darlongs who are of the Kuki clan. The Longtharai range forms the boundary of Kailashahar and Kamalpur subdivisions and is about 48 kilometres long. Its highest peak is Longtharai (515 m).

There are many rivers in the state which rise from these hill ranges and, after being fed by innumerable small *cherras*, flow through the valleys into the mighty rivers of East Bengal. They are fed only by rain water, most of them drying up during the winter and swelling dangerously during the monsoons, causing destructive floods. The Lungai, Juri and Deo rivers rise from Jampui range. They are respectively 98 kilometres, 79 kilometres and 132 kilometres in length. The Longai runs north between Jampui and Mizo Hills and then enters Assam near Damcherra.

The upper portion of the river is known as *Saisilui*, Tulianpui and Sai Lutlai. It has many tributaries of which the more important ones are Kalagang, Manachhara, Damcharra on the left bank and Boaraibui and Gabaicharra on the right. The Juri meets the Ragna of Dharamnagar and flows along the western boundary of that subdivision towards Bangladesh.

The Deo runs northward from Jampui towards Kumarghat where it meets the Manu river forming an arc behind it. This is a ferocious river during the rains and causes great erosion on its banks. The Manu, known as Chaumanu in its upper portion, rises from the Sakhan range and meets innumerable small streams as it flows southward towards Kumarghat till finally it passes into Bangladesh by the side of Kailashahar town after a course of 167 kilometres. This also usually overflows its banks during the rainy seasons causing heavy floods.

The Dhalai and the Khowai rivers have their source in the Longtharai range, the latter being called *Maricherra* in its upper portion. They are 117 kilometres and 166 kilometres in length respectively. The Khowai river flows towards the northwestern direction up to Teliamura and then turns north till it enters Bangladesh near Khowai town. The source of Hawra river is the Baramura range and it runs for a length into Bangladesh. A sharp shower of a few hours is enough to bring this river in spate at which time it threatens the Agartala town.

The historic Gumati river is probably the most important in Tripura. The ancient capital of Tripura was situated at Udaipur which is washed by its waters. It flows almost along the centre of the state dividing it into two equal parts. It is navigable for small country rafts and barges and serves to open up the huge hinterland of Amarpur to river trade. Many towns were flourishing along its banks in ancient days as is evidenced by the ruins at Udaipur, Maharani and Amarpur.

It rises from the range connecting Longtharai and Atharamura. Raimacherra flows from the confluence of Kalyansingh and Malyansingh near Kanti Charan Para in the eastern part of Amarpur subdivision till it meets the Thermanadi near Duchaibari. The Therma then flows from north to south and after some distance assumes the name of Gumati and runs in a singularly serpentine course up to the Dumbur fall of Amarpur subdivision. The length of the Gumati is about 133 kilometres. It is a big river and runs across Amarpur, Udaipur and Sonamura subdivisions and then flows towards Bangladesh by the side of Sonamura town.

Geology

Tripura was covered by the sea during the earlier part of the Tertiary period. The shore line was said to be running in a wide arc from Garo to Mikir hills, the sea continuously receiving sediments formed by the denudation of soil from the shore. The drying up of the sea in the Oligocene period was followed by earth movements as a result of which the shore line resumed its original position during the Miocene period due to subsidence. The water, however, became shallow receiving sediments all the time. Extensive swampy and boggy areas are still found in Tripura, especially in the south. Towards the end of this period there were intensive earth movements resulting in the formation of high hills.

The present form that we find in this territory is entirely the result of weathering and erosion by rivers and streams.

Some of the rocks were deposited under shallow water conditions and are of fresh water origin. Some others were deposited under deep and tranquil water conditions and are of marine origin.

Soil

The soil of Tripura is sandy loam to loamy sand, clay loam to pure clay or lateritic. It is grey to brown in colour. Large tracts of soil is alluvium consisting of sand, silt and clay, pure sand being exclusively confined to the river beds. Except the sandy loam, all other varieties of soils become very sticky even after a shower, but they dry up very quickly.

Forestry

Over 95 per cent of the territory of Tripura was covered with luxurious forests about 50 years ago. It was this fact that got the princely State of Tripura the name of Hill Tipperah. But now, due to the extensive immigration of both tribal and non-tribal people from Bangladesh and due to the practice of *jhum* cultivation, unregulated and unrestricted fellings, grazing and repeated fires, much of these valuable forests have been destroyed and replaced with a vegetable cover like bamboo and savannah over extensive areas.

Wildlife

Not too long back, it is said, elephants used to graze in the fields where now the imposing structure of the Secretariat stands at Agartala. About 10 years ago a District Collector shot a huge tusker a few yards from the MBB College. At present, however, due to deforestation and extension of agricultural lands, wildlife has become scarce. But, in many of the forest areas like the Jampui, the Sakhan, Gandacherra, Raima, etc., herds of elephants are still found. Other varieties of wildlife found in Tripura are tigers, leopards, samber, barking deers, wild pigs, and monkeys. Wild buffaloes and bisons also exist, but they are on the verge of extinction.

Mineral Resources

The mineral resources of Tripura are meagre, apart from the clay found near Agartala, which is being used locally — Traces of lignite, coal, limestones and ochre have been reported, but the quality is poor and reserves too low to be of any commercial value. There is, however, a good possibility of striking oil in Tripura as the formations in which oil is found in Assam and Bangladesh occupy much of the territory here; it is optimistically stated in some knowledgeable circles that Tripura is floating on oil. Gas has already been found in test drilling.

The exposure of workable building material laterite have been found near Bagpasha, Silbari, Pabiacherra and Sindhukumarpara. Sandstones which can be suitably used as a road metal are found in the Gagracherra area and near Gorar Tila. The conglomerate beds from Bahuricherra quarry and near Atharamura range are also suitable for use as road metal.

Lignite deposits were traced at a place in Quarercherra branch of Ratikraicherra in continuation of the lignite deposits of Ujan Thangna. Some lignite has also been noticed near Hiracherra Tea Estate in Dhatuacherra and Indolacherra, near Natingcherraa Tea Estate.

Superficial nodules of ochre have been found in a dark grey clay seam in a valley below Bindapa-*tilla* hill in Belonia.

Petroleum

The rocks in Tripura are similar to the Burma strata where petroleum has been found. The Oil and Natural Gas Commission has carried out a detailed survey and they have found that the strata running into Tripura is the same as in nearby areas of Bangladesh where huge reserve of natural gas has been recently discovered.

Test drilling has been taken up. It is reasonably certain that natural gas will be found here in commercial quantities and there may be sufficient reserves of oil to run a refinery of 3 million tonnes capacity in the course of time if the expectations of the experts are fulfilled. It is likely that the economy of Tripura in future, like that of Kuwait, will be interlinked with its oil and natural gas resources.

Climate and Rainfall

Tripura is situated within the southwest monsoon belt. Usually the heaviest rain is between May and October, more than 90 per cent of the annual rainfall being received during these months. However, there is intermittent rain throughout the year, not a single month passing without rain. The average rainfall over the past 50 years has been over 250 centimetres.

Mosquitoes are very common in the valleys and also in the hills except in Jampui and Sakhan. The valleys are usually hot and humid though in the winter they tend to become exceedingly cold due to a thick mist over it. The sun succeeds in piercing it by 11.00 a.m. and 2 or 3 hours later again vanishes behind the hills.

Probably the coldest place in the plains of Tripura is Anand Bazar, located as it is between the Jampui and Sakhan hills.

The weather on the other hill ranges, apart from the Jampui and Sakhan hills, is not very pleasant. These hills are full of mosquitoes, flies and parasites of all sorts. Jampui hills, however, are very pleasant during the winter, a chilly breeze blowing across the hill top. It can easily be converted into a health resort in case transport facilities can be developed.

Climate

General Aspects: The State of Tripura experiences Humid Sub-tropical type of climate. The features of climate, however, vary between its different parts of the state. There are only two Meteorological Observatories at Agartala and Kailasahar in Tripura having the facility to record temperature and other weather information. Some of the important features of regional variation of climate with regard to temperature, rainfall, humidity and wind speed are described below.

Temperature

The normal temperature at Agartala and Kilasahar is 25.2°C and 25.0°C respectively. The temperature shows a declining trend from west to east. The daily maximum temperature and minimum mean temperatures are 30.70°C and 19.50°C respectively during summer months. The cold weather starts from about the end of November when the temperature of both day and night decreases steadily. January is the coldest month when mean daily minimum temperature is only 8.9°C and maximum temperature is 25.2°C. Average temperature in different years is given in following table.

Table: Average temperature in different years (in °C)

Year	Agartala		Kailasahar	
	Highest	*Lowest*	*Highest*	*Lowest*
1987	33.9	16.7	NA	NA
1988	33.4	16.3	NA	NA
1989	33.3	16.5	NA	NA
1990	34.1	16.1	NA	NA
1991	33.6	15.5	NA	NA
1992	33.2	16.0	NA	NA
1993	32.9	15.6	NA	NA
1994	33.4	15.9	NA	NA
1995	34.0	15.4	NA	NA
1996	34.2	14.8	NA	NA
1997	32.8	14.9	33.1	16.25
1998	32.1	16.7	33.3	17.5
1999	33.7	17.2	34.1	17.3
2000	NA	NA	NA	NA

Rainfall

A more sensitive element of climate is the variation in rainfall. It varies not only from place to place or from year to year, but also between seasons. Variation of rainfall between the districts over some years is shown in following table. Annual rainfall ranges from 1922 mm to 2,855 mm. The rainfall generally increases from southwest to northeast. There is a big gap in the rainfall content in southern central part around Amarpur, which is surrounded by 1,500 mm isohytes. The northeastern part of the state around Dharamnagar gets maximum rainfall.

Most of the rain comes during the months April-June and July to September. This period is generally referred to as the kharif season this is the major agricultural season of the whole State. The variation of kharif rainfall between the districts as also shown in following table.

The Factors governing rainfall are the seasonal changes in the direction of wind and the presence of cool upper air current over the given parts of the state. During the kharif season, large depressions develop over one or the other parts of the state.

Table: Average rainfall in different years (in centimetre)

District	1987	1988	1989	1999	1991	1992	1993	1994	1995	1996
West Dist.	271.6	333.0	200.7	254.6	297.5	172.8	269.1	146.3	207.8	192.2
North Dist.	228.8	325.3	255.1	260.8	337.6	226.8	373.4	226.6	223.8	222.5
South Dist.	249.7	337.8	230.5	313.5	373.8	173.8	372.6	182.4	251.1	209.4
Dhalai Dist.	NA	NA	NA	NA	NA	NA	NA	NA	323.7	285.5
Tripura	250.0	332.0	228.8	276.2	336.2	191.1	338.4	185.1	251.6	227.4

Table: Quarterly average rainfall in different district in 1996 (in Centimetre)

District	January- March	April-June	July-September	October-December
West District	11.4	88.2	69.6	23.0
North District	22.9	86.4	97.6	15.6
South District	11.1	92.2	77.9	28.2
Dhalai District	16.3	130.5	122.8	15.9
Tripura	15.4	99.3	92.0	20.7

Humidity: Humidity is generally high throughout the year. In the summer season the relative humidity is between 50 per cent to 74 per cent whereas in the rainy season it is over 85 per cent.

Wind Speed: The mean wind speed is 7.1 km per hour, with maximum of 13.1 km per hour in May and minimum of 3 km per hour in December.

Climate and Agriculture: The relationship between rainfall, temperature and farming is suitable to grow paddy crops in the plains, and bamboo trees and jhum cultivation on hills along with the scope for plantation of rubber, coffee, cashewnut, coconut and other evergreen and deciduous plants on the hilly and tilla land.

The state represents hypothermic soil temperature regime. On the basis of variation in rain fall, potential and actual evapotranspiration and length of crop growing period and their interrelationship, the state of Tripura has been divided into eight agroecological zones.

Table: Agroecological Zones in Tripura

Climate	Physiography	Soil Type	AWC	LGP	Moisture
Perhumid Hyperthermic	Northeastern hills/Purvachal	Red & Lateritic	150-199 mm/m	>300 days	
Humid Hyperthermic	Northeastern hills/Purvachal	Red & Lateritic	150-199 mm/m	>300 days	
Humid Hyperthermic	Northeastern hills/Purvachal	Red & Lateritic	150-199 mm/m	>300 days	80-100%
Humid Hyperthermic	Northeastern hills/Purvachal	Red & Lateritic	150-199 mm/m	>300 days	60-80%
Humid Hyperthermic	As above with high structural hills	Red & Lateritic	150-199 mm/m	>300 days	
Humid Hyperthermic	Northeastern hills/Purvachal	Red & Lateritic	150-199 mm/m	>300 days	40-60%
Humid Hyperthermic	Northeastern hills/Purvachal	Red & Lateritic	250 mm/m	<300 days	
Humid Hyperthermic	As above with high structural hills	Red & Lateritic	250 mm/m	<300 days	

Flora and Fauna

Flora

The flora of Tripura, Assam, Mizoram, Manipur, Meghalaya Arunachala Pradesh and Bangladesh are mostly common. The greater part of the territory of Tripura was, even 60 years ago, densely covered with primeval forests. Even today the mountainous eastern part of the state is covered with deciduous and evergreen forests. Different types of plants, herbs, grasses, creepers, bamboos, trees, vegetables, roots and fruits are available in both primeval forests and cultivated fields. Pineapple, mango, lichi, guava, betel-nut and leaf, lemon, banana, jackfruit, orange and black berries are abundantly available. The trees commonly\available in the forests are: Amalaki (Emblica myrobalan), Amda (hog plum Spondias piunata), Balda (Terminalia balerica), Chalita (Dillenia Indica), Chamal (Artocarpus chaplasha), chhatim (Alstonia scholaris), Dongar (Ficus hispida), Gamir (Gmelina,arborea), Garjan (Dipterocarpus turbinatus), Hargaial (Dillenia pentagyna), Jir (Ficus retusa) Karai (Albizia procera), Mandar (Erythrina indica). popatoon (Toona liliata), Royna (Aphanomixis polystachya), Udal (Sberclllia villosa), Vat (Ficus bengalensis), etc.

In plant composition the state may be divided mainly into two regions: (a) evergreen and (b) most deciduous forests. The former is characterised by a large number of species whose lower middle and top canopies remain evergreen with tall clear trunks. The other species in the forest may be deciduous or semi-deciduous but their presence does not affect the evergreen nature of the forest as a whole. Bamboos and canes are grown in abundance and small palms are common. There are numerous climbers in such type of forests. The undergrowth is often a tangle of canes.

A large number of herbaceous species comprises ground vegetation. Evergreen forests which once covered almost the entire area of the state were in the past practically inaccessible, and, therefore, had an unhindered growth. Most of the areas in Dharmanagar, Kailasahar, Bilonia, Sabrum and Kamalpur subdivisions, and the portion of the Sadar subdivision including Teliamura were covered with these luxuriant tropical evergreen forests. But the depletion of the forests began with World War II to meet the increasing demand for wood products.

The primitive method of shifting cultivation by the tribals *(jhooming)* also contributed greatly towards decimating the forest areas. At present, the evergreen forest is limited only to areas not suitable for *Jhoom* and plough cultivation, viz., in patches of stiff non-cultivable hill slopes and rocky river-banks. Most deciduous forest can be subdivided into two categories, viz., those characterised by the presence of *Sal (Shorea Robusta Gaertn)*, and those by the absence of it, called moist deciduous mixed forest.

The former category is found in the Bilonia, Udaipur, Sonamura and Sadar subdivisions. In certain areas particularly in Sonamura and Sadar subdivisions, the *Sal* forest areas have been reduced to a secondary savannah where much of the area Considerable breakthrough seems to have been achieved with the successful introduction of rubber plantation in Tripura· since mid-sixties. While in 1965 rubber plantation was confined to an area of 49 hectares only, in December 1975, the area was extended to about 575 hectares and in 1995-96 the Forest Development and Plantation Corporation has brought 6,641 hectares of land under rubber cultivation.

The production of rubber has gone up from 28.18 metric tons in 1977-78 to 1,850 tons in 1995-96 enabling the Corporation to earn Rs. 6.51 crores. The Corporation has set up 43 rubber processing centres in the state, and hopes to achieve a target of producing 10,000 tons of rubber bringing 55,000 hectares of land under its cultivation by the year 2000. Apart from increasing production, the scheme also aims at the rehabilitation of the shifting cultivators. The Tripura Rehabilitation Plantation Corporation claims to have rehabilitated already 1966 families by 1995-96. The State Government and the Tripura Tribal Area Autonomous District Council have taken a joint initiative to rehabilitate about 15,000 tribal shifting cultivators in rubber plantation scheme.

In fact rubber has been identified as one of the thrust areas in Tripura, in view of its suitability to the terrain and the acceptability amongst the people. Studies have shown that about 1,00,000 hectares of area in the state can be brought under rubber plantation. The area under rubber cultivation at present is estimated to be about 23,500 hectares, which is the second largest, after Kerala. The yield @ 1,500 kg per hectare and the quality of rubber are also comparable to Kerala's plantations. In fact, Tripura has recently been declared the "Second Rubber Capital of India" by the Rubber Board.

The State Government has taken up an ambitious programme to increase the area under rubber plantations by another 20,000 MT by the end of Ninth Plan, i.e., by 2001-02 AD, with assistance from the Central Government, the Rubber Board and the World Bank. As a result, it is expected that the rubber production, which is presently about 5,000 MT per annum, will increase to about 20,000 MT.

The State Government is very keen to promote processing of rubber and setting up of rubber-based industries in the state. TFDPC (a State Government undertaking) has already set up a Centrifugal Latex Processing factory, with installed capacity of 5.76 TPD, which is being increased to 13.44 TPD. The State Government is also setting up a Process-cum-Product Development Centre at a cost of Rs. 12 million, with a view to create basic infrastructure for promotion of rubber-based industries. The availability of good quantity of high quality rubber offers ample scope for setting up of rubber-based industries in the state.

Fauna

Fishes: The dominant form of life in all the water covering the surface of the earth is the fishes, the largest class of vertebrates. There is hardly a lake, stream, river or pond that does not contain some kind of fish. The rivers in Tripura flow into the river Meghna in Bangladesh, and this has somewhat reduced the scope of availability of river fishes in the state.

However, during monsoon (June-August) when the rivers swell enormously and inundate the adjoining low-lying areas, certain fishes, viz., cartelagenous rays and large-sized catfishes migrate from the major rivers of Bangladesh into the territory. One important migratory fish, Hilsa is not generally found. In the rivers and *jheels* of Tripura are found fishes of the species *chital* and *pholui* belonging to the group *Notopteridae*. Fishes related to the group *cytariophysi*, viz., carps, catfishes and loaches are also commonly found in almost all rivers. Small in size but bright and silvery in colour, some of their species like *chela, laltari, chapkhori* (or *chapila*), etc., are popular among the common people for their taste and moderate price.

The major carps of the subfamily *cyprininae* belonging to the species *laltla, rui, lallibaush, ghania, bhagna, mrigal,* etc., are also raised by the households in their own ponds and tanks. Smaller varieties of the same origin like *sarputi, puti,* etc., and different varieties of *pabda* (silvery white fish) belonging to the *Silundae* family are also found in abundance in *jheels,* tanks and rivers. These fishes are quite tasty and nutritious, and are often a good source of income. 'Aristocrats' among them are *rui, katla andpabda*. Other fishes having their common habitat in shallow waters and small streams found throughout the state are *tangra, gulasha, aeer, bojori,* all belonging to the family *Bagridae; singh* or *singhee* of the family *saccobranchidae, kakaya* (or kai), *chanda,* the only species representing, respectively, the families of *xenentodontidae* and *centropomidae.* Most of these fishes make excellent dishes and are liked much by the people.

The state's large marshy and water areas offer ample scope for a good crop of closed-water fishes every year. The State's fishery department has taken steps in this direction. Training facilities are offered to the actual pisciculturists in technical aspects and material assistance is extended for induced breeding of high-yielding varieties of crops. The production of fish has exceeded 21,000 metric tons in 1990-91 from 12,000 in 1986-87. The Gumti reservoir is exploited for pisciculture by members of fishermen's cooperative societies which include the tribals of the adjoining areas. The marketing of fish collected from the reservoir is done through five permanent fish stalls established in five major towns of the state.

The Birds: The perching birds considered as the most advanced group of birds, they account for more than one-half of all modem avian species. An important distinguishing feature is their keen sense of organs, a highly efficient nervous system and a high rate of body activity that produces the highest body temperature found in the animal kingdom. Small to medium sized, and feet adopted for holding onto branches, most of these birds have a well-developed voice apparatus and are distinguished by their songs and calls.

The most important species of perching birds found in Tripura are: the jungle crow or Dora kak (c. Macrorhynchus), red bulbul (Pycnonotus cafer and jocosus), green bulbul (c.aurifrous), king crow or pechya (Dicrurus adsimilis), Mynah (Acredotheris tristis), house sparrow (Passer domesticlls) or chorai, Indian Tree Pie (Dendrocitta vagabllnda) or taroka, and common babbler (Turdoides caudatlls) or chilchil. Also found in the same group are Jerdon's chlorpsis, a grass green bird of an approximate size of a bulbul, the song birds shama (*copsychus malabaricus)* having almost the same size as that of a bulbul, with a bit long tail, magpie robin (c.saularis) or doyel and the tailorbird (Orthotomus sutorius) or tuntuni, as it is popularly known, the crop-raiding baya weaver bird (Ploceus philippinus) or babui which move about in flocks and the black-headed oriole or haldi pakhi, etc.

Babul birds are of the size of a sparrow with its upper parts streaked heavily with dark brown and the breast with yellow colour. The haldi pakhis are of the size of a mynah and are sometimes found near human habitations.

It is quite interesting to see the making of a nest by the green-coloured little tuntunif with a few pieces of leaves and grass. Like any other bird's nests, their attempts in building a nest display a fine workmanship; it is indeed remarkable in view of the fact that the birds have only their beak and legs to serve as tools. The forests in the vicinity of Rudrasagar beel are the nesting grounds of a variety of birds.

Noted for their beauty, colour and variety and some for their call or song are tuntuni, bulbul, mynah or maina, haldi pakhi, slim but long-tailed bhating, glossy steel coloured and sparrow-sized migratory species of swallow (Hinmdo rustica) or balia and munia. During the summer months, one hears the songs of the Indian cuckoo (Cuculus micropternus), popularly known as bou-katha-kao. It has derived this name as its call sounds somewhat like this which, if translated literally into English, means 'My lady, speak out'. In Rudrasagar beel of Sonamura subdivision is seen pancowri, a cormorant-like water bird of the size of a kite. Its colour is black with silvery streaks on the back and soft brown head and neck and whitish chin and throat. With a long and pointed bill, slender and snake-like neck, the bird feeds on fish, crabs, frogs, etc.

The other avian fauna of Tripura include jungle fowl, owl, kite, parrot, kingfisher, woodpecker, vultures, flowerpicker, duck, pigeon, etc. Besides myriads of protozoans, there are spongilla, coelenterates, helminth-parasites, butterflies, locusts, scorpions, centipedes, millipedes, musseh, slugs and snails. The common wild mammalia at present on the wane due to economic development and urbanaisation are elephant, bison, deer, leopard, jackal, monkey, cat, pig, dog, etc. By far the most valuable wildlife of the state is the elephant which are sometimes seen in herds in the forests.

Two-thirds of the state is forested where different species of trees, orchids, birds and wildlife are found. There are four sanctuaries in the state namely, Rowa wildlife sanctuary, Sepahijala wildlife sanctuary, Trishna wildlife sanctuary and Gumti wildlife sanctuary.

Rowa wildlife sanctuary is situated in the north of the district. It is a small wildlife sanctuary covering an area of 85 hectares. This sanctuary is easily accessible to the tourists from all around the world.

The Sepahijala Wildlife Sanctuary in Tripura has 456 plant species of monocotyledon and dicotyledonous plants. Trees of Sal, Chamal, Garjan and Kanak exist predominantly. The secondary species consist of Pichla, Kurcha, Awla, Bahera, Hargaja, Amlaki, Bamboos and grasses. Sanctuary has abundant Rauwalfia serpentina and home to other endangered and endemic species. There are 5 species of primates in this sanctuary. The crab eating Mongoose, which was last, sighted before 72 years ago in India has been discovered again in this sanctuary. There are about 150 species of birds in this sanctuary. During winter a large number of migratory birds visit the sanctuary. There are more than 150 species of residential birds and migratory birds are found here. This sanctuary is also a beautiful picnic spot.

Gumti Wildlife Sanctuary is the second sanctuary of the South Tripura district located. There is a vast water reservoir covering almost 300 sq km of an area. This water reservoir attracts many migratory water birds. This Sanctuary has Elephants, Bison, Barking deer, Wild goat apart from many other animals and reptiles. This is an ideal destination for tourists interested in eco-tourism. There are numerous medical and therapeutical botanical species in abundance in the surroundings of the sanctuary.

Wildlife

Gumti Wildlife Sanctuary: Gumti Wildlife Sanctuary is the second sanctuary of the South Tripura district located in the southeast corner of the state. Its area is 389.54 km. Close to the sanctuary, there is a vast water reservoir covering almost 300 sq km of an area. This water reservoir attracts several resident and migratory water birds. Gumti Wildlife Sanctuary in Tripura has Elephants, Bison, Sambar, Barking deer, Wild goat or Sarow apart from many other animals and reptiles. This is a very ideal destination for the tourists interested in eco-tourism. The sanctuary boasts of a rich flora and fauna. One can find numerous medical and therapeutical botanical species in abundance in the surroundings of the sanctuary.

Rowa Wildlife Sanctuary: The Rowa Wildlife Sanctuary, situated in the north of the district, can be approached from Panisagar and is adjacent to the National Highway. Rowa Wildlife Sanctuary in Tripura is a small wildlife sanctuary covering an area of 85'85 hectares and it is one of the few remains of the natural forests left. This sanctuary is easily accessible to the tourists from all around. Rowa Wildlife Sanctuary provides plenty of scope for study by the botanists, ecologists, environmentalist and students of wildlife system. The Tripura Rowa Wildlife Sanctuary houses more than 150 species of birds, wild beasts and primates. The sanctuary with bountiful of forest reserves, including both botanical and zoological is worth a visit. It is the most ideal destination for the tourists, who are more inclined towards eco-tourism. The forest is rich with a large number of economic plants such as medicinal and aromatic, treat fodders, fruit producing trees, oil-seed producing trees, spices and orchids and other ornamental plants.

Sepahijala Wildlife Sanctuary: The Sepahijala Wildlife Sanctuary in Tripura is at a distance of 35 km from Agartala and the NH 44. Tripura Sepahijala Wildlife Sanctuary is spread over an area of 18.53 sq km and boasts of a rich collection of wildlife particularly of birds and primates. One can appreciate both in-situ and ex-situ conservation of flora and fauna at Sepahijala Wildlife Sanctuary. The Sepahijala Wildlife Sanctuary in Tripura is the hot spot of biodiversity with abundant stock of flora, fauna, birds, etc. It has 456 plant species of monocotyledon and dicotyledon. Trees of Sal, Chamal, Garjan and Kanak exist predominantly. The secondary species consist of Pichla, Kurcha, Awla, Bahera, Hargaja, Amlaki, Bamboos and grasses. Sanctuary has the 4,489 cum per ha of timber biomass. Sanctuary has abundant Rauwalfia serpentina and home to other endangered and endemic species. There are 5 species of primates in this sanctuary. The crab eating Mongoose which was last sighted about 72 years ago in India has been discovered again in this sanctuary. Presbytis, or spectacled langur, an endemic species of Tripura is abundant here. There are about 150 species of birds in this sanctuary. During winter lots of migratory birds visit the sanctuary. It is absolutely thrilling to watch them. Wonderful habitat of Sepahijala attracts lot of migratory birds of which lesser whistling teal, white ibis, open billed stork is of prime importance.

Trishna Wildlife Sanctuary in Tripura: Covering an area of 197.7 sq km, the Trishna Wildlife Sanctuary in Tripura is a rich in vegetation and fauna. Trishna Wildlife Sanctuary Tripura can be approached either from Belonia in the south or from Sonamura in the northern part of the state. The Trishna wildlife Sanctuary was notified in the year November 1988. The sanctuary is rich in forest reserve with abundant patches of virgin forest reserve. The sanctuary has the unique educative value to the school going children, academicians, Botanists, environmentalists, taxonomists and visitors. The Trishna Wildlife Sanctuary is one of the most conserved forest reserve with rich biodiversity. The forest reserve is ideally planned for Education and Awareness and Entertainment and Amusement.

Indian Gaur (Bison) is an attraction of this sanctuary. Apart from it, there are varieties of birds, Deer, Hooklock Gibbon, Golden Langur, Capped Langur, Pheasants and many other animals and reptiles. Bison is the main attraction in this sanctuary, in addition to the resident and migratory birds. The dense forest covers 62 per cent of the total area, 18 per cent is covered by degraded forest and the rest 20 per cent is covered by bushy forest. Sanctuary also has a numbers of perennial water rivulets, water bodies, grass land.

The sanctuary has Tropical Semi Evergreen Forest, East Himalayan lower Bhabar sal, Moist mixed deciduous Forest and Savanah wood land. One species of Bamboo Oxtenanthera Nigrocilliate locally known as Kaillai is found in abundance at this place, leaves of which are liked by Bison. This bamboo is said be endemic. The vegetation of the Sanctuary is unique through out its area. There are numbers of tree species, herb, Shrubs, climbers, grass, etc. in the Trishna Sanctuary Tripura. There are 230 nos of trees species 400 nos herbs, 110.

Nos shrubs and 150 nos climbers available in the Sanctuary. Among the floral diversity there are good nos of species of having medicinal value. Kurcha, Tulsi, Vasak, Sarpaganda, Rudraksha, Bel, Chirata, Kalamegh, etc. are medicinal plants available in plenty. The sanctuary is famous for Bison locally known as "Gaba" and home to several species of "Primates". Some of the species found here are — Bos gaurus (Indian Bison), Trachypithecus phayrie(Spectacle langur), Hylobates hoolock (Hoolock Gibbon), Macacca mulatta (Lalmukh Bandar), Trachypithecus pileatus (Capped Langur), Sus scrofa (Wild boar), Felis chaus (Wild cat), Panthera pardus (Leopard).

Major Rivers

The Gumti, the Khowai, the Manu, the Haorah, the Muhuri and are some important rivers of Tripura. The first one, Gumti or Gumti, is the largest river which "receives a number of south-flowing streams and cuts across the ranges in a steep-sided valley from east to west before emerging out of the hills near Radhakishorepur. There are a number of waterfalls in its channel through the Dombur hill, and the landscape in the neighbourhood is exceedingly picturesque. The Gumti is considered to be the most sacred of all the rivers in Tripura. As in north India, the Ganges is loved and respected by all and considered to be the symbol' of hopes and fears. In Tripura the river Gumati is believed to gush down the earth from its heavenly abode. As legends has, the elder of the two daughters of a priest fall in love with the coursed Prince in disguise of python, who got married with him. This angered priest father, killed the python, who in the eyes of elder daughter used to be a handsome Prince got shocked and sadden by this, and killed herself, by drowning in the water flowing where the head of python was buried, and the younger sister also followed the same path. The two sisters formed two rivers namely Raima and Saima, the two joins to form the river Gumti.

The place where head of python was buried, sweetest fragrance flower Khumpui had grown from this place the Gumti river is considered to have originated. From this Khum (flower) +Twi (Water) > khumtwi > gumtwi > gumti > gomoti and derived that is why Gumti is most sacred river to Tripuri People. The source of the river is taken to be Tirthamukh, where in lies the beautiful Dombur falls believed to be one of the most important holy places. On *Pous Sankranti* (or *Makar Sankranti)* day, which is Hangrai to Tripuri people, hundreds of thousands gather at the river mouth and take a holy dip in the sacred river. The religious sentiment has found expression in the name of the river Gumti and its source Dumbur. The latter has derived from the Tripuri Word *dungur* meaning deep water fall.

According to some, the names of the two rivers, Gumti and Manu, suggest early colonisation of Tripura by the Aryans. But in truth is not so, it is only the recent phenomenon and corrupt pronunciation of Tripuri names. For Gumti is said to be a tributary of the river Saraju over whose bank the capital of Ayodhya stood. But this has no basis and authenticity, like the Haorah river is corrupt form of Tripuri word Saidra (saidra > haidra > haodra > haorah) to which the indigenous Tripuri still call by this name. This clearly shows the influence of the indo-aryan influxes in Tripura.

The famous pilgrim spot in Tripura, Unakoti, is only about ten kilometres away form Kailasahar. Further, a few names in hills of Tripura like Hryshyamukh, Tirthamukh, etc., also suggest a link with Sanskrit language. Thus from the names of the hills and rivers of Tripura it seems the Tripuri had come in contact in the distant past with the indo-Aryans. None of the rivers of the state is said to have undergone any sudden or abrupt change. In different places river banks appears differently. In the hills they are of steep and rugged rocks covered with fern and other plants; in the plains they are abrupt but not very high. The riverbeds are usually sandy in the hills and clayey in the plains. There are no artificial canal systems in the state. In the low-lying areas there are numerous swamps and marshes. Inland water-traffic is conspicuous by its absence.

Feni River

Feni River is a river in the Indian state of Tripura and southeastern Bangladesh. It is a trans-boundary river with an on-going dispute.

Course of the River: Feni River originates in South Tripura district and flows through Sabroom town and then enters Bangladesh.

It enters Bangladesh at Belchhari in Matiranga Upazila of Khagrachari District. It flows through Ramgarh Upazila (Khagrachari), Fatikchhari Upazila (Chittagong) and then flows along the border of Chittagong (Mirsharai Upazila) and Feni (Chhagalnaiya Upazila, Feni Sadar Upazila, Sonagazi Upazila) districts and discharges into the Bay of Bengal near Sonagazi. The length of the river is 108 km. The river forms the international boundary at some points.

Muhuri River, also called Little Feni, from Noakhali District joins it near its mouth. The river is navigable throughout the year by small boats up to Ramgarh, some 80 km upstream.

Dispute: The question of sharing of the waters of the river between India and Pakistan was discussed way back in 1958.

Reports from Pakistan say, "India is trying to withdraw water from Feni River for irrigation projects in exchange of resolving erosion problem in Bangladesh side of this bordering river."

According to statement on sharing of river waters with Bangladesh, released by India, "Feni River has been added to its mandate in the 36th JRC meeting. A decision was taken in the meeting that the Ministers of Water Resources of both the countries would visit the sites where developmental works have been held up. This Joint Inspection of various locations of developmental and flood protection works on common rivers was held from September 14-21, 2006."

Feni Closure Dam: A 3.41 km long closure dam was constructed across the river in 1965-66 at a cost of 593.5 million takas to divert the flow through the Feni regulator. It is located between Mirsharai and Sonagazi, in the Chittagong and Feni districts respectively. It was constructed to prevent saline water intrusion from downstream and retain fresh water upstream for use in the Muhuri Irrigation Project.

Inland Port in Tripura: Sabroom in South Tripura, in India, is only 18-20 km from Bay of Bengal, but it is a virtually a land locked territory. There is a thinking that an inland harbour could be built at Sabroom, connected to the sea through a canal, if Bangladesh allows it. The construction of such a harbour could reduce considerably the cost of transportation of goods from the rest of India to Tripura and the North-East of India. However, it is all at the thinking stage and no proposal have been tabled.

Gumti River

Gumti River originates from Dumbur in the northeastern hilly region of Tripura state of India. From its source it flows about 150 km along a meandering course through the hills, turns west and enters Bangladesh near Katak Bazar (Comilla Sadar). Then it takes a meandering course again and passes through the northern side of Comilla town and east of Mainamati. Keeping Burichang upazila on the north, it cuts through Debidwar upazila and reaches Companiganj Bazar. The distance from Mainamati to Companiganj Bazar is about 60 km. From Companiganj it turns west and finally falls into the Meghna at Shapta in Daudkandi upazila. The segment between Companiganj and Daudkandi is about 50 km long. The Gumti is about 135 km long within Bangladesh. The dakatia is one of the important tributaries of the Gumti and the Buri river is its distributary.

The Gumti is a hilly river having a strong current. Its flow varies from 100 to 20,000 cu ft/s at Comilla. During the rains its average breadth is about 100 m, it is full from bank to bank and the current is rapid. But during the winter it shrinks and becomes fordable at most places. In a year of normal rainfall the river rises to above 1.5 m than the level of the surrounding areas. Flash floods are common phenomena of this river and it occurs at regular intervals.

Haora River

The Haora River flows through the Indian city of Agartala, it is the major river which flows in the Sadar subdivision of the Western District of Tripura. It is called *Saidra* in Kokborok by the original inhabitants of the state.

Origin of Saidra: The Saidra or the Haora originates from the Boromura hills in central Tripura and flowing through the foothills passing through important towns like Champaknagar, Jirania, Khumulwng, Khayerpur and the capital city Agartala it goes to merge with the famous Padma river of Bangladesh crossing the international border.

Khowai River

Khowai River originates from the eastern part of the Atharamura Hills of Hill Tripura in India. Flowing west and northward, the Khowai enters Bangladesh at Balla in Sylhet district. The river further flows beside the east of Habiganj town and debouches into the Meghna near the mouth of the Kalni at Nabiganj.

Manu River

There are a couple of important rivers in the state of Tripura and the Manu River is one of them. Along with the other rivers of the region, that is, Khowati, Muhuri, Haorah and Gomati, Manu helps to drain the district. The rivers of the state of Tripura can be classified into two main types; these are the rivers that flow towards the north and those that flow towards the west. The Manu River is one of the north-flowing rivers of the place. The other north-flowing rivers of the state are Khowai, Juri, Doloiand and Langai. The Manu River of Tripura has its origin in the mountainous region of the state. Its course runs through quite uneven surfaces including stiff clips and gorges. After running through these rough regions, River Manu of Tripura flows through a wide plain. In this plain, the speed of the river slows down and it has a winding course.

It finally moves towards the north into the plains of Sylhet. River Manu finally leaves the country of India and enters the neighbouring country of Bangladesh through the district of Maulvibazar. In this region, the river meets another river called River Kushiyara. One of the most important facts related to the Manu River is the fact that the Geological Survey of India is the proposed establishment of the Manu Earth Dam on the Manu River. The Geological Survey of India and the Government of Tripura are involved in this project. This dam is to be built at the high-altitude stretches of the river. The main aim behind the construction of this dam is to facilitate irrigation and control excessive floods in the region.

Forests

Forest resources play significant role in both socio-economic development and environment of any area. The Forest ecosystem is now known to serve a multiple function in absorbing carbonload, generation of oxygen, moderating climate, preventing soil erosion, recharging groundwater, etc. Forest, through the process of photosynthesis, trap solar energy, which can provide biomass for energy production. Besides producing timber and fuel, forest offer a wide range of non-timber forest produces like leaf, fruits, flowers, gums, resins, medicinals. Above all, forests harbour 80 per cent of the biodiversity on the planet earth.

Forest Types

The forest in Tripura may be classified into three different types of classificatory system.

Table: Forest type of Tripura

Sl.No.	Classificatory System	S. No.	Forest Types
A.	Climatic Types		
		1.	Evergreen forest
		2.	Moist deciduous forest
			a. Sal forest
			b. Mixed forest
B.	Seral Types		
		3.	Swamp vegetation
C.	Edaphic Types		
		4.	Bamboo forest
		5.	Cane forest
		6.	Garjan forest
		7.	Savannah forest
		8.	Grass land vegetation

Grasslands

Grasslands are formed as an edaphic climax on wet soils. Besides the natural grassland, grassland succeeds activities of shifting cultivation, forest fire and areas of other human activities. Aquatic grasses often occupy silted marshland enriched by silt and organic debris.

Swamp Vegetation

Swamps cover a large part of the geographical area of the state. The swamp areas harbour herbaceous species, few shrubs and trees dominated by *Albizia, Baringtonia, Lagerstroemia, Macaranga, Mullotis* species; herbs and grasses include *Clinogyne, Phragmites* and *Saccharum* species.

5

Society

On the whole the state of Tripura covers 0.318 per cent of the total geographical area of the country and carries about 0.3 per cent of country's total population. As would be seen from the table the spatial distribution of population in the state of Tripura is highly uneven.

The District of West Tripura which accounts for about 20 per cent of the total geographical area of the state carries 47.16 per cent of the state's population.

The Districts of North Tripura and South Tripura are inhabited by 26.6 per cent and 26.2 per cent people of the state respectively. Economically as well as socioculturally it is the District of West Tripura which is the most developed part of the state.

Pain topography, renewal of soils by the criss-crossing streams, sufficient rainfall, provision of irrigation facilities, growing period all the year round, developed means of transport and communications; fertility of soils, concentration of most of the manufacturing industrials units, location of important towns and cities because of historical reasons, etc. are those physical and economic factors which have led to the concentration of nearly half of the state's population in an area which merely accounts for about one-fifth of the total geographical area of the state.

Nevertheless, the historical factor needs elaboration here. As has already been seen the seat of the government (whether it be Agartala or Old Agartala or Udaipur of some other settlement for a short period), *i.e.* capital has always been in this region. Naturally, as the charity begins at home, this region has always received preferential treatment as far as the socio-economic development is concerned.

Apart from that when the native rulers found it that Jhuming has been a serious impediment in the way of speedy economic development and the tribal people did not respond to the pleas, arguments and even entreaties to give up the slash and burn based shifting cultivation, the rulers thought of immigrating the people well versed in settled agriculture.

The rulers were of the opinion that the tribals may emulate the agro-pastoral practices of the immigrants and may thus opt for a settled living based on permanent agriculture.

The immigrants who came from the Brahmaputra valley for obvious reasons chose to settle down in plain tracts, *i.e.* Western Tripura, Moreover, after population when Hindu refuges from the erstwhile East Pakistan (now Bangladesh) shifted to Tripura, they also settled in the District of West Tripura. As a result of these historical reasons the population was likely to be concentrated in West Tripura.

Moreover, world over, these are the lowlands which support a major chunk of the population. Broadly speaking nearly 80 per cent of the world population lives in areas characterised by elevations ranging less than 500 metres above sea level. Naturally, Tripura is no exception to the universal pattern of population distribution.

Even among the lowlands the lowest possible tracts support an overwhelming section of the swarming humanity. If the relief and population distribution maps are superimposed one shall find that the highlands are areas of sparse population and the lowlands are densely peopled. In other words, the relief maps, seen purely from cartographic angle, appear to be inverted population maps, *i.e.* relief and human numbers are conversely related.

The average arithmetic density of population in Tripura as a whole in 1981, was 174 persons per square kilometre. As compared to the national picture (221 persons per sq km) the arithmetic density in the state is fairly low. However, detailed look at the last column of the aforesaid table one finds that the arithmetic density of population varies from part to part.

At the district level the density is the highest (326 persons per sq km) in West Tripura which carries the highest percentage of the state's population with the lowest percentage of the state's geographical area. North Tripura is characterised by the lowest (139 persons per sq km) density while South Tripura (148 persons per sq km) falls in between.

But going to subdivision level one finds that the arithmetic density of population varies markedly and ranges between 81 (Amarpur subdivision of South Tripura) to 419 (Sadar subdivision of West Tripura) persons per square kilometre. This means that the highest density figure is almost double of the national density while the lowest density of population is nearly one-third of the country's average density of population.

The three subdivisions which carry higher arithmetic density figures are Sadar (419), Sonamaru (277) and Udaipur (244). The first two subdivisions fall in the West Tripura District, the most developed part of the stage otherwise situated on the western plain tract. The subdivision of Sadar includes Agartala and Old Agartala, towns which have been associated with governmental affairs.

The town of Agartala is still the seat of the State Government, while earlier Old Agartala has also enjoyed that position for a pretty long time. Coincidentally, the Udaipur subdivision contains the town of Udaipur which housed the administrative headquarters of many old native rulers for quite long a period. The subdivision of Amarpur adjoining the neighbouring country of Bangladesh in the east, is a hilly region very badly denuded and degraded as a result of the removal of forests here excessive rains and steep slopes promote a higher rate of soil erosion which have progressively been reducing the cultivable hectarage and even shrinking the Jhuming domain.

Growth

The first estimates for the population of Tripura were made in 1874-75 and vide these estimates the population then it was 74,528 persons. The first proper census count was held in 1881, and it recorded the population of Tripura at 95,637 persons.

It means that during half a decade it rose by 28.33 per cent. In the next decade when the census data was released in 1891, the population of Tripura had risen to 1,37,575 persons. The decadal growth during 1881-91 amounted to 43.83 per cent. In 1901, the population of the state had risen to 1,73,325 persons registering a decadal positive charge of 25.98 per cent.

The table affords a peep into the growth pattern of the population till the beginning of the present century.

From the table it is clear that the population during eight decades has grown for more than nine times. In arithmetic terms it has risen by 954 per cent. A one very distinct feature of the growth of population in Tripura has been that even during the decade 1911-21 when the population of the country fall by about 0.30 per cent that of Tripura rose by 32.59 per cent. Such a situation may be the result of the following factors:

- The base of population in Tripura as compared to the national scene is too small. In such conditions in the case of Tripura even a slight increase in absolute numbers shall show a magnified percentage.

- During 1911-21 the decrease in India's population was due to the spread of epidemics and contagious diseases. In Tripura, where because of mountainous relief and then greatly forest covered landscape the diseases could not make a headway where already thinly peopled and scattered hamlets dominate the population distribution scenario.

- Some people from the adjoining plain tracts also retired to the isolated valley in the high hills where because of relatively salubrious climate and peculiar topography they could be saved from plain borne diseases and epidemics.

- Above all it was also the period when the native rulers had been promoting immigration of Bengali people to these forested hills.

Thus the increase, in Tripuras population through all the decades in general and the 1911-21 decade in particular has not entirely been the outcome of the interplay of fertility and mortality alone but the mobility factor (immigration) has also played a significant role.

The decadal rate of population growth in Tripura with the sole exception of 1971-81, decade has always been higher than the all India rate of population growth. The growth rate has however, been usually high during 1951-61 and unusually low during the census decade of 1971-81 and thus these facts need explanations.

In the state of Tripura, the princely rulers have been promoting immigration of plainsman of Bengal with the purpose of popularising settled agriculture so that the Tripuri highlanders should also slowly and gradually give up eco-degrading practice of Jhuming and take to settled and permanent agriculture. Besides, there being acute shortage of literate and skilled personnel among the tribals the rulers had to promote the immigration of skilled and educated Bengalis to run the administration and help in establishing industries and other sectors of economy.

As a result of this factor the decadal growth rate of population in Tripura had to be higher than the all-India rate. However, the unusually high rate of growth during 1951-61 was the aftermath of partition. No doubt in the wake of partition some non-Muslim people from the erstwhile East Pakistan out migrated to Tripura during 1941-51 but a majority of them left their earlier opted country after 1951 when atrocities and brutalities on the non-Muslim people increased manifold.

Even a large number of tribals living in the Chittagong Hills felt insecured and sneaked into Tripura during the decade. The political unrest and social chaos increased markedly towards the close sixties and early seventies when Zulfiqar Ali Bhutto dominated political order in the then Western Pakistan and refused to hand over the reins of power to Mujibur Rehman a Bengali Muslim from the erstwhile Pakistan who had swept the majority in the polls. To suppress the popular uprising continuous atrocities and brutalities were committed on the people of then East Pakistan.

Consequently, a very large number of people from the erstwhile East Pakistan migrated to the adjoining Indian territory including Tripura. The independent nation of Bangladesh came into being in December 1971. But as a result of Shimla agreement a large number of them went back to their native land.

Resultantly, the decadal growth rate which was higher in Tripura during 1961-71 came down drastically in the next census decade of 1971-81. However, after Mujibur Rehman when the political order with a secular outlook and pragmatic approach was replaced by fanatic and theocratic order the non-Muslims and tribals from Bangladesh continue to sneak into the adjoining Indian States including Tripura.

Although, negotiations between the Indian authorities and Bangladesh have been held many a time yet the problem of illegal immigration of Bangladesh nationals to the Indian territory has not come to end. No wonder during the next census count the total population of Tripura shall be between 21 to 22 lakh persons.

Sex Ratio

The percentages of male and female population of the states as per 1981 census, work out to be 51.34 and 48.66 respectively. The average sex ratio of Tripura (number of females per thousand of males) of 948 is relatively high as compared to the sex ratio of 935 (as per 1981 census enumeration) for the country as a whole.

In the year 1971, when the country's average sex ratio was 930 in Tripura it was still higher, *i.e.* 943. Nevertheless, from 1901 to 1961 Tripura was characterised by low sex ratios in relation to the all India scenario. The reason is not far to seek. Earlier for want of socio-economic development in general and the lack of public health and medical facilities the death rate of woman at the time of delivery of child (natal Mortality) was quite high.

Moreover, as a result of the lack of general awareness, the females were a neglected lot and no wonder female infanticide was practised among Hindus and children diseases heavily preyed upon the uncared female children. Above all on the inducement of the native princes when Bengali immigrants reached Tripura they entered as "business bound immigrants."

Among the business bound immigrants all over the world the stream of new comers has always been age and sex specific. But once they succeeded in planting their roots they started bringing their spouses and children also and such an occurrence is bound to raise the sex ratio.

District-wise, the West Tripura district has the highest sex ratio (956) and is followed by South Tripura (945) and North Tripura (935). It has also been found that particularly after 1961 the sex ratios in all the districts has shown happily rising trend. Such a development is a happy sign the lowering sex ratio has very far reaching implications for a population of a region.

Literacy and Urbanisation

As per 1981 census data, as against the national literacy rate of 36.23 per cent the state of Tripura is characterised by an average literacy of 42.12 per cent. Among all the states of the Indian Union on the literacy from Tripura is preceded by the states of Kerala (70.42), Maharashtra (47.18%), Tamil Nadu (46.76%), Nagaland (65.57%) and Himachal Pradesh (42.48).

But when compared to the Union Territories excepting the UT of Dadra and Nagar Haveli (26.67) all other UTs were far ahead of Tripura. At that time Arunachal Pradesh too was a Union Territory and it had also a lower (20.79%) literacy rate.

Spatially, it shall be observed from the table that the District of West Tripura (46.21%) excels the districts of North Tripura (41.96) and south Tripura (34.83 per cent) at the literacy front. Both the latter districts fall below the state average while the last district lags behind even the national literacy rate. A decade earlier also by and large a similar literacy mosaic existed in the state. In 1971, the state of Tripura had a literacy of 30.98 per cent which was slightly higher than the national literacy rate of 29.95 per cent. District-wise it was West Tripura which with a literacy rate of 32.61 per cent was at the top and was followed by north Tripura (32.17%) and South Tripura (26.69%) districts.

Coming to subdivision-wise literacy it was found that Sadar with a literacy rate of 49.75 per cent, topped all other subdivisions. Out of 10 subdivisions, only three subdivisions, *i.e.* Sadar, Khowai (42.71%) and Dharmanager (46.14%) were characterised by literacy rates higher than State's average literacy rate.

The subdivision of Sabroom had the lowest (28.72%) rate of literacy among all the subdivisions. The level of literacy is one of the yard-sticks of measuring the duality aspect of human population. Literacy and educational attainments provide an idea about the quantum of such human resources which can be employed in diversifying the occupational structure and removing more and more people from the traditional primary economic activities and absorbing them in secondary and tertiary economic sectors. Viewed from that angle we find that even sex-wise literacy rates have shown upward trends.

As per 1981 census data, the male and female literacy rates in Tripura were 51.05 per cent and 31.60 per cent respectively. The particular increase in the female literacy is a welcome achievement because by educating a female child, potentially one complete family shall be educated. And such a development goes a long way in initiating and sustaining different schemes related to the social welfare.

In the year 1981, out of the total population of 18,27,490 the number of city and town dwellers was only 2,25,568. Thus only 12,34 per cent of the people of Tripura were urbanites. The degree of urbanisation in the state is far less than the national rate of 23.31 per cent. The degree of urbanisation in Tripura is lower than all the states and Union

Territories barring Arunachal Pradesh (6.56%), Dadar and Nagar Haveli (6.67%), Himachal Pradesh (7.61 per cent), Assam (10.29%) and Orissa (11.79%).

Out of the total urban population of Tripura nearly 58.8 per cent lives in the capital town of Agartala (1,32,186) alone. No other town of the state nears in its population to Agartala. The second town as per its population to Agartala.

The second town as per its population is Dharmanagar (20,806) town in North Tripura. In all there are only 10 census towns in the state. These are Agartala, Khowai Sonamura (West Tripura), Dharmanagar, Kailashaher, Kanialpur (North Tripura), Radhakishorepur, Belonia, Alnarpur and Sabroom (south Tripura). Out of these ten towns, the towns of Sonamura, Kamalpur, Amarpur and Sabrooin emerged as census towns in the year 1981 only.

In the year 1971, about 10,4317 of Tripura's population lived in its six urban centres. Of the total population of the scheduled castes (Harijan) and scheduled tribes (Girijan) only 6.2 per cent and 1.31 per cent, respectively live in urban areas, meaning thereby that the urban population of Tripura predominantly consists of the non-Harijan and non-Girijan people.

Coming to the countryside one finds that there are only 864 villages in the state out of which 856 are inhabited. But villages in the hilly, sub-mountainous and mountainous areas are not compact and concentrated settlements. In fact, in such areas every census village consists of many hamlets separated from each other by rivulets, trees groves and such other physical features. On the whole there are 5,215 hamlets out of which 483 were uninhabited in 1981. In a state where a section of the populace practices shifting cultivation some hamlets do remain uninhabited, although, the same hamlets may not remain uninhabited every year.

Ethnic Groups

In Tripura, there are not only people hailing from different regions but also people constituting different ethnic groups. As has been asserted by historians and other social scientists many of the Harijan groups living in northern India come from the original Dravidian stock while majority of the caste Hindus and Muslims fall in the lineage of the Aryans.

On the other hand a majority of the tribal groups living in north eastern India come from the original Mongoloids. Hence, Tripura is characterised by ethnic diversity. Going by religions, as per census data available, in Tripura, there are people of all the major religious groups found in India as shown in the table.

It shall be seen that Tripura has been a Hindu dominated stage. In the year 1981, its 89.66 per cent of the total population consisted of Hindus. The next dominant religious groups has been Islam which in 1981, accounted for 7.6 per cent of the total population.

Buddhism has always been at number three and in 1981, nearly 2.9 per cent of the people of Tripura hailed from this religion. Christianity has been next on the ladder of religious composition but the numbers of the Christians which stood at merely 328 in 1941 rose to 24,872 in 1981, showing an increase of 748 per cent during four decades.

It has been the outcome of conversation of tribals to Christianity by the missionaries. The dwindling as well as rising and falling numbers of the Sikhs and Jains clearly reveal that they constitute a part of that floating population which has been entering the region as business bound immigrants to be periodically replaced by others who may and may not be the followers of same faiths. In 1971, the share of major religious groups was 89.55 per cent Hindus, 6.68 per cent Muslims, 2.72 per cent Buddhists and 1.01 per cent Christians in the population of Tripura.

Out of the seven states of North Eastern India, only three, *i.e.* Tripura, Assam (71.04%) and Manipur (58.97%) are the Hindu majority states. The only valid reason for Tripura being a predominantly Hindus inhabited state is historical. The rulers being Hindus, their faith must have affected the religion of their subjects and no wonder slowly and gradually some of the tribals confessing animistic order might have started showing themselves as Hindus.

Moreover, in the wake of partition many Hindus immigrated to Tripura from the erstwhile East Pakistan. That is why the total numbers of Hindus have rapidly risen during the intercensal decades of 1951-61 and 1961-71 when as a result of highly discriminatory attitude of the authorities and atrocities committed on Hindus by the authorities of then East Pakistan a large number of them moved to the adjoining Indian territories including the state of Tripura.

The Muslims were never in majority but their numbers also swelled steeply during 1951-61 when the atrocities were unleashed on Bengali Muslims by the Martial Law authorities backed be the West Pakistani based politicians and statesmen. Nevertheless, once the socio-political conditions stabilised with the birth of Bangladesh in the erstwhile East Pakistan the over-riding majority of the Muslim refugees went back to their homes and this way the Muslim population declined by about 54 per cent in 1981. The Chakma and Mugh tribals claim themselves to the Buddhists.

It is also interesting to note it here that, whereas, the proportion of Hindus in Tripura is higher than the all-India proportion (82.72%), in case of Muslims (India 11.21%), Christians (India 2.60%), Sikhs (India 1.89%) and Jains (India 0.47%) it is relatively low. However, the proportion of Buddhist population in Tripura is significantly higher when compared to the national percentage of 0.70 per cent.

Scheduled Castes

The scheduled caste population in Tripura forms a fairly good chunk. This section accounts for 15.12 per cent of the total population. It is higher than the all-India figure.

This percentage has increased from 12.40 per cent in 1971. It also appears that a number of scheduled caste people have come from outside the region.

That is why nearly half of the scheduled caste people of the state (47.2%) are found living in West Tripura district wherein the population numbers have risen more by immigration than the natural rate of growth. However, as per cent of the total population in a subdivision it is the subdivision of Sonamtaru (West Tripura) which outranks all other subdivisions of the state with 22.32 per cent of its total population consisting of the Harijans.

Dharmanagar subdivision (North Tripura) with the percentage of 7.80 per cent is at the lowest rung of the related ladder. As already stated only 6.2 per cent of the scheduled caste people live in urban areas meaning thereby that a majority of them pursue primary economic activities of cultivation from jungles. The overall scheduled caste literacy in the state is quite low (33.89%) as compared to the state's average literacy rate. Functional non-relevance is the major cause for such a sad state of affair. In the subdivision of Sabroom it goes as low as 27.94 per cent. In no subdivision the scheduled caste literacy even nears the state's average literacy rate.

Scheduled Tribes

Mahatma Gandhi preferred to call our tribal brethren as Girijans (giri means jungles and/airy means folk), *i.e.* forest dwellers. What an apt nomenclature! Till recently, most of the tribals have not only been living in forests but their economy, their culture, their way of life, their fairs and festivals and even their superstitions were woven around the forests and hills.

As against the all-India figure of 6.4 per cent, 28.44 per cent of the total population of Tripura consists of the Girijans. The tribal population has been a very significant and vital attribute of State's population, though, its percentage is gradually falling with the continued influx of not tribals as immigrants and floating population.

In a real spread the district of South Tripura with 35.83 per cent of its population belonging to scheduled tribes ranks first and is followed by the districts of North Tripura (27.32%) and West Tripura (25.01%). Subdivision wise as per cent of the total population of the subdivision Amarpur (64.07%) subdivision tops in the state while Sonamuru (West Tripura) subdivision (11.29%) is at the lowest rung of the ladder.

The subdivisions of Sabroom (South Tripura), with 43.06 per cent, and Khowai (West Tripura) with 38.68 per cent of their respective population belonging to Girijan folks are other two subdivisions where tribals definitely form majority groups. With only 1.31 per cent of the Girijans living in urban areas of the state they form the most ruralistic section of the population. Their literacy rate (23.07%) is also lowest in the state. Whereas, the lowest tribal literacy (11.68%) has been noted in sabroom subdivision the highest (33.92%) is found in Khowai subdivision, meaning thereby that in no subdivision the tribal literacy nears the state's average rate of literacy.

As shall be observed from the shows on table, although, in absolute numbers the tribal population has been progressively rising over the decades yet their proportion to the total population has been, some times gradually and sometimes rapidly falling from one census decade to another. One more thing evident from the table is that the rate of growth of the Girijan populace in Tripura has been the highest during 1911-21 and 1951-61.

During the former decade many tribal groups from the different parts of the erstwhile province of Assam moved to the parts now forming Tripura. However, during 1951-61 the then authorities of East Pakistan in a bid to turn the erstwhile East Pakistan as an Islamic Republic created such conditions that a large number of tribals living in Chittagong Hill Tract migrated to Tripura.

The table it is clear that the proportion of the scheduled tribe population in the total population of Tripura has decreased from 64 per cent in 1875 to 28.44 per cent, in 1981. It is further expected that by the Census of 1991 it may account for only one-fourth of the state's total population. It may not be out of place to add some meaningful lines about the major tribes living in Tripura.

Most of the tribal groups living in Tripura belong to the Tibeto-Burmese languages speaking groups and are supposed to be the earliest inhabitants of Tripura. They are believed to have entered India from Tibet and Burma froth the northeastern, and Southeastern directions and later on spread to the entire Northeastern India, which now has seven states. Thus strictly speaking they too are not the original inhabitants or aboriginals of Tripura. They are as good immigrants to Tripura as the Bengalis are. It is only a matter of time; the tribal groups entered Tripura hundreds of years ago while Bengali immigration has been relatively recent. Thus, there is no sanctity in calling the Bengalis as outsiders and creating terror — some conditions against them in this ground.

At present people of 18 different tribal groups are found living in Tripura. The Chaimal group entered the state during 1951-61 and left the region during the next decade. The Bhutias, Lepchas, Bhils, Santhals, Oraons and Mundas do not belong to this region. They have migrated to Tripura from other parts.

Although, some families of some of these tribes have settled down in Tripura yet they are numerically insignificant, politically unorganised, and socioculturally isolated from the local tribes. They migrated very recently from the states of Bihar and Bengal, whereas, the autochthon tribes migrated from Burma and Tibet long long ago.

The Tipperalls are numerically the largest tribe of Tripura and this tribe has also the credit of ruling over the region for centuries. The sociologists regard them an offshoot of the ancient Kirats who were originally Mongoloids and entered India from Tibet through the Brahmaputra valley about three millenniums ago.

The hair-knot tied on the top of their head is an evidence of their being Kirats originally. In good old days they are an animistic tribe and subsisted on tubers, roots, fruit, flowers and other forest products and led a stone-age life. For quite a long time they spoke Sino Tibetan dialects but at a later stage they showed a preference for living in plain areas. Thus coming in contact with the plainsmen they underwent changes and a vast majority among them embraced Hindu faith.

The Kukis have also come out of the Kirats but have a close affinity to the Chins of Burma and later on migrated to India are the present-day Kukis. From Burma they came to the Mizo Hills they arrived in Tripura through Chittagong Hill Tracts and Manipur.

From Mizo Hills they were ousted as a result of a massive Burmese attack about two centuries ago. The Kukis are further subdivided into the Darlongs, Halains, Rupinis and Lushais based upon their habitat. For instant Darlongs are named such because their habitat was located on the Darlong Hang range of the Mizo I-Tills.

The Halams branched out of the southern Kukis who were named Halams by a Tripura ruler. He named them so for their habit or roaming about on footpaths. The word Halam in a local tongue refers to footpath. The then princely ruler exploited their instinct of roaming about. They were employed by the Maharaja as tax collectors.

During war also because of being swift walkers they proved their mettle in extending a thrust in the enemy ranks. Being closer to the ruling house, they slowly and gradually got alienated from the Kukis and started preferring Hindu faith than their animistic faith. Many of them coming under the Vaishnav cult of Hinduism gave up taking flesh.

The Lushais constitute the most advanced group among the Kukis Chin groups. Their hamlets are mostly found on the ridges of the Jampui and Sakhang hill ranges. Some sociologists opine that they derived their nomenclature from a sub-tribe Lushei or Lusei that is supposed to have ruled over them.

Others dispute the derivation and assert that this head hunting tribe (Lu means head while Chai refers to cut) was named after their major activity. These people left western Burma when they were ousted by a more ferocious tribe. Omesh Saigal has mentioned that in their original habitat in Western Burma (Khanpat Village) they planted a banyan tree and believed that when the branches of that tree would touch the ground the Lushais would retreat to their original homeland.

In 1921, the branches of that banyan tree touched the earth surface and many Lushais including some persons in active service of the forces returned to Burma, where they now number more than twenty thousand.

The mautam, *i.e.* famine, consequent upon the profuse flowering of bamboos, of 1911 brought the Lushais to Tripura from the Mizo Hills. The immigrants to Tripura were headed by Hrungbhunga. Maharaja Birender Kishore Manikya was naturally upset over the influx of a ferocious group. He thus planned to follow a policy of appeasement to keep the danger at bay. He conferred the title of Raja on their chief who in turn pledged peace.

Phuldungsei was the first hamlet settled by them on the Jumpui hill range. The entire socio-economic life of the Lushais in Tripura revolves around Jhumming. Though, the Manikya ruler offered them to abandon the shifting cultivation yet they did not leave it. This tribe of roaming head hunters has developed a very effective device of communication.

Torch signals, Mirror flashes and whistling are used. A very powerful drycell battery-operated torch is held horizontally on the right shoulder. Long and short flashes are flashed to denote the dash and dot Morse codes. No wonder an imported message gets flashed within an hour over the entire Lushai habitat. Similarly, long and short whistles are blown to denote dash and dot. Mirror flash method can be employed only on sunny days and it needs higher degree of deftness.

The Rupinis assert themselves as the original residents of lake side village. The Rih tank near the international border with Burma adjoining Mizoram is taken as that lake. They believe that they came to Tripura long ago and their Chief in fact was the first Manikya ruler.

They have also become vegetarians and that may be the impact of the Vaishnav cult. Well to do Rupinis dominate the foothill zone of the Baramura Range in Sadar and Khowai subdivisions. Earlier, they used to live on machan types of hut but after coming in contact with the plainsmen they shifted to mud wall and thatched roof houses.

The Darlongs came to Tripura from eastern Burma more than three centuries ago. They also came via Mizo when the Darlong Hang Range is a mute witness to this fact. They dominate the hill tract lying between the Unakoti and Telimura ranges.

It is said that the city of Kalashahr (earlier called *Kulashor*) was named after Kula, a brave and warrior son of a Darlong chief. About seven decades ago this city was inhabited by Darlongs alone barring a couple of Bengali families. For quite a long time the Darlongs were governed by their hereditary chiefs. Nupa, an elected village council functioned under the Chief.

However, the decisions related to Jhumming were solely rested with the chief. One of the traditional and unique customs is being meticulously observed by the Darlongs even now. When some body dies, no villager is supposed to leave the village. It is believed that the departed soul haunts the settlements for 24 hours and it is the duty of every villager to appease it. Cucumbers, sugarcane and some other eatables are hung along walls of every dwelling for this purpose.

The Jamatias (Jamait in Urdu refers to a class) are said to the successors of a class that provided an over-riding number of soldiers to the royal army.

Besides being dauntlessly deft warriors they also proved highly loyal to the ruler. In recognition of their meritorious services the ruler accorded honours on them and also exempted them from the family tax payment, *i.e.* gharchukti. No wonder among all the tribal groups of the state they came to enjoy a very commanding position. They were also granted very fertile lands around Udaipur. Majority of them are now followers of the Hindus religion.

The Reangs constitute another such group that enjoyed nearness to the ruler. Originally, employed as planquine carriers, in due course of time by dint of their industrious nature, loyalty and sacrificing spirit they found their way to the royal army. As a result of their contact with the armed forces their cultural life underwent some drastic changes.

However, in spite of their best efforts they could not win the royal confidence to the extent the Jamatias had succeeded. They were also required to pay the tax like gharchukti. Resultantly, after some time they gave up their fine traditions and turned to be rebels.

In 1924, heir revolt had far reaching echoes in the ruling family when the ousted royal representative, *i.e.* Rai from their area. Since then, it is the Reang Village Councils which reign supreme in their settlements.

The Mughs and the Chakmas are Buddhist-tribal communities of Tripura. They were originally shifting cultivators who after the soil fertility in their original. Land had completely exhausted, came out in search of fertile land.

At one stage the Chakmas created a Chakma State in East Bengal (now Bangladesh) and ruled over it through the offices of Raja, Dewan, Talugdak and Karbari. Lewin is of the opinion that Mughs (also spelt as Mogs) are the offsprings of Burmese by the Bengali women. These noble and upright people are known for their cooking skill throughout the metropolis of Calcutta.

The Mughs are a classless and a free society with their concentrations in the Sabroom subdivision. In matters of food, dress and customs they appear to have been under the impact of Chakma life style. Though Buddhists they love and cherish meat dishes. They form that community which has abandoned Jhuming completely.

The round nosed, small headed and short statured Oraons are brown to dark in colour. Similar to the hair of some negroes their hair to have a tendency to be curly and jet black. The beard and moustaches develop among their quite late. Superstitious like most of the tribals they believe in ghosts and spirits.

But they are found of flute blowing and brook no rivalry in their love or matrimonial affairs. The flute and wife are the two most inseparable belongings of an Oraon although, on the contrary side they neither mind a divorce nor a widow remarriage. They have proved to be very good agricultural as well as casual labourers.

The Mundas were once a wandering people, but later on took to Jhuming. Of late they have shown interest for settled agriculture. Unlike most of the tribal groups the Mundas have very favourably responded to well meaning changes. They also pursue fishing and hunting to supplement their earnings from farming.

They have come to this region from Chhotanagpur plateau. Brown to dark brown in colour they are short in stature but possess sturdy body. They are mostly monogamous and have no taboos about divorce, separation, remarriage and widow remarriage. However, their origin and particularly, the related place are still controversial.

The Santhals too are short in stature but have a broad flat nose with a sunken nose-ridge. They have woolly and curly hair. Although, now on being persuaded they have taken to settled cultivation, till recently, they practiced Jhuming.

Nonetheless, they opted for permanent cultivation when they could comprehend the abuses of soil erosion. Poultry farming is an obsession with them. The female Santhals are more hardworking than males.

The Bhutia's migrated from Tibet. They belong to the Tibeto-Burman stock and practise a combination of pastoralism and semi settled agricultural practices. They are also excellent image makers who make many images during Durga Pooja season for the Bengalis.

Besides, some Bhutias are also engravers, carpet makers and wood carvers. Till recently, the Bhutia's were polyandrous although, monogamy and polygamy were not unknown among themselves.

People

The majority of the state's population comprises of Bengalis, Manipuris and 19 different tribal communities. In fact, Tripura is also home to thousands of migrants from West Bengal and Bangladesh. The tribal people follow their customs and religion with the highest regard. Tripura, despite having 19 Scheduled Tribes that form about 40 per cent of population, is largely a Bengali community. Regardless of practicing different religions and notions, the people live in harmony with each other.

The Habitats

The issues of habitat are considered the vital indicators for assessing the living condition of human population in an identified geographical area. The State of Tripura, remains predominantly rural with 84.70 per cent population living in the rural sector.

The rural population of Tripura is distributed over census 856 villages in four districts. The village size, classified on the basis of basis of population indicate that largest number of villages (274) have 2000-4999 population and only 3 villages have more than 10,000 population. About 265 villages have less than 1,000 population.

A total of 4,39,101 households are identified in these 856 villages of the state; more than 80 per cent of these households are located in "Kutcha" houses; of the kutcha houses 42.85 per cent remain non-serviceable. The living condition of vast majority of human population in Tripura remains much below the national average both in terms of percentage of kutcha houses (33.76%) and percentage of non-serviceable kutcha houses (9.24%). The number of village classified by population (1981) and number of rural households and classification of rural households are given in following tables.

Table: Number of Village Classified by Population Size in Tripura: 1981

1. Total Number of Inhabited Village		856
2. Total Rural Population		1,827,490
3. Average Population per Village		2,135
4. Village wise Population	<200	34
	200-499	91
	500-999	140
	1000-1999	253
	2000-4999	274
	5000-9999	56
	>10000	3

[*Source:* Census of India, 1981]

Table: Number of Rural Households and percentage occupying Pucca, Semi Pucca and Kucha houses, 1991

	Total Number	Percentage of various type of houses			Kutcha%	
		Pucca	Semi-Pucca	Kutcha	Servicable	Non-Servicable
Tripura	439,101	1.91	17.35	80.74	37.89	42.85
India	111,539,448	30.59	35.65	33.76	24.52	9.24

With regard to the service sector, only 30.60 per cent of the total housing have access to safe drinking water in the state of Tripura as against national average of 55.34 per cent. This again reflects the present status of living condition of more than 80 per cent of the people of state remain much below the desired level.

In terms of toilet facilities, 62.43 per cent of rural households in Tripura are reported to have access to such facilities as against Indian average of 9.48 per cent; if this data is authenticated, Tripura stands second to Lakshadweep.

The urban centres of the state can be classified into 6 categories, viz. Class I (100,000 and above), II (50,000-99,999), III (20,000-49,999), IV (10,000-19,999), V (5,000-9,999) and VI (less than 5,000). The census data of 1991 show that a total of 18 urban centres are known from Tripura, of which only one belongs to class I category (Agartala) and the largest number (7) belong to class II categories. Census data of 2001 show that total number of urban centres have increased to 23, of which West Tripura district has the largest number of urban centres, i.e. 13 followed by South and North and Dhalai district.

Table: Number of Urban Centres by Size Class

	Total Number	Number of Urban Centres by size Class					
		Class I	Class II	Class III	Class IV	Class V	Class VI
India	3696	300	345	947	1167	740	197
Tripura (1991)	18	1	0	4	7	4	2
Tripura (2001)	23	1	0	6	8	8	0
West	13	1	0	3	5	4	0
South	4	0	0	1	2	1	0
Dhalai	3	0	0	0	0	3	0
North	3	0	0	2	1	0	0

The rural and urban populations break up of the state shows that West Tripura district has the highest population in both the categories while Dhalai district reflects the lowest in the state.

Table: District Wise Rural & Urban Population and Urban Centre

District/State	Rural Population	Urban Population	Total Population	Percentage of Urban population
West Tripura	11,23,030	4,07,501	15,30,531	26.62%
South Tripura	7,08,498	54,067	7,62,565	7.09%
Dhalai	2,88,546	18,871	3,07,417	6.14%
North Tripura	5,28,000	62,655	5,90,655	10.61%

In 1991, of the total urban population of 0.42 million, the number and percentage of people living in the slum were 0.07 million and 17.6 per cent respectively, the latter figure being much lower than the national average of 21.21 per cent. The respective figure for 2001 are not available till date.

In 1991, of the 85,054 households in urban Tripura, 24.02 per cent lived in Pucca houses, the rest in semi pucca (38.06%) and Kutcha houses (37.42%); this shows that urban living condition remained much below the national average; of the total population only 5.5 per cent people have pucca houses. The respective figure for 2001 however are not available till date.

Table: Urban Housing in Tripura and India

	Percentage of various type of houses			Kutcha%	
	Pucca	*Semi- Pucca*	*Kutcha*	*Servicable*	*Non-Servicable*
Tripura	24.02	38.06	37.92	6.68	2.88
India	72.75	17.69	9.56	12.04	25.89

Table: Rural and Urban Housing (Combined) in Tripura and in India

	Percentage of various type of houses		
	Pucca	*Semi-Pucca*	*Kuncha*
Tripura	5.50	20.71	73.79
India	41.61	30.95	27.44

In terms of accessibility to safe drinking water, 71.12 per cent people are reported to have the access as against national average of 81.38 per cent. Taking urban and rural population together only 37.18 per cent people of Tripura have access to safe drinking water as against 62.30 per cent on a national average.

Table: Percentage of household with access to safe drinking water (Rural –Urban combined)

	Urban	Rural	Total
Tripura	71.12	30.60	37.18
India	81.38	55.34	62.30

The livelihood pattern of urban population, like the rural ones, demands a clean sanitation system for better environment. While 63.85 per cent of Indian urban population have toilet facilities, the figure for the state of Tripura stand at 96.32 per cent; taken together with the rural population, the total percentage of population with toilet facilities stands at 67.93 per cent as against 23.70 per cent for India.

Tripura is one of the four amongst all Indian States and Union Territories (in 1991) with 60 per cent and above people having toilet facilities, the others being Mizoram (70.73%) Chandigar (70.80%), Delhi (63.38%) and Lakshadweep (71.02%) [Source: Office of the Register general of Census Commission, 1995].

It may be noted that a study conducted by National Institute of Urban Affairs (1991) on 398 urban household, shows that 65 per cent of population have private toilet and 22 per cent have community toilet facilities, making it 87 per cent instead of 96.32 per cent mentioned earlier.

Tribes in State

Bhim Tribe

Bhim tribe is settled in the eastern state of Tripura. Little is known about their specific lifestyle and culture. The main source of income comes from agriculture.

They are animistic people believes in ancient traditions and religions. Usually the members follow the endogamous (marriages within the same clan) system.

Bhutias

Bhutias are a race of Mongoloid origin. They permanently settle in Bhutan and are mostly found in Sikkim in India. Bhutias came for the sale of woollen garments and temporarily resided in the North East. In Tripura they form a minority group.

Chaimal Tribe

Chaimal is a sub-caste of the Kuki community. The Kuki community had migrated to Tripura from Mizoram. The Chaimals are mainly found in the subdivisions of Dharmanagar, Kailashahar, Amarpur, and Udaipur. The main source of their living is Jhum cultivation. Like the Kukis, people of Chaimal community also wander from one place to another in search of Jhum land. The community constitutes of only a few families, which has had the negative effect that they have been nowhere in the census reports since 1961.

Hrangkhawl

Hrangkhawl is one of the 21 scheduled tribes of Tripura state of India. They are mainly dwelling in the Teliamura subdivision of West Tripura and the Ambassa subdivision of Dhalai districts. Hrangkhawls are also found in the North Cachar Hills in Assam. They speak the Hrangkhawl dialect of Kuki language which is of Tibeto-Burmese origin. Their appearance is mongoloid.

Garo

Garo is a tribal group of Tripura. They are mainly found in the districts of South Tripura and Dhalai. This tribal group was migrated to Tripura from Garo Hills of Meghalaya. According to ethnologists, the language spoken by Garos belong to the Tibbetan-Burmese linguistic groups. They live in houses made of mud wall and roofed with 'Chan' grass.

Sangnakma is the name given to the head of the community. The main dance performed by the group is called *Wangala*. Dama and Aaduri, made of buffalo horn are two main musical instruments accompanying this dance.

Halam

Halam is a tribal group of Tripura. Originally it belonged to the Kukis, another older tribal group of Tripura. The Halam tribe is subdivided into 16 sects. The main source of living of the Halams is jhum cultivation. They make various sacrifices and offerings to avoid disasters causing crop failure and epidemics. A community dance form called *Hai-Hak* is performed after the harvest to satisfy Goddess Lakshmi.

Jamatia

Jamatia is the third largest tribal group of Tripura. A Mongloid countenance is the outstanding feature of their person. They are a well-organised tribe. Jamatias are hard working agriculturalists. Kokborok is their major language. Many rituals and rites are carried out as part of their culture. Hoda is the main subsect of the Jamatias. Artistic and cultural activities such as song, dance and acting add colour to their lives.

Khasi Tribe

Khasi is a tribal group inhabiting Meghalaya and Tripura. They are mainly found in Datuchhera of Kailashahar subdivision. The major source of living is betel leaf or pan cultivation. Pass-tea-a is the name of the dance form performed by the tribal group. It is similar to the Noagerem dance of the Khasis of Meghalaya. Only male members will participate in this dance form.

Koch Tribe

Kochs are the primitive tribal group of Northeastern India. They live in the states of Assam and Tripura. The tribe is believed to be an offshoot of the Garo. They speak a language known as 'Koch,' a Baric language that belongs to the Tibeto-Burman language family. The community members are hard-working and peace-loving people. Traditionally, they practice 'plot rotation' type farming. Kochs are also adept carpenters, blacksmiths and merchants.

Kochs reside in small village settlements, which are divided into clans and castes, and are run by a village chief. Their various geographical groups are known as 'jai'. These groups are divided into several subsections that branch into local lineage groups. They allow marriages within the same clan.

Koch sleep in huts made of mud or bamboo with thatched roofs. Kochs practice some type of ethnic religion, which revolves around an extensive number of village and household gods. They worship the gods of fire, water and the forest.

Kuki People

The term *Kuki*, in literature, first appeared in the writing of Rawlins when he wrote about the tribes of the Chittagong Hill Tracts. It refers to "Hillsmen" comprising numerous clans. These clans share a common past, culture, customs and tradition. They speak in dialects that have a common root language belonging to the Tibeto-Burman group. Kuki have Mongoloid features and are generally short-stature with straight black hair, Dark brown eyes and brown skin.

The different kuki clans are recognised as schedule tribe of India. They spread out in a contiguous region in Northeast India, Northwest Burma (Myanmar), and the Chittagong Hill Tracts in Bangladesh. They are most prominent in Manipur, Nagaland, Assam and Mizoram. Kuki is composed of many different entities/Clans: Aimol, Anal, Baite, Changsan, Chiru, Chongloi, Chothe, Darlawng, Doungel, Guite, Halam, Haokip, Haolai, Hangsing, Hmar, Hrangkhawl, Kipgen, Koireng, Khelma/Sakachep, Kolhen, Kom, Lamkang, Lenthang, Lhanghal, Lhouvum, Lhungdim, Lunkim, Lupho, Lupheng, Thangeo, Lhangum, Maring, Mate, Misao, Monsang, Moyon, Paite, Purum, Simte, Singsit, Sitlhou, Tarao, Touthang, Vaiphei, Zou, etc.

Though the term Kuki can be thought of as been synonymous with Mizo and Chin tribes, predominantly all Zo groups other than those who are in Mizoram and Chin refer to themselves as Kukis.

History: Kuki country was subjugated by the British and divided between British India and British Burma administrations following the 'Kuki Uprising of 1917-19'. Up until the fateful defeat in 1919, the Kukis were an independent people ruled by their chieftains. During WW II, seizing the opportunity to regain independence, Kuki fought with the Imperial Japanese Army and the Indian National Army led by Subhash Chandra Bose. The success of the Allied forces over the Axis group dashed the aspiration of the Kuki people.

Today the Kukis are dispersed in northeast India, northwest Burma and the Chittagong Hill Tracts in Bangladesh. With regard to Kuki identity, Prof. J. N. Phukan writes, If we are to accept Ptolemy's "Tiladae" as the Kuki people, as identified by Gerini, the settlement of the Kuki in the North-East India would go back to a very long time in the past. Prof. Gangumei kabui states, 'Some kuki tribes migrated to Manipur Hills in the pre-historic times along with or after the meitei advent into the Manipur valley'. This hypothesis will take us to the theory that the Kukis, for that matter, The Mizos, at least some of their tribes, have been living in North-East India since pre-historic time.

In the second century (AD 90-168), Claudius Ptolemy, the geographer, identified the kukis with Tiladai, who are associated with Tilabharas and place them "to the north of Maiandros, that is about the Garo Hills and Silhet". Stevenson's reference to Kuki in relation to Ptolemy's also bears critical significance to its existence in this period. The Rajmala or Annals of Tripura refers to Shiva falling in love with a kuki woman around AD 1512. The *Encyclopaedia Britannica* records, "Kukis, a name given to a group of tribes inhabiting both sides of the mountains dividing Assam and Bengal from Burma, South of the Namtaleik river ". Concerning the origins of kuki, in 1893, E. B. Elly, a British official, wrote, the terminology 'kuki', meaning 'hill people' originated in Sylhet, in former East Bengal.

Historian such as Majumdar and Bhattasali refer to the kukis as the earliest people known to have lived in pre-history India, preceding 'the "Dravidians" who now live in south India.' The Aryans, who drove the Dravidians towards the south, arrived in the Indian subcontinent around BC 1500. In the Pooyas, the traditional literature of the meitei people of Manipur, 'two kuki chiefs named kuki Ahongba and kuki Achouba were allies to Nongba Lairen Pakhangba, the first historically recorded King of the meithis (Meiteis), in the latter's mobilisation for the throne in 33 AD'. Cheitharol kumaba (Royal chronicles of the Meitei Kings) record that in the year 186 Sakabda (AD 264) Meidungu Taothingmang, a kuki became King.

The Kukis in particular were widely known as "war-mongers". They have been in minor ethnic wars within the kuki clans and subclan, Hmars fought with Singson (Thadou) in 1960s, This was a result of social change among the Hmar people, whose Chiefs were Singson one of the Kuki clan and the paites in 1997 with KNF(p), which is led by Kipgen; other related kuki subclan joined in the fray. The Kuki had an ethnic war with the Nagas in the early 1990s which predominantly was due to the ethnic cleansing propaganda of the NSCN (IM) militants. The Kuki share the same culture, traditions, and genealogical affinity with their brethren of the Chin state in Burma and the Lushei or Mizo of Mizoram.

Culture: The Kukis have a rich culture and numerous tradition that are unique, interesting, and impressive.

Daily Life: Rice is their staple food. They domesticated a number of animals. Of these, Se'l(mithun) is the most prized possession, while a dog is considered a faithful animal.

Festivals: Kuki festivals include:

- Lawm Se'l Neh (a celebration by young people of the community after the season's work is over).

- Chavang Kut (a celebration by the whole community after rice harvest).

- Mim Kut (related to maize harvest and similar in content to Cha'ng Kut).

- Sa-Ai (a celebration of a successful big game hunt of big animals).

- Chaang-Ai (a celebration of bounteous rice harvest).

- Hun (an occasion of worship in ancient times).

- Chawn le Han (hosting of this occasion involved feasting and holding of sporting events).

- Ka'ng ka'p (a game in which disc-liked seed is rolled) besides many others.

Music: There are different musical instruments to enhance these festivities.

- Kho'ng-pi (big drum).

- Kho'ng-cha (small drum).

- Dah-pi (gong).

- Pe'ngkul (trumpet).

- Gosem (bagpipe).

- Theile (flute).

- Theiphi't (whistle).

- Se'lki (horn).

- Lhe'mlhei (a peculiar mouth instrument).

These instruments were useful not only for raising the festival spirit, but also for adding solemnity to certain serious occasions.

Folklore: The folklore of the people abounds with the heroic adventures of Galngam le Hangsai, Chemtatpa, Lengbante, Jamdil, Sangah le Ahpi, etc. The poignant romances of Khupting le Ngambom, Jonlhing le Nanglhun, Changkhatpu le Ahshijolneng, Khalvompu le Lenchonghoi; and folktales, such as Chipinthei le Mailangkoh, Lhangeineng and others, represent the rich variety of the Kuki culture.

Customs and Traditions: The land of the Kukis is blessed with rich customs and traditions. Sawm, a community centre for boys – was the centre of learning in which Sawm-upa (an elder) did the teaching, while Sawm-nu took care of chores, such as combing of the boy's hair, washing of the garments and making the beds, etc. The best students were recommended to the King's or the Chief's service, and eventually would become as Semang and Pachong (ministers) in the courts, or gal – lamkai (leaders/warriors) in the army.

Lawm (a traditional form of youth club) was an institution in which, boys and girls engaged in social activities, for the benefit of the individual and the community. It was also another learning institution. Every Lawm has lawm-upa (a senior member), To'llai-pao (overseer or superintendent), and Lawm-tangvo (assistant superintendent). Besides being a source of traditional learning, Lawm was also useful for imparting technical and practical knowledge to its members, especially with regard to farming methods, hunting, fishing, and sporting activities such as- Kung – Kal (high jump, especially over a choice mithum), Ka'ng Ka'p, Ka'ngchoi Ka'p (top game), Suhtumkhaw (javelin throw using the heavy wooden implement for pounding-de-husking-paddy) and So'ngse (shot put). The Lawm was also a centre where the young people learned discipline and social etiquette. After harvest season, 'Lawm meet' is celebrated with a Lawm-se'l (on the occasion, a mithun is slaughtered for the feast) and, as a commemoration, a pillar is erected. The event is accompanied by dance and drinking rice-beer, which sometimes continues for days and nights.

The Kuki male traditionally wore his hair in the form of a Tuhcha (long hair rolled up in a bunch at the nape). His clothing consisted of a Boitong-Sangkhol (a half-sleeve jacket) and a Pheichawm (short lungi). They are renowned hunters and reputable warriors. Their hunting kit consists of Se'llung-bawm (a leather waist-pouch for pellets), Se'lki meiloupai (an animal's horn for storing gunpowder) and a knife.

Watchful waiting on a machaan for the game also did a favourite past time hunting. Often, many kinds of traps and snares are also set. The fishing equipment consists of Len (fishing net), Bawm (basket trap), Ngakoi (fishing hooks). Ngoituh (a method of using dams and baskets in a flowing river), Ngalhei (draining out water) and Gusuh (a method of temporally stunning fish by using toxic herbs) were also common methods of catching fish in small streams.

The Kuki men took great pride in big-game hunting and a killing of big animals was followed by somber celebration. The Kukis believed that the big game hunted in a man's lifetime would accompany him in his after-life journey — the spirits of animals would clear the onward path for him. It was therefore believed that a man was not complete unless he was also successful in big game hunting; he would not be entitled to partake in Lalju, a special drink meant for those who have killed big game.

The Kuki women traditionally wore their hair in two plaits braided around the head. They wore a Nih-San (a red slip) underneath a Po'nve (a wrap-around), which was worn from above the chest. The ornaments included Bilba (earrings), Hah le Chao (bracelets and bangles), Khi (necklace), and occasionally Bilkam (a type of ring-shaped earring worn to stretch the earlobes). Cha'ngsuh (grain-pounding), Cha'ngse'p (winnowing), Ponkhon (cloth-weaving) and looking after domestic animals were some of the daily chores of the women folk.

The woven designs of the Kuki women are unique and appreciated the world over. Cha'ng-ai, the place of honour for a good harvest was given to the lady of the house. This formed the highest honour accorded to the Kuki woman. The men folk occupied themselves with cane and bamboo crafts and house building. They were blacksmiths and also engaged in carpentry and other such like jobs. The manufacture of guns and gunpowder were a very specialised profession among the men. Twi-cha'ngsu (water mill)' and Chotle'p (a sea-saw mechanism), are some of the ingenious methods used for pounding rice with minimum use of human energy. Sawh and Ke'ngke (noise creating instruments) functioned as the scarecrow and were placed in the cultivated fields. Twisawh was another inventive contraption, which used running water from a stream making continual sounds to scare away birds and pests from standing crops.

Laws and Government:

Governance: With regard to governance, Semang (Cabinet) is the annual assembly of a Kuki village community held at the Chief's residence represents the Inpi (Assembly). In such an assembly, the Chief and his Semang and Pachong (Cabinet members and auxiliary of Inpi) and all the household heads of the village congregate to discuss and resolve matters relating to the village and the community.

Legal System: The legal system – arrangement of a girl's marriage, bride-price, and the Chief's administrative system, relief for widows and orphans – are elaborately and systematically defined in the Kukis' way-of-life. Traditionally, polygamy is not permissible. Capital punishment was never in practice. The maximum penalty was 'bultuh' (stockade in which the guilty was kept outside the village and provided food until death). This reflects the high ethics of the Kuki people.

Judicial Process: The Kukis also practiced Twilut, a judicial process of judgement by going under water. Twilut is a phenomenon in which the litigants are subjected to go under water to determine the culprit. It is an ultimate and decisive recourse for cases where the normal processes of trial by court does not reach a conclusive end. In the event of resorting to twilut, certain customs are strictly adhered to. The chief and elders of the community call upon the thempu (magic-medicine man/priest) to conduct the proceedings. For instance, in a boundary dispute, the two litigants are brought into the presence of the public. The 'thempu' then recites rituals, which includes the invocation of 'Pathen' (God), followed by the litigants being submerged in the water. The culprit becomes immediately apparent because she/he cannot remain underwater at all. Of the two litigants, the defaulter would be in absolute agony, experiencing extreme sensations of being inflamed from within, and therefore emerge to the surface. In contrast, the innocent person able to remain under water, quite normally.

Language: Kukis speak multiple dialects, all denoted as Kuki language.

Writing: It is known that the Kukis were in possession of some documents, inscribed on leather, known as *Savun Lekhajo'l* (scroll). These scrolls were lost in the passage of time and along with this, the Kukis also lost their script. Therefore, there is no known Kuki script. Today, the Roman script forms the basis for Kuki literature.

Literature: The academic and Kuki National Organisation spokesman Seilen Haokip has written a number of articles and books about the Kuki and tribal relations in Northeastern India.

Education: Although the existence of formal learning institutions is not available, the Kukis were not unfamiliar with astronomy and astrology. They were able to study the stars and the phases of the moon and could forecast for themselves certain aspects of nature, particularly rainfall, drought and the seasons.

Lusai Tribe

Lusai is a tribal group of Tripura, mainly inhabiting the Jampui Hills situated on the Kanchanpur subdivision of North Tripura District. Jhum cultivation is their main source of living.

Their number is very insignificant compared to the total population of the state. Their social life and customs have been objects of great attraction to others. The principal means of livelihood of the Lusai still remain to be Jhum cultivation. The Lusai believe in the eternal nature of the soul. The name of their imaginary heaven is 'Piyalral'. These who can reach there get delicate food. When a man dies his soul starts for Rih lake, at a distance of 3 miles from Mizo Hill border. After three months the soul comes back and begins to live nearby the village. His relatives keep an empty place for him and offer food. After three months the soul is bidden adieu through a ceremony known as 'Thitin Achai'.

Cher, Khaulam, Solakia, Pawanto are the main dances of the Lusai.

Mag Tribe

Mag (Mogs or Maghs) is a tribal group of Tripura. It is a mixed tribe with characteristics of Arakaness, Burmese and Chinese groups. The word Mag is said to have originated from Magadh of Bihar state. The actual native land of the Mag tribe is not yet known. But the Mag groups of Sabroom or Belonia subdivisions are said to have drifted from the Chittagong Hill Tracts of Bangladesh.

Superstitious by nature, they believe the cause of illness as the effect of evil spirits. Various food items are offered to appease these spirits. The Mags are mainly followers of Buddhism. One of the most important festivals celebrated is the Sangrai. As part of the celebration various cultural programmes are conducted. Water will be poured on the roots of a tree called *Bodhi Briksha*. The Boat festival, Water festival, Byuhachakra Festival are the other important occasions. Besides these, there are other festivals associated with the worship of Lord Buddha.

Meiteis

Meitei, also known as Meetei, is a tribal community found in Imphal valley of Manipur. Some of them have settled in the states of Assam and Tripura. Meiteis speak Manipuri, a Tibeto-Burman language. Their main occupation is agriculture. For additional income, they engage in business, fishing, weaving and basket making. The community members are considered as the strong and heavy members of Mongolian type. Men folk wear white kurta, dhoti and pagari, while women like choli and fanek.

Meiteis live in small houses, which are constructed using bamboo and wood. The roofs are thatched, supported by bamboos. A bamboo pillar is placed at the southwestern corner which is the place for worshipping Sanamahi (the Meitei deity).

Virtually Meiteis are followers of Vaishnavite Hinduism mixed with traditional beliefs. Some follows ancient Meitei religion called *Sanamahi laining*. A small section known as Meitei Pangal follows Islam.

Khong kangjei, lamchel, hockey and kangand polo are their traditional games. Ningol Chakouba is an important festival celebrated by the female member of the tribe.

Mogh Tribe

Mogh is a tribal community of Tripura. The people of the group are said to have migrated from Arahan due some insurgency. The members of this community are disciplined and hard working people with no inter group dissimilarity. The Moghs are jolly and carefree by nature, and are known for their simplicity and hospitality.

The community activities are looked after by a headman. Moghs follow Buddhism.

Women folk are stout and assiduous and weave their own garments. They are fond of dazzling ornaments and dresses.

Jhooming is the main occupation. But some indulge in plough cultivation other than jhooming.

Noatia Tribe

Noatia is a tribal group of Tripura. Noatias are believed to be a branch of the Tripuries. It is interesting to note that none of the Noatias uses Noatia as their surname. Instead they use Tripuri after their names.

Their sociocultural rites, rituals and customs are very much identical with those of the Tripuri.

Reang Tribe

Reang comprise the second largest tribe of Tripura. Even though the customs and living style are different from Tripuris (the largest tribe of Tripura), they are considered as the kinfolk of the Tripuris. They speak Kokbarak. It is believed that the Reang tribes had migrated from Bangladesh to Tripura. The group mainly believes in animism. Hindu deities are also worshipped.

Mataikatar is their chief god. The supreme dance form of the tribe is called the *Hozagiri* which is performed by the women folk. It is performed to worship the deity Lakshmi.

Savaras

The Savaras are an ancient tribe of hunters widespread in Orissa. They are also found in Bihar, Andhra Pradesh, Madhya Pradesh, Maharashtra, Assam, Tripura and West Bengal. They are called by various names: Sabara, Saur, Sora and Saura. The name 'Saura' has been derived from two words namely 'Sagories' (meaning an axe) and 'Saba Raye' (carrying a dead body.) Savaras are referred to in Aitareya Brahmana, the Ramayana and the Mahabharata. They believe in forest spirits. Savaras worship their ancestors and Goddess Sarvasavaranam Bhagavati (Goddess Durga). They are best known for their wall paintings called 'ikon'. Their language is an uncultivated one and varies from individual to individual and region to region. Their dress consists of loin cloth of about six ft long. Savaras build their houses on the slopes or foothills. Houses are rectangular in shape, built of bamboo and wood plastered with mud. The walls of the houses are made of stone and are coloured red with red earth. Hunting, cultivation and fishery are their chief occupations.

Tiperas

Tiperas are among the aboriginal tribe groups of the Northeastern India. They are the largest tribe in Tripura. A majority of this nomadic tribe are also settled in the states of West Bengal and Assam. Tiperas speak 'Kok Borok', a Baric language belonging to the Tibeto-Burman language family.

Agriculture is the main occupation of this community. Major crops cultivated include jute, rice, wheat and sugarcane. Some also work in the state's industries, which include weaving cloth, milling rice and flour, canning fruit and producing bamboo and leather items.

Tiperas live in tiny, one-roomed houses near the river valleys. The houses are made of temporary materials — usually mud or bamboo. The community members reside in small village settlements, which are divided into clans and castes, and are run by a headman.

They allow marriages within the same clan. Polygamy is tolerated, but not common. The womenfolk are especially fond of wearing jewellery, which can be bought from Bengali craftsmen.

They practice some type of ethnic religion. The gods of fire, water and forest are worshipped commonly.

Uchais

Uchais is one of the smallest tribal group of Tripura. Duapathar in Chittagong Hill tract of Bangladesh is considered as their native land.

They are very similar to other tribes of Tripura and are also of Mongloid origin. Jum cultivation is their main source of living. Vegetables, fish, meat of different domestic and wild animals, and homemade wine are their main food.

The rituals and customs followed are similar to that of the Tripuris. In the sphere of religion they are influenced by Buddhism and Hinduism. Rantak, Ker, worship of Ganga and Naksumatai are the major fairs and rituals.

Usipi Tribe

Usipi is an ethnic community found in the eastern states of Assam and Tripura. They are commonly characterised as Garo tribe. But little is known about their exact routine and culture. The tribe members speak Usipi language (also Kok Barok), which is a part of Sino-Tibetan language family.

Agriculture is the main occupation of this tribe, with about seventy per cent of the population involved in it. The raising of livestock, particularly horned cattle, buffalo, horses and mules, is also a central feature of their economy.

Usipis are predominantly ethnic religionists. They believe in animism and ancestral worship. Due to the influence of Hinduism, Usipis now worship Hindu deities such as Brahma, Shiva, Vishnu and Shakti.

Style of Living

Food

Rice is main food. Cooking oils commonly used are mustard oil and used for both deep-frying and cooking. Other vegetable oils are also used. Ghee is used for cooking special occasion foods. Important spices and ingredients are mustard seeds and paste, chillies (both green and red), Paanch Phoran (a mix of five spices – white cumin seeds, onion seeds, mustard seeds, fennel seeds and fenugreek seeds). Yoghurt, coconut, maize and gram flour are also common ingredients. Milk and dairy products play a huge role in the preparation of sweets in Eastern India. Popular dishes are Momos (steamed, meat or vegetable-filled wontons) and Thukpa (a clear soup), Tomato Achaar (tomato pickle), Machcher Jhol (fish curry), Jhaal-Muri (a spicy snack made with puffed rice and mustard oil), Sandesh, Rasgulla, etc.

Dress

Tripuris have their own traditional dresses. This dress is similar to rest of the North-East Indian people in terms of the type. But it is totally different from rest of the people in terms of the pattern and design.

Female Dresses

The dress women for the lower half of the body is called *Rignai* in Tripuri and for the upper half of the body cloth has two parts Risa and Rikutu.

Risa covers the chest part and the rikutu covers whole of upper half of the body. In the yesteryears these garments were used to be woven by the ladies by home spun thread made from the cotton. But nowadays the threads are bought from the market and the risa is not worn, instead blouse is worn by most of Tripuri women because of convenient. In present-day young girls are wearing rignai with tops also.

Rigwnai

Each of the clans of Tripuri has their own rignai pattern and design. The pattern of the rignai are so distinct that the clan of a Tripuri woman can be identified by the pattern of the rignai she wears. Nowadays there is inter-mingling of the 'rignai' and different clans are wearing 'rignai' of other clans freely and new designs are being woven differently. 'Rikutu' is a plain cloth of different colour and shade woven by the Tripuri ladies.

Rigwnai Designs

Different types of designs fashion that are woven in the rignai borok by the Tripuri women are as follows:

- Anji
- Chamthwibar
- Khamjang
- Kuaiphang
- Kuaichu bokobom
- Malibar
- Muikhunchok
- Muisili
- Phantokbar
- Salu
- Takhumtei
- Thaimaikrang
- Tokbakbar
- Toksa
- Toprengsakhitung
- Rignai mereng
- Rignai khamchwi
- Rignaibru
- Kwsapra
- Sorbangi and many more.
- Banarosi
- Jirabi
- Khumbar
- Kuaichu
- Kuaichu ulta
- Miyong
- Monaisora
- Natupalia
- Sada
- Similik yapai
- Temanlia
- Thaiphlokbar
- Tokha
- Toiling
- Rignaichamwthwi
- Metereng trang
- Kwsakwpra
- Rignaikosong
- Songkai

It is said that at the time of Subrai Raja, the most famous and legendary King of Tripura, through his 250 wives he had invented two hundred fifty designs of rignai. He married those woman whoever invented a new design. But all these design had lost in time and only few are retained till date. The effort to rediscover the lost designs is in process.

Male Dresses

Male counter part used to wear 'rikutu' for the loin and 'kamchwlwi borok' for the upper part of the body. But in the modern age very few people are wearing these dress except in the rural Tripura and working class. The male have adopted the modern dress of international style.

Costumes

Tripura, the frontier hilly state of the North-East, is the land of skilled weavers, gifted with proper know-how. The women of the local tribes, such as the Khakloo, the Halam, the Lushei and the Kuki-Chin tribe, excel in the art of weaving, as is attested in the diligent traditional costumes, which they diligently preserve.

There is a striking resemblance in the traditional costume of the Khakloo and the other fellow tribes. The plain dressing style is apt for the hilly climate, and for regular work. The infants are hardly given clothes except when it becomes essential in the winter and rainy season. The children put on a loincloth.

The daily work-costume of a full-grown male is a towel-like sheet of loin cloth, called Rikutu Gamcha, topped off by a self-woven shirt, called *Kubai*. To combat the blazing heat of the sun and to continue working in the open heat, the men resort to a pagri, i.e., a turban. Western influence is prominently visible on the young boys of today's because they prefer wearing shirts and pants.

The infants are normally kept undressed, although in winter and monsoon season, garments suitably shield them. Children, covers themselves in a loin-garment.

The Khakloo, and at large the Tripuri women, envelop themselves in a greater size of cloth-piece, known as Rinai. This long as well as broad cloth is draped around the waist and reaches the knee. She dons herself in a shorter piece of cloth called *Risa*. This upper-attire passes under the arms, and conceals the entire chest-region of the body. Risas are often invested with beautiful embroideries.

Nowadays, the younger generation of girls prioritise blouses over Risa, as being more management-friendly. However, still among few clans, the wearing of Risa during wedding is mandatory. Women folk also are found to use some kind of headdresses while at work outside.

The neck areas of women are adorned with plethora of beads and coin strands. The element of finery is dim in the costume of the women of the Lushei tribe. Every woman wears a dark blue cotton fabric, to serve as a skirt or petticoat. This cloth, wrapped around the waist, is held firmly by a corset of brass wire or string. The Rinai-like cloth, which falls down to the knees, is associated with an upper-attire; a short white jacket and a cloth to invest in their appearance the sobriety.

In the mirthful times of revelry, the female costume, gets an extra item, a dignified headgear, specifically during dance-performance. This headdress is a coronal, made of brass and coloured cane, further embellished with porcupine quills. Moreover, the upper edges of these quills are studded with the green feathers of the parrot's wings, decorated at their tips, with tussocks of contrasting red wool.

The earlier costumes of the Kuki-Chin women had deigns, imitated from the patterns, seen on the hide of snakes. They bore several names, such as Thangang, Saipi-khup, Ponmongvom, and Khamtang. However, these clothes were previously the prerogative of the women of the aristocrat background, like those from the chief's family and other noble-blood.

Indeed, the simplicity yet attractiveness of the traditional costume of Tripura, is attributed to the artistic fervour and weaving-talent of the natives.

Cuisine

Once again, the strong influence of Bengali community is visible in the cuisine of Tripura, as Rice and Fish make the essential ingredients. People prefer eating non-vegetarian delicacies on top of vegetarian food. In most of the families, one can see preparation of authentic Bengali food. Pork, chicken, mutton, beef, turtle, fish, prawns, crabs, and frogs are consumed profusely by the non-vegetarians. Some of the traditional Tripuri delicacies are Chakhwi, Mwkhwi, and Muitru.

Marriage

The Tripuri marriage follows some steps and beliefs.

Hamjwk Tubui Kaimani: In this system of marriage the negotiation between two families is made by a marriage broker. He is known as Raibai or Andra in Reang dialect. In finalising a marriage the parents or the guardians play the sole role. The bride or the groom has no choice. This type of marriage always takes place in the house of the bridegroom.

If the girl is chosen by the parents of the boy, the guardian of the daughter demands dowry of money, ornaments, etc. Among the Tripuris the bride does not bring any dowry to her father-in-law's house. The Tripuri society is free from the dowry system. There is a trend towards expectation of a dowry at present, however.

Koksurma: Koksurma is the preliminary proposal for marriage, coming from either side of the parties. Generally the raibai performs the brokerage in the koksurma. If the proposal is accepted by both parties then they fix a date for a final settlement called *Kokswhngmung.*

Kokswhngmung: Kokswhngmung is the finalisation of marriage where both sides of the party commit to get their wards marriage. The guardian of both sides sit side by side in front of two pots of rice beer called *bwtwk.* A bell-metal plate containing some cotton, durba, copper coin, rice, soil, etc., is put in front of them to perform the rituals of dangdua, performed by each person three times. The would-be bride then comes before the assembled persons and bows before the elders. The dates and times, terms and conditions of the marriage, bearing of expenditure, etc., are finalised in this kokswhngmung.

Khum Phunukmung: After the finalisation of the marriage, there are rituals of invitation by offering betel leaf, nut and flower, etc., to every family of the village. It is started from the house of the Chokdori, the village head. On the fixed date the bride is brought into the groom's house and received with much enthusiasm, and dangdua.

Aya and Ayajwk: Aya is the helper and assistant of the groom, in dressing, make up, and procedural follow-up. Similarly Ayajwk is the counter part for the bride. Throughout the marriage ceremony they are to remain nearby the respective person.

Bedi: A bedi is a platform on which the marriage ceremony is performed. It is made of bamboo, cane, wood, etc. Over the bedi seven layers of plain pieces of cloth are tied one over the other like a tent. Jari is a pot made of brass, somewhat like a kettle but elongated, that is used in carrying the secret water to be sprinkled over the bridegroom, first by the priest then by the parents and other elders. The morning rituals are performed by Ochai the priest. The ritual is called *Lampra uathop.* A deity is worshipped along with the Twisangrongma. After the ceremony the new couple bow down before and touch the feet of each senior person in attendance, and the aged person blesses the couple with gifts called Heli. Following this ceremony on the same day a grand marriage feast is served to all. The next day of the marriage is called *Dolan* when a post-marriage ceremony is observed by the close relatives of both parties. The non-vegetarian dish that is served on this occasion is an important part of Tripuri marriage ceremonies.

Maitwrang Beraimani: Maitwrang beraimani is the first visit after the marriage to the bride's parents. It generally occurs after three days of marriage.

Different Kinds of Marriages

Nok Kaisa Kaimung (Marriage by Exchange): Sometimes marriage is arranged between two families by exchanging a boy and a girl and thus avoiding the payment of bride-price. The rituals and procedure remain almost the same.

Kharlai Kaijakmani (Marriage by Elopement): If a couple do not get the approval of respective parents for their desired marriage they may decide to elope. The boy generally takes the initiative and runs away from home. The marriage ceremony would be conducted in a supportive relative's home by performing the *wathop* worship.

Phuisai Tubuma (Marriage by Purchase): In this form of marriage the bridegroom or his parents pay a sum of money in cash to the bride's family as her price. Subsequently, the bride's parents have less say in the marriage ceremonies than the groom's parents.

Koklam Kwrwi Kaimung (Marriage by Capture): This form of marriage is not very common with Tripuris. No wedding rituals are maintained except the uathop worship.

Hamjaklai Kaijakmani (Marriage by Love): This form of marriage is very common among the Tripuris and is becoming increasingly more popular. When a boy and girl fall in love they bring their desire to marry to the notice of their respective parents and obtain consent, then the parents arrange the marriage. All the rituals of the wedding are observed.

Sikla Sogya Kaimani (Child Marriage): This type of marriage among the Tripuri was practised in the past. It is becoming rare, and found in remote villages only.

Chamari Omor (Marriage by Service): This type of marriage was prevalent in Tripuri society. In this form of marriage the groom leaves his house and goes to live in his would-be father-in-law's house. He and his bride remain there for a lifetime. All the usual wedding procedures are followed.

Chamari Ompa: This form of marriage is identical with the marriage of chamari omor, the only difference being that the bridegroom is obliged to serve the parent-in-law's house for a certain period of time, generally two or three years. All other rituals remain the same.

Sundul Phulmani (Widow Remarriage): Widow remarriage is commonly practised in Tripuri society. A widow, widower, divorced person, deserted woman is allowed to remarry. This type of marriage is also settled by the Raibai. The guardians of each party settle the marriage in the presence of the raibai and fix for the date. The worship of the uathop is done by the ochai. The arrangements for the ceremony are low profile.

Performing Arts

Music

Music is integral to the tribal lifestyle. Some of the aboriginal instruments, developed in Tripura, are Sarinda, Khamb (Drum), Lebang, Do-Tara, Chongpreng, Khengrong, and Sumui (a kind of flute). Be it the occasion of marriage, religious ceremony or other festival, songs are sung to commemorate each event in the state. The renowned musicians, Sachin Dev Burman and Rahul Dev Burman, belonged to Tripura.

Dance

Dance is a vital constituent of the tribal way of life. Where some dance forms are exclusive to some occasions, there are many others to mark celebration of different events. For example, Garia dance symbolises the prosperity of the people, Hai Hak and Cheraw dances depict the confinement of Lusai woman. In Tripura, Basanta Raas is a delightful dance form of the Hindu Manipuris. Apart from the above-mentioned, there are many other dance forms, like Hojagiri, Bihu, Wangala, Sangraiaka, Chimithang, Padisha, Abhangma, Gajan, Dhamail, Sari and Rabindra, which belong to and are performed by different communities.

Religion

The main Tripura religion is considered to be Hinduism. The people who belong to the ethnic groups of Tripura are immensely influenced by the religion of Hinduism.

Some of the significant deities of Tripura are Matai-Katar, San-Grama, Lam-Pra, Mailu-ma, Ganga or Uima, Thari-rao and Bani-rao, Burha-cha and Khuluma. These deities are an important part of the religious life at Tripura.

Most of the tribes of the state like the Tripuris, the Jamatias, the Reangs, the Halams and the Noatias are actually followers of the Hinduism. The Noatias and the Halams have faith in the Sakti cult. The Rupini and Kalai subgroups of the Halams are believers of Vaishnavism.

The people of Tripura take part in a number of religious ceremonies. A few popular religious ceremonies celebrated at the place are Kharchi, Maikwtal and Mamta, Hojagiri, Ker, Ama, Bisu and Sena and Hangrai.

These people have faith in animism. One of the major tenets of animism is that God resides in all natural objects. The people who have faith in animism consider all places to be sacred and they believe that all places on earth contain either bad spirits or good spirits. They believe that by pleasing these spirits, they can save themselves from any kind of natural calamity like flood, famine or even an epidemic.

Goddess Tripura Sundari is an integral part of the religious life. Tripura Sundari, are Tara, Kali, Bhuvaneshwari, Chhinnamasta, Bhairavi, Bagalamukhi, Dhumavati, Kamalatmika and Matangi.

Other than Hinduism, Christianity is also one of the prominent religions at Tripura. This state has a number of structures that hold a lot of importance to the Christians of the region. The Baptist Christian Union, the Sadar North Baptist Association and the Khowai-Ompi-Kamalpur Baptist Association are some of them.

Christianity

Christianity is one of the most important religions but few people believe in Christianity.

Tripura hoses many a structures that are closely associated with Christianity. These man-made structures form an important part of the religious life of the state.

The Khowai-Ompi-Kamalpur Baptist Association is a major baptist association of the subdivisions of Kamalpur and Khowai in the districts of Dhalai and West Tripura. This association is a segment of the Tripura Baptist Christian Union. It is a very important part of the Christian life.

The Baptist Christian Union is one of the major unions associated with Christianity in state. It is the biggest body of protestant church. The head office of this union is located at the capital of the state, Agartala.

The Sadar North Baptist Association or SNBA is one of the significant associations linked with Christianity. There are about a hundred churches under this association. It is an association of the Tripura Baptist Christian Union.

Sundari

Tripura Sundari is one of the most popular deities that are worshipped in the state. Tripura Sundari is also referred to as Shodashi, Rajarajeshwari or Lalita. She is actually one of the ten goddesses associated with the Hindu religion who are together called the *mahavidyas*.

This goddess is described as being the mate of lord Shiva. It is commonly believed that the Tripura has derived its name from Tripura Sundari. One of the major temples of the state is dedicated to the worship of Tripura Sundari.

This popular temple is situated at the top of a hill close to the village called *Radhakishorepur*. This place is not very far away from the prominent town of Udaipur. There is a hymn dedicated to Tripura Sundari.

The importance of Goddess Tripura Sundari can be understood from the fact that it is considered one of the 51 pithasthanas associated with the religion of Hinduism.

Goddess Tripura Sundari is often referred to as Shodasi. Shodasi is commonly reperesented in the state as a girl of sixteen years. She represents sixteen different types of urges. The Shodasi Tantra is an important source of information about Tripura Sundari. According to this source, Tripura Sundari is actually the illumination in the eyes of Lord Shiva.

Buddhism

Mog (Burmese origin), Chakma, Barua and Uchai are the followers of Buddhism in Tripura. The total Buddhist population in Tripura is around 2,00,000 (0.2 million) of the total population 3.1 million.

There are around 200 Buddhist monasteries and 250 Buddhist monks in the state. Almost all the monasteries are small, made of bamboo and straw. The Buddhists are financially very weak and most of them live in villages. Almost all the Buddhists are the followers of Theravada Buddhism. Their cultural background and customs resemble with that of Burmese and Thai Buddhist tradition.

The Mog Buddhists have close affinity with Burmese Buddhism in all sociocultural and religious aspects. Though they live in Tripura, almost all Dhamma books [Tipiiaka, Aiihakatha, Burmese (Myanmar) Translations, etc.] are brought from Myanmar and Dharma teaching is done in Burmese (Myanmar) script. The dialect that the Mog people speak is similar to that of Burmese (Myanmar) and Arakanese (Rakhine) language with little variation in pronunciation, but the script is the same [Burmese (Myanmar) script].

The Chakma and Barua are also followers of Theravada Buddhism. Their language and cultural background find close affinity with that of Bengali. The three major Buddhist communities of Tripura, viz. Mog, Chakma and Barua, have close relation with each other and observe *vassa*, Buddha Purima, Kaihina Civara Dana, etc. in uniformity. The Buddhists of Tripura have been preserving Buddha Sasana in the state amidst fierce missionary wave of Christianity and majority Hindu culture.

The Christian missionaries are very rampant in the state. They visit almost each and every village and try to convert people into Christianity by offering money, clothe, medicine, etc. As most of the people in Tripura are poor, they get easily carried away by the tempting offers of Christian missionaries. Many Buddhist families have converted into Christianity and many more are opting the same route as they have been convinced that Jesus is the only saviour of poor people which the Christian missionaries have practically demonstrated. The Buddhists are the minority community in Tripura. They are merging slowly into majority Hindu culture, causing a threat to the survival of Buddha Sasana in Tripura.

There is no Buddhist educational institute in Tripura to impart monastic education to monks and train them on Dhamma. Most of the monks are not educated and as a result the monks have low profile and are not competent enough to safeguard Buddha Sasana from the influence of Christian Missionary and eclipsing majority Hindu Culture. Books on Buddhism are also not available in Tripura. Until recently, there was no meditation centre in the state. The Buddhists have somehow been preserving Buddha Sasana in the state. They practise Buddhism mechanically as it is a part of their culture. There is an urgent need to set up a Buddhist educational institute with well-equipped infrastructure to impart Buddhist education to both monks and lay people. A good Buddhist library and meditation centre is also required to provide Pariyatti and Paiipatti base of Buddhism to the Buddhists of Tripura.

Hinduism

Hinduism is the most practised religion in Tripura. Both Bengalis and Tripuris follow Hinduism with ardent fervour. The main gods worshipped by the people are Lord Shiva and Goddess Tripureshwari. Besides, many fertility gods are also worshipped.

Tripuris are under Hindu inspiration. They had their tribal religion modified by Hinduism. The Cantais (the Tripuri high priests) and the Deodais are regarded as the custodians of the Tripuri religion and still occupy as exalted a position in society as the Brahmins in Hindu society.

Majority of the tribes in Tripura — the Tripuris, Reangs, Jamatia, Noatias and Halams — are Hindus and practise all the Hindu religious rites. The Halam and the Noatias are generally the followers of the Sakti cult, but most of the people belonging to the Kalai and Rupini sections of the former tribe follow Vaishnavism.

Tribal Faith

The following are the names of various gods worshipped by the Tripuris and other major tribes of the state.

- *Matai-Katar:* The supreme deity of Tripura is identified with Shiva Mahadev. The word Matai means God and Katar mean great or supreme.
- *Lam-Pra:* The twin deity of sky and sea. Lam means sky or earth and Pra means sea or water.
- *San-Grama:* Deities personifying the sky, the sea and the mountains.
- *Uima or Ganga:* It is especially worshipped in the month of Agrahayana. Tuima means water-mother or water-goddess.
- *Mailu-ma* or the goddess of corn is identified with Sri or Lakshmi.
- *Khuluma* or the goddess of cotton plant.
- *Burha-cha* or the god who is worshipped specially to cure illnesses.
- *Bani-rao and Thari-rao* — sons of Burha-cha.
- The *seven goddess* of witchcraft.
- The two brothers *Goraiya* and *Kataiya* worshipped on the last day of the Hindu year (chaitra sankranti).

Health Care

Health and environment have been interlinked in more than one area of study. While human development index, as adopted by UNDP, consider non-economic indicators to assess development, health indicators can clearly indicate the quality of air, water, sanitation, noise vis-a-vis state of human health.

Health Care Facility

The State of Tripura, till date, seems to suffer significantly in terms of health care delivery system. The available data of 1999-2000, published by Directorate of Economics and Statistics in Tripura shows that total number of Public Health Clinic is only 59, total number of Hospitals 28 and dispensaries 621. While these figures have improved between

1985-2000 and may not sound alarming, the figures for available number of doctors (905), nurses (920) and midwives (95) shows the extreme inadequacy of health care delivery. While Indian figure for doctors stands at 48 per 100,000 persons, for nurses 58 per 100,000 persons and midwives 30 per 100,000 persons, the respective figures for Tripura stands at 32, 32.9 and 3.6 per 100,000 persons.

Table: Health Care System 1999-2000

Year	No. of PHC	No. of Hospitals	No. of Dispensaries	No. of Doctors	No. of Nurses	No. of Midwives
1985 *	39	12	NA	NA	NA	NA
1999**	68	24	538	905	920	95

Folk Dances

Tripura has rich cultural heritage of 19 different tribal communities, Bengali and Manipuri communities. Each community has its own dance forms which are famous in the country.

Tripuri Community

The Tripuris constitute the weightiest section of the entire tribal community, representing more than 50 per cent of the total tribal population of the state. The Tripuris live on the slopes of hills in a group of five to fifty families. Their houses in these areas are built of bamboo and raised five to six feet height to save themselves from the dangers of the wild animals. Nowadays a considerable section of this community are living in the plains and erecting houses like the plains' people adopting their methods of cultivation and following them in other aspects of life, such as dress, manners and cosmetics. Tripuri women rear a scarp, called *Pachra*, which reaches down just below the knee. They weave in their loin-loom a small piece of cloth, which they call 'Risha', and they use this small piece of cloth as their breast garment.

Garia Dance

The life and culture of Tripuris revolve around Jhum (shifting) cultivation. When the sowing of seeds at a plot of land selected for Jhum is over by middle of April, they pray to the God 'Garia' for a happy harvest. The celebrations attached to the Garia Puja continue for seven days when they seek to entertain their beloved deity with song and dance.

Lebang Boomani Dance

After the Garia festival is over, the Tripuris have a time to rest awaiting the monsoon. During this period, folks of charming colourful insects called '*Lebang*' use to visit hill slopes in search of seeds sewn on it. The annual visit of the insects renders the tribal youths to indulge in merry-making. While the men-folk make a peculiar rhythmic sound with the help of two bamboo chips in their hand, the women folk run tottering the hill slopes to catch hold of these insects called *'Lebang'*.

The rhythm of the sound made by the bamboo chips attracts the insects from their hiding places and the women in-groups catch them. With the change of time jhuming on hill slopes are gradually diminishing. But the cultural life that developed centering round the jhum delved deep into the society. It still exists in the state's hills and dales as a reminiscence of the life, which the tribal of today cherish in memory, and preserve as treasure. In both the dances Tripuris use the musical instruments like Khamb made of Bamboo, Flute, Sarinda, Lebang made of bamboo and bamboo cymbal. Tripuri women generally put on indigenous ornaments like chain made of silver with coin, Bangle made of silver, ear and nose rings made of bronze. They prefer flower as ornaments.

Reang Community

Next to Tripuris, the Reangs constitute the second biggest group among the tribal population. It is generally believed that this particular community migrated to Tripura from somewhere in the Chittagong hill Tracts in the middle part of the fifteenth century. The Reangs are very disciplined community. The head of the community enjoys the title 'Rai' word is supreme in all matters of internal disputes and hence to be obeyed by all belonging to the said community. They generally avoid normal court for justice. The Reangs are very backward both educationally and economically and, therefore they are still considered to be the primitive group.

Hozagiri Dance

While the theme of the dance remains almost to be the same as of other tribes, the dance form of the Reang community is quite different from others. The movement of hands or even the upper part of the body is somewhat restricted, whereas the movement beginning from their waist down to their feet creates a wonderful wave. Standing on an earthen pitcher with a bottle on the head and a lighted lamp on it, when the Reang belle dance twisting rhythmically the lower part of the body, the dance bewilders the onlookers. The Reangs also use the musical Instruments like Khamb, Flute made of bamboo and bamboo cymbal. The Reang women prefer to put on black Pachra and Rea. Reang women put on coins ring, which generally covers their entire upper region. They also put on rings made of coin in their ears. They are fond of fragrant flowers as ornaments to metal things.

Chakma Community

People of Chakma Community in Tripura are found normally in the Subdivisions of Kailashahar, Amarpur, Sabroom, Udaipur, Belonia and Kanchanpur. They are followers of Buddhism. Although the Chakmas are divided into several groups and subsections, no major difference is noticed in the manner and customs indifferent groups. The Chakma chiefs are generally called 'Dewans' and they exercise great authority and influence within the community in all internal matters. The Chakma Women, like all other tribal women are experts in weaving. The Chakmas are very neat and clean in their domestic life.

Bizu Dance

This popular form of dance is characteristic of the Chakma community. Bizu means 'Chaitra-Sankranti'. 'Chaitra-Sankranti' denotes end of Bengali calendar year. It is during this period when the Chakmas sing and dance to bid good-bye to the year just being ended and welcome the new year. The dance is beautifully orchestrated with the rhythm playing of what is known as 'Khenggarang' and 'Dhukuk' sorts of flutes. The Chakma women are fond of flower, which they often use in their hair. They also use metal ornaments.

Halam (Malsum) Community

Malsum is one of the 12 groups belonging to the Halam community of Tripura. Halam, again, originally hailed from one of the branches of Kukis. It is said that Kukis had lived in Tripura even before the Tripuris came in to conquer the land. Those of the Kukis who had submitted to the Tripura 'Raja' came to be known as Halams. Originally the tribal was divided into 12 subgroups of 'Dafas' but in course of time these subgroups have split into sections and new as many as sixteen clans are found to be making up for the whole Halam community. Malsum belongs to one of these 12 groups. The Halams are followers of the 'Saka' cult, but the influence of 'Vaishnavism' is quite marked, particularly, in two sections of the community. They believe in the existence of spirit too. Their worship is solemnised with offerings and sacrifices so that nothing calamitous befalls the community in the form of crop failure or epidemic or any other natural disaster. During the festival, they sit together to settle all internal disputes, try cases or crime and inflict punishment on the offenders which make the Puja a useful social gathering in keeping peace and harmony within the community.

Hai-Hak Dance

Like other tribal community of this State the social and economic life of the Halam community also revolve around jhum cultivation. At the end of the harvesting season the Malsum traditionally adore Goddess Laxmi. They enjoy this festive occasion for their famous Hai-Hak dance. It is also a community dance with exquisite beauty. Rhythms of the dance reflect the tradition inherited from distant past.

Garo Community

The people of Garo community live in the South and Dhalai District of Tripura. Originally they use to live in Tong Ghar made of bamboo to save themselves from wild animals like the other tribals of Tripura. But now they prefer houses made of mud wall with 'Chan' grass as roof. They are believed to have migrated to Tripura from Garo Hills. The life style of the Garo living in Tripura is almost like the other tribal. The Heads of the community is known as Sangnakma and the priest of the community is known as Kama. They put on the dress as good as that of the Khasis.

Wangala Dance

After the happy harvest 'Wangala' (1st rice eating ceremony) is performed in every houses. The Sangnakma, head of the communities visits every house and cuts a pumpkin as a part of worship. This pumpkin is sacrificed on this occasion. After that the women dance to the beat of 'Dama' and 'Aaduri' made of buffalo horn. The dance projects the rehearsal for war.

Lusai Community

The Lusai were originally inhabitant of the hills lying with east and northeast of Tripura and also to the adjoining hilly areas. They have settled down on Jampui Hills situated on the northeast boundary of the state under Kanchanpur Subdivision in North Tripura District. Their number is very insignificant to the total population of the state. Their social life and Customs have been objects of great attraction to others. The principal means of livelihood of the Lusai still remain to be Jhum cultivation. Of course, this can be considered chiefly to the dearth of plain land in the hills. They prefer living in high altitude of the hills.

Welcome Dance

The Lusai girls are well dressed. They generally wear their colourful cloth. They performed welcome dance whenever any visitor pay visits to their house. This is very colourful dance where young girls of the entire community take part. Their dress is so colourful that the ornaments are not very much required except fragrant flowers.

Darlong Community

The Darlongs are the sub-caste of the Lusai community. They live mostly in Kailashahar Subdivision in North Tripura District. Their main livelihood is cultivation of pineapple, orange and cotton.

Cheraw Dance

The Darlong reposes faith in after life. They believe that man is destined to go to Haven after death. Incidentally, they think that if a pregnant woman dies, she feels it very difficult, with all her physical strains, to track the long journey to Heaven. Hence, at the last stage of her pregnancy - in fact just at the time or immediately prior to delivery all her relatives perform this 'Cheraw' dance in-group throughout day and night so as to instill confidence in the mind of that woman. They are firm in their belief that even if the woman dies at this juncture. It will be possible for her to go Heaven with the courage and confidence together with joy gained through the sound of bamboo as the rhythm of the dance produced till her death.

Mog Community

There is a controversy over the origin of the word 'MOG' or 'MOGH'. In a periodical magazine of the Burmese Research Society, this 'word' has been desired to originate from Bengali. But in the model Bengali Dictionary of Bangiya Sahitya Parishad, the origin of this word is 'unknown'. In another Dictionary this word is claimed to have originated from a Burmese word 'Mogh' which is generally used as an epithet before the name of a gentleman.

Some others of course referred to the ancient Mogadha Empire for its origination. But it is sad that when the domination of Hindu religion began to thrive in this ancient centre of Buddha religion, a branch of Mogadha dynasty left for Chitagong and subsequently settled down in Hill Chitagong. Probably the Word 'Mong' came from 'Mogadhi' (one who hails from Mogadhaor one who is a resident of Mogadha).

In English dictionary the words Mog, Mogen, Mouge have been shown as surnames to the inhabitants of Arakan in 15th and 16th centuries. Bangalees of course refer to the inhabitants of Arakan as 'Mog'. The people of 'Mog' community claimed to have come from Arakan and settled down in Tripura in 957 AD. Almost all the people belonging to the Mog community are the followers of Buddhism.

Sangrai (last day of the month of Chaitra, which is the last month of the Bengali Calendar Year) is the occasion of special festival. The people of the Mog community in general and the young boys and girls in particular celebrate the day through cultural programmes to invite the new year. Cakes are prepared at every home and denisens move from house to house to take cakes. On this day water is carried through auspicious pitchers and respected persons are allowed to take bath with this water.

The young boys and girls indulge in aquatics traditional Khouyang is played on bet. Paste of fragrant sandalwood and water of green coconuts are sprinkled in every house. There is myth and merriment everywhere and in the midst of pomp and grandeur fragrant water is poured on the root of 'Bodhi Briksha'. The festival continues for three days. The youths of Mog community on this auspicious occasion move about from house to another dancing and singing with pious 'wish Yielding Tree' (Kalpataru) on head.

Way (Lamp) Festival

The people of Mog community observe austerity from the full moon of Bengali month of Ashad down to the full moon Bengali month of Ashwin. Generally no auspicious occasion of Ashad down to the full moon of Bengali month of Ashwin. Generally no auspicious occasion like marriage is celebrated during the period. Even the married women do not go to their parents' house during this time. 'Way' festival is celebrated on the day of full moon of the Bengali month of Ashwin.

Lamps dedicated to the Lord Buddha are launched on this day. The young boys and girls stand in rows with lamps in hand to worship the Lord Buddha. The youngsters indulge in merriment through songs and dances in the premises of Buddha temple. The traditional dance of the Mog community is known as 'Way Dance' or 'Lamp Dance'.

Art and Craft

The novelty of the state's art and craft comes alive in its handicrafts and handlooms. Handloom products make the vital part of the economy of Tripura. Silk, cane and bamboo works are some of the main industries. Here skilled artisans craft a fascinating variety of handiwork using simple materials, such as, bamboo, cane, palm leaves and ordinary yarn. Some of the popular handicraft items are bamboo screens, lamp stands, baskets, ivory work, tablemats, sitalpati, woodcarving, silver ornaments and other crafts.

Festivals

Tourism Festival:

- Tourism Festival at Vanghmun,
- Unokuti Tourism Festival,
- Neermahal Tourism Festival,
- Pilak Tourism Festival.

Cultural Religious Festival:

- Makar Sankranti at Thirthamukh and Unokoti,
- Holi,
- Ashokashtami at Unokoti, Brahmakunda (Mohanpur),
- Rash
- Bengali New Year,
- Garia, Dhamail, Biju and Hozagiri Festival,
- Boat Race and Manasa Mangal Festival,
- Ker and Kharchi Festival,
- Durgapuja,
- Diwali,

- Christmas at Jampui Hills,
- Budha Purnima,
- Rabindra-Najrul-Sukanta Utsav,
- Street Drama Festival,
- Chongpreng Utsav,
- Khumpui Festival,
- Wah Festival,
- Folk Cultural Festival (Loka Utsav),
- Murasing Festival,
- Sanghati Festival,
- Baishakhi Festival (Sabroom), etc., are celebrated annually.

Various Occupations

Out of the total population of the state 6,08,589 and 53,860 were classified as "main workers" and "marginal workers" respectively in 1981. This means that less than one third of the total population of the state consists of workers and more than two third are dependants. If the numbers of the marginal workers are excluded (who are partly dependants) the volume of working force shrinks still further.

In statistical terms as against the all-India participation rate of 33,417 in Tripura only 2,96,117 (far less of even one-third of the total population) of the people participated in economically productive activities. Nonetheless, this rate is higher than 1971, when it stood at 27.79 per cent. But the male participation rate in relation to 1971 has gone down from 49.43 per cent to 49.069 while the female participation rate has marched ahead from 4.83 per cent to 9.05 per cent.

Of the total main workers 43.57 per cent were recorded as cultivators, 23.92 per cent as agricultural labourers, 1.6 per cent were found to be engaged in house hold industry and 30.907, were engaged in other services. In relation to 1971 the percentage of agricultural labourers has gone up while that pertaining to cultivators has come down.

In urban areas only 26.66 per cent of the people (All India 29.2%) and in rural areas 29.97 per cent (all-India 34.8%) of the people were found to be engaged as workers. In the absence of detailed data it is difficult to trace the definite factors responsible for the changing occupational scenario in relation to 1971. However, it can be conjectured that changing social and moral values, reaction of the landlords to land reform measures, growing literacy and consequent rising level of general awareness are the possible causes. It has also been observed that the educated youth and particularly the educated tribal youth get alienated from the soil and the shows preference for a white collar job for which the enjoy the concession of reservation.

On the other hand the progressively rising population and concomitantly rising unemployment force many a non-Harijan and non-Girijan youth to opt for agricultural labouring at least as a transitional measure. On the whole the problem of unemployment has grown out of all proportions in Tripura. Although, this has now become a global problem and more acute in developing countries but it play raise a very ugly head in a sensitive and strategically located state.

As per 1983 statistical Abstract, 82,312 persons were shown as unemployed on the Live Registers of Employment Exchange of the state in 1983. How about those persons who did not get their names renewed either out of ignorance or out of frustration and those who are not registered with employment exchanges?

In 1977, this number was 56,758 and it may be inferred that by the end of 1990 the number must be around one million. The absorption of unemployed youth in schools, offices and other such institutions is no solution for the ever growing problem. As asserted by Chib such infrastructural services give a sharp spurt in money income without a corresponding increase in economic output and thus aggravate the problem at many a front.

Moreover, there is a limit of expanding jobs in this sector. The only answer is to develop the household and cottage industry sectors which with increase in production also expand job opportunities. Agro-pastoral based industry, agriculture, scientific forestry, pisciculture, beeculture, horticulture, sericulture, food processing, etc. hold a promising future in the region. The threat and attack on the social peace and communal harmony in Tripura have basically sprung from the economic backwardness and the growing bane of unemployment in the state.

6

Education

Tripura schools are run by the State Government or by private organisations, including religious institutions. Instruction is mainly in English or Bengali, though Kokborok and other tribal languages are also used. Secondary schools are affiliated with the CISCE, the CBSE, or the Tripura Board of Secondary Education. Under the 10+2+3 plan, after completing secondary school, students typically enrol for 2 years in a junior college, also known as pre-university, or in schools with a higher secondary facility. Notable higher education institutions of Tripura are MBB College, National Institute of Technology, Tripura Institute of Technology, Tripura University, and ICFAI University all located in Agartala.

Education in Tripura has developed at a very fast pace since its formation on 21st January 1972. The beautiful small state of Tripura offers immense opportunities for students from within and outside the region. To carry on the smooth operation of the education system at all levels in the state the Department of Education was formed. The department was further divided into three sections such as School Education, Higher Education and Social Welfare and Social Education Department.

As per the census of 2001, literacy rate of Tripura was 73.66 per cent. The Government of the state has taken a number of steps to develop the educational set up of the region. A free and compulsory education policy was introduced by the government that caters free education to the students who fall in the age group of 6 to 14 years of age. The education system of Tripura can be divided into four stages, they are the primary stage which comprises of Classes I-V, the middle stage consisting of Classes VI-VIII and the secondary stage comprising of Classes IX-X. Classes XI and XII are the higher secondary stage of education.

The state of Tripura has two medical colleges, one university, one pharmacy college and wide number of engineering colleges and polytechnic colleges. Compared to the population the number of educational institutes is less but the government is taking special measures to solve the problem.

Schools

Tripura Schools plays a vital role in spreading education in the region. The Schools are either affiliated to Indian Certificate of Secondary Education (ICSE) and the Indian School Certificate (ISC) examinations of Delhi, Tripura Board of School Education, or Central Board of Secondary Education (CBSE) board. While some of the schools are exclusively for boys, some are just for girls, the others are coeducational schools.

Colleges

In the Tripura Colleges many eminent scholarly professors and lecturers impart knowledge to the pupils. A number of undergraduate, graduate, post-graduate, medical, engineering, law, polytechnics and ITI institutes are established both by the State Government and private organisations.

All the colleges are affiliated under Tripura University, while the technical institutes are approved by AICTE. The courses offered by the colleges are B.A. (English, Hindi, History, Bengali, Political Science, etc.), B.Sc. (Maths, Botany, Physics, Chemistry, Zoology, etc.), M.A. (English, Hindi, Economics, Bengali, History, Political Science, etc.), M.Sc. (Maths, Physics, Botany, Zoology, Chemistry, etc.), etc. The specialised colleges offers courses in Pharmacy, Journalism, engineering, medical science and many more. The infrastructure of the colleges are well developed with good laboratories, libraries, modern equipments, etc.

University

Tripura University was established on 2nd October 1987. To a great extent it fulfils the aspirations of the people for their quest for higher studies. Before the establishment of the university the colleges had to seek affiliation from the Calcutta University, which was becoming difficult for the colleges and also the students. The demand of the students was finally fulfilled on the fateful day of 18th May 1985 when the then education minister Dasharath Deb laid the foundation for Tripura University on the sprawling 75 acres of land that was donated by the State Government, at Suryamaninagar near Agartala.

Presently, Tripura University offers post-graduate courses on sixteen subjects. The subjects that are offered for the post-graduate degree are Political Science, Geography and Disaster Management, History, English, Philosophy, Analytical and Applied Economics, Sanskrit, Physics, Commerce, Hindi, Zoology, Bengali, Kokborok, Botany, Chemistry,

Human Physiology and Mathematics. A number of Departments, Directorates and Centres under the supervision of the university provide 38 degree courses. There are in all twenty-four general and technical colleges which are affiliated with Tripura University.

Tripura University enjoys the highest autonomy in all matters of higher education in the state. Some of the other facilities provided by Tripura University are NSS Unit, Computer Centre, Sports Board, Students amenities' centre with a canteen and mini gym, 100-bedded hostel for boys and 40-bedded hostel for girls, a branch of State Bank of India, a Post-office, etc.

Distance Learning

The distance learning courses in Tripura are provided by the universities of Tripura and other Tripura Distance Learning Institutes. These Distance Learning Courses are highly in demand as they allow the students to nurture other interest along with their studies. The initial hesitation of pursuing education through distance learning mode has gradually evaporated. On the contrary, today, distance education is looked forward as a suitable mode of pursuing higher education. It is easier for the students to pursue a correspondence course from the universities of Tripura as the course fee of these distance learning courses are much lower as compared to that of the regular courses.

Moreover the distance learning Institutes also offer necessary study materials to the students. Thus, Tripura Distance Learning Institutes offer fair amount of flexibility to the students.

The Directorate of Distance Education, Tripura University is the leading provider of distance education. As the course fee of these distance learning courses are quite low, large number of people can pursue these courses at their own time and pace. Thus the Distance Learning Institutes are playing a very important role in so far as the democratisation of higher education in the state is concerned.

7

Language and Literature

Bangla is the official language of Tripura, It is also a medium of instruction in a majority of schools although English besides being used in offices is also the medium of instruction in institutes of higher education and the public schools catering to the elite.

On the whole notwithstanding a stiff opposition from a section of the Tripura population, it is Bangla and Bangla alone that has come to be the *lingua franca* in the sense that in schools, colleges, offices, clubs, theatres, cities, towns and even in a majority of the newspapers and other periodicals Bangla dominates the scenario. All most daily, weekly, fortnightly and monthly newspapers, journals and magazines appear in Bangla language. In English and Tripuri languages only some appear, while in the Manipuri languages 3 such publications.

Thus it shall be relevant to dwell upon the Bangla language and literature as pursued in Tripura. Out of the Austric-Dravidian group of languages, Bangla is believed to have emerged, first as a separate dialect somewhere during the medieval period (ninth to twelfth century AD) of the history. The Shaurseni and Prakrit as old languages and Sanskrit as a supreme and towering language have greatly contributed to the development of Bangla. Slowly and gradually Bangla came to be developed as an independent language with a script of its own. It has thirteen vowels and thirty-nine consonants in its alphabet. Apart from that, similar to the Devanagari script, joint alphabets, by combining vowels with consonants or vowels with vowels and consonants with consonants can be formed.

The sphere of Bangla, slowly and steadily, became so vast, that today one finds many variations in the Bangla as used in different areas. Above all, for its enrichment and speedy development Bangla kept its door wide open for alien influences. Arabic, English, Urdu, Hindi, Sanskrit, Turkish, French, Japanese, Burmese, Chinese and Malayan are those principal languages which have left their mark on Bangla. It has been observed the world over, that the development of literature in any language starts with the development of poetry, which has been rated as the finest and most appealing way of expressing human emotions. The Bangla literature has been no exception to this norm. Nonetheless motives behind the development of language and literature can be diverse, as economic, social, cultural or religious.

In the case of Bangla poetry although no body can deny the fact that socio-economic and cultural factors had played their roles in their own way, yet it was religion which inspired and accelerated the development of Bangla poetry. It was Charyapada a collection of devotional songs composed somewhere during the Pala period that laid down a very stable, solid and concrete anchor sheet upon, which a magnificent and imposing edifice of Bangla poetry came to be raised. The Siddhagurus, religious leaders of the period, are believed to have been the original compositors of the Charyapada. During the tenth century AD another two religious movements lent a supporting hand to Bangla poetry for its rapid development. The Nath cult of the Shaivite Hinduism and Sahijya cult of Buddhism through their reforming movements came forward during the tenth century AD and indirectly extended support for the development of Bangla poetry. These ash screaming ascetics with bored ears and an alms receiving bowl in their hands roamed about chanting and singing devotional hymns. But such a device had also its limitations. Although it could provide the bed rock but was unable to provide bricks, lime and mortar for building the edifice of everlasting poetry. Thus it was the great Bengali poet Chandidas who brought the Bangla poetry on a strong footing. His writings imported a wave of romanticism in the Bangla poetry and in Tripura till present times Chandidas poems are read with fond love. Chandidas, himself a Brahman priest in a temple fell in deep love with a washer-woman whom he eulogised through his poetry.

Today when Tripura society is in a transitional phase in respect of its, sociocultural characteristics many a building poet have followed his themes and styles of composing romantic poetry in Bangla Language. Mangal Kavya is another dimension of the Bangla poetry being deeply cherished in Tripura. As already narrated the religion as a force has been a dominant factor behind the development of the Bangla poetry. These persons who were uprooted from their hearths and homes and were haunted for a long time by the miseries, privations and brutalities they faced at the time of partition turned many Bangla immigrants settling in Tripura towards religion and religious poetry. No wonder sensing the mood and taste of such people there emerged a wave of mangal kavya in Tripura, a wave witnessed in Bangal centuries ago. For quite some time Vijaya Guptas Manasmangal, Mukand Charvarty's Chandi Mangal Kavya and Bharat Chandra's Anand Mangala were those works which found favour with the general readers in Tripura.

Krittidasa's translated Ramayana, from Sanskrit to Bangla, is very popular in Tripura. Similarly Kashiram Dasa's translated Mahabharata, from Sanskrit to Bangla, finds favour with the people of Tripura. This translation was rendered somewhere in the sixteenth century but the rendering into Bangla has been so fine that the common people prefer it overall renderings into Bangla.

The beauty behind this title is that it was inspired and supported by Muslims like Pargali khan, Chhutti Khan and Hussain Shah. Similarly the fifteenth century renderings of Bhagvat into Bangla are liked by the people of Tripura. This title in Bangla is known as Shri Vijayadashami and it is gathered that its translator Maladhar Basu was awarded the title of Gunraj Khan, a fact again supporting the contention that most of the best Bangla renderings of principal Hindu scriptures during the medieval period were inspired by the Muslim patrons.

Some of the Muslim poets of that period themselves contributed in this regard. For instant the works of the famous Hindi Poet Malik Muhammad Hayasi were translated into Bangla by a Muslim Bangla poet Alaul on the instance of Magan Thakur. The Bangla prose which came in usage in Tripura also entered from Bengal where the prose writing in Bangla was inspired, motivated and supported by the foreigners. In fact, the foreign missionaries, whose one of the aims was to convert people to Christianity needed prose for the propagation of their religion.

Dome Antanio, a Portuguese missionary, was the first to write Brahman Roman Catholic Samvad in Bangla prose. George Thomas, William Carry and William Morsh were other foreigners who not only wrote Bangla prose but even set a trend and style for the indigenous authors to follow. Raja Ram Mohan Roy a missionary in his own right has been that person whose prose writings were read with keen interest in Tripura. Similarly the prose works of another Bengali social reformer, Ishwar Chandra Vidyasagar have been liked and loved in Tripura. Pyari Chandra Mitra's Bangla novel Alaler Ghareduala has been that piece of prose which has been read time and again by thousands of Tripuris. Bankam Chandra Chatterji, Sharat Chandra Chattopadhyaya, Bimal Mitra, Rabindranath Tagore are among those authors who are held in very high esteems among the people of Tripura.

In Tripura, there has been a relative dearth of creative writers. In fact, natural calamities, class turmoil and political instability have been the responsible factors. Moreover, with growing degree of awakening among the different religious and ethnic groups there has been an under current flowing in favour of developing the tongues of the indigenous sections of the populace. Tripuri and Manipuri are already on their way to development. Even the state authorities have been compelled by the circumstances to assist and promote the development of not only the Tripuri and Manipur languages but even some other tongues used by different tribal groups.

The protagonists of this move have started writing articles in some of the newspapers and periodicals appearing in these languages. Nonetheless, it shall take a long easy and long time for these writings to gain maturity and effectiveness among the people.

So far most of the articles pertain to the problems of the tribal pockets and the tribal people residing therein. But it has been seen that all facets of the newly produced literature in these languages have been largely influenced by the Bangla literature.

Although there is a section among the non-Bangla writers who disfavour the borrowings from Bangla but such a move is against the natural laws. It is but natural that the literature being produced in Manipuri and Tripuri languages gets the impact of Bangla and Assamese or some Bodo group of dialects than the languages of some distantly located places.

The Backdrop

Languages in Tripura comprises Bengali and the different dialects of Tripuri. The influence of Bengali in the languages of Tripura is remarkable. The Chakma language, spoken in Belonia and Sabrum subdivisions, stands as an exemplar of the influence of Bengali on the languages of Tripura.

The official language of Tripura is Bengali. Bengali, also known as Bangla, Banga-Bhasa, etc., is one of the most predominant languages. It is estimated that about 80 per cent of the people speak Bengali. In fact, a large number of the population consider Bengali as their mother tongue. It is noteworthy that Tripuri is also written using the Bengali script. Another major language is Tripuri. Tripuri is the language of the community and is mostly found in Khowai, Kailashahar, Sadar, Amarpur subdivisions. Tripuri is also spoken in the adjoining areas of Chittagong Hill Tracts. The mother tongue of the people is Halam and their dialect is known as Rankhal. Rankhal is said to be an offshoot of Halam.

Besides, the dialect of the Tripuri, also known as Kak-Barak, belongs to the Tibeto-Burman group of languages. The root of the dialect can be traced from Sino-Tibetan speech family. It is interesting to note that Kak-Barak does not possess any script: it is written using the Bengali script.

Bengali

Bengali is the official language of Tripura. About 80 per cent of the total population speak Bengali. Under the branch India, Bengali belongs to Indo-European languages.

Bengali is written in Bengali script, a Brahmanic script. The Brahmanic script is similar to the Devanagri script used for writing Sanskrit and Hindi. In the Brahmanic script, the syllables are represented through the base symbols. To change the vowel of a particular syllable, other symbols are added to it. Two symbols are ligated to form a consonant cluster.

It is noteworthy that the Bengali alphabet is a syllabic alphabet. In the Bengali alphabets, the consonants usually have an inherent vowel with two different pronunciations. But, it is not always easy to determine the difference in the pronunciation.

Moreover, the vowels are written as independent letters. On many instances, the vowels are also written using diacritical marks. Special conjunct letters are used, when too many consonants occur in clusters. The use of conjunct reduces the letter of the consonants. The final consonant remains intact, as the inherent vowel is only applied to the final consonant. The Chakma language is an instance of the influence of Bengali on the languages of Tripura.

Tripuri

Tripuri is one the principle languages of Tripura. Tripuri belongs to Tibeto-Burman group of languages. The root of the language can be traced from the Sino-Tibetan speech family.

Tipuri is also known as Kak-Barak in Tripura. 'Kak' implies 'words' and 'barak' means 'men'. Thus, the literal meaning of Kak-Barak is the language spoken by the people. It is noteworthy that the Kak-Barak possess any script.

Occupying a position next to Bengali, Tripuri is spoken in Sadar, Kailashahar, Amarpur and Khowai subdivisions. Tripuri is also spoken in the adjoining areas of Tripura, such as the Chittagong Hill Tracts. The mother tongue of the people residing in these areas is Halam. The dialect spoken by them is Rankhal. It is interesting to note that Rankhal is a branch of the dialect.

The words of the language can be divided into five categories, viz.:

- Original words;
- Words with suffixes;
- Composed words;
- Loan words;
- Naturalised words.

Tripuri is related to the Bodo language. Dimasa language has a close association with Kak-Barak. Initially, Kak-Barak was written in 'Koloma'. 'Rajratnakar', a chronicle of the Tripuri Kings, was written using the Koloma script. Kak-Barak was recognised as the official language of Tripura around 1979 AD.

Kokborok Literature

Kokborok language, the language of the Tripura state has gone through considerable development/evolution during the 20th century. There have been many Royal Tripuri Princes and Government Officials and also common people who have contributed to the language's development in the last century. Tripura is a state in North East India.

Novels

"Hachuk Khurio" (In the lap of Hills) by Sudhanya Deb Barma is the first modern Kokborok novel. It was published by the Kokborok Sahitya Sabha and Snskriti Samsad in 1987 AD. Also "Tongthai Naitungnani" (In search of above) by Shyamlal Deb Barma was published serially in *Lama* a literary magazine.

Short Stories

Dundurkma a compilation of 12 short stories by Shyamlal Deb Barma in 1984 and also Adong in 1987 edited by him. Nakhwrai a compilation of four stories by Benoy Deb Barma in 1987. Elemni Bibi a compilation of eight stories by Haripada Deb Barma in 1989.

Poetry

Kok-Borok Koklob Bwchab (A collection of poems) in 1983 edited by Naresh Chandra Dev Varma and Shyamlal Deb Barma; Chhimalwng Chhakao Molongni Khum (Flower of stone on a crematorium) in 1984 by Nanda Kumar Deb Barma; Kogtang-Koklob Bwtang (collection of poems and rhymes) in 1983 and Muktwi by Santimoy Chakraborty. Luku Sochama Rwchabmung (Songs of the masses) by Mahendra Deb Barma in 1984. Ha Kwchak (Red Soil) 1983 and Nwng Hamjakma Rwya 1988 and also Ang bai Kwkharang twini khorang in 1986 and Rwchapmung by Sudhanya Tripura. Haping Garingo Chibuksa Ringo 1986 and Kolomtwi Kishi Mwkhang 1986 also Bolong Kwkhrang 1987 by Chandra Kanta Murasing. Sonnet Koktangrog by Benoy Deb Barma 1988. Kokila Nwng twmani aswk pung by Narendra Deb Barma 1988. Horni boro or Sangh tram panchali by Alindralal Tripura. Bolongni Bwsajwksong Nwsao by Nanada Kumar Deb Barma 1988 and Kok-Borok Gono Sangit by Shyamlal Deb Barma 1988.

Ani Ganao Ang and Ani Rwchabmung 2000 by Nanda Kumar Deb Barma, Himalayni Bedek Buprao 1991 and Love-ism 1995 by Chandramani Deb Barma, Dormo Lam boy Kok-Borok Baul 1992 by Khajual Jamatia, Khumpui Barrwrwk 1995 by Kokborok tei Hukumu Mission, Vakharai 1996 by Kumud Ranjan Deb Barma, Nono Rikha Khumpui 1997 and Jaduni Khorang 200 by Sudhanya Tripura, Bolong Muphunjak Yakbai 1998 by Bikashroy Deb Barma, Longtrainin Eklobyo 1998 by Bijoy Deb Barma, Lok Chethuang Lok 1999 and Pindi Uatwi Pin 1999 by Chandra Kanta Murasing, Sinijak Kwrwi Bumui 2000 by Kunja Bihari Deb Barma and Kokthiarog Swngo Bonbonia 2000 by Shyamlal Deb Barma.

Sana Muchungbo Sajakya Kokrok 2002 by Sona Charan Debbarma.

Others

Tripurani Kereng Kotoma 1980 by Santimoy Chakraborty and some of the translated books were Kok-Borok Geeta by Nanda Kumar Deb Barma 1988, Nok Arini Kothoma and

Kok-Borok Bai Rabindranath in 1987 by Shyamlal Deb Barma also Takhumsa Bodol by Narendra Chandra Deb Barma. Also many literary magazines were popular in this decade such as *Lama* of the Tripura Upajati Ganamukti Parishad, *Chati* of Kokborok Sahitya-O-Sanskriti Samsad and *Dangdu* of Tripura Rajya Kokborok Sahitya Sabha.

Novel

Hachuk Khurio (In the lap of Hills), 2nd part, 1994 by Sudhanya Deb Barma. Khong in 1996 by Shyamlal Deb Barma.

Short Stories

Belonia, 1994 by Nagendra Jamatia, Mokol Bwskango 1994 and Biyal 1997 and Chethuang Tolao 2000 by Snehamoy Roy Choudhury, Bolongni Khum 1996 and Busu 2000 by Sunil Deb Barma, Swkal Jwkma 1998 by Bijoy Deb Barma, Naphurai Jamatia and Rabindra Kishore Deb Barma. Osthirog 2000 by Biswa Kumar Deb Barma, Jalai Tokpuku 200 by Haripada Deb Barma and Naithok 1998 by Naphurai Jamatia and Ashok Deb Barma.

Yamroksa 2002 by Binoy Deb Barma, Holong Beserni Khum 2002 by Rebati Debbarma, Toksa Tiyari 2004 by KOHM.

Others

Some of the translation books were Komola Kantoni Doptar 1992 by Nagendra Deb Barma, Mangni Uansokthani Geeta 1997 by Annaprasad Jamatia and Lobmung Bwchab (Psalms) by Tripura Baptist Christian Union. Other prominent books are Kwrak Kothoma 1995 by Krishnadhan Jamatia, Anglo-Kokborok Dictionary 1996 by Binoy Deb Barma, Phukmung 1994 by Kokborok tei Hukumu Mission, Kokboroni Rangchak-Richak 1994 by Binoy Deb Barma, Gandhiji 1995 by Sukanta Deb Barma, Kokborokni Kokrok Kisa 1996 by Nitai Acharjee, Sachlang Jorani Imangni Kumpui 1997 by Bimal Deb Barma, Kokborok Sikhum 1997 by Rabindra Kishore Deb Barma and Bemar Tai Bini Hamrimung 1999 by Nilmani Deb Barma.

General

Twiprani Laihbuma (The Rajmala — History of Tripura) translated by R. K Deb Barma and published in 2002 AD by KOHM. Dr. B. R. Ambedkor 2001 by Chandra Bala Deb Barma also by KOHM, Thangphlaihni Bithilwng (The Borok herbal medicine) 2002.

Present Scenario

The present trend of development of the Kokborok literary works show that the Kokborok literature is moving forward slowly but steadily with its vivacity and distinctive originality to touch the rich literature of the rich languages.

Newspapers, Radio and Television

The following table shows, in relation to its total population, rate of general awareness and levels of education Tripura has a fairly good number of newspapers and periodicals have started appearing in the region. The table reveals that whenever there occurred variation in the total number of periodicals it were the weeklies that were affected most.

Similarly coming to language of the papers, the Bangla periodicals exhibited ups and downs. Where as the numbers of the daily papers have shown a fair degree of uniformity. The newspapers and periodicals appearing in the Bangla language too showed fewer fluctuations. Although certain sections of the populace have been quite vociferous with regard to the introduction of Tripuri language as an official language as also the medium of instruction but the number of newspapers and periodicals appearing in this language have been dismally low.

It appears that for a long time to come the Bangla language shall reign supreme. No doubt the numbers of newspapers and periodicals appearing in Bangla have fluctuated but such a degree of fluctuation can be seen in any language and any part of the country.

In fact some educated unemployed persons having some interest in journalism make an initiative for self employment but the vagaries involved in this field force closure or suspended animation. Nonetheless, as inferred from the table, the future of newspaper industry and Journalism is not bleak but promising in the region.

Number of Periodicals in the State of Tripura

Year	Number of periodicals	Daily	Weekly	Others	English	Bangla	Manipuri	Tripuri
1975-76	53	12	39	2	3	46	2	2
1976-77	61	14	46	1	4	53	2	2
1977-78	64	13	48	3	4	56	2	2
1978-79	47	12	33	2	2	41	2	2
1979-80	56	12	37	7	4	47	3	3
1980-81	55	12	37	6	2	48	3	2

8

Economy

Tripura (land adjoining water) is located in the extreme Southwest corner of the North East. This hilly land locked area spreads over a total area of 10,492 sq km, covering approximately 0.29 per cent of the Indian landmass and 3.9 per cent of the entire North East. This land of hilly slopes, flat lands, rivers, lakes, hillocks and forests stretches between 91.09 degree to 92.22 degree East longitude and 22.56 degree to 24.32 degree North latitude.

The state of Tripura was merged with the Indian Union on October 15, 1949 after Independence of the Country as a 'C' category state and became a Union Territory in July 1963 before being conferred full Statehood on January 21, 1972. Tripura shares an 856 km of international border with Bangladesh.

Despite being geographically the smallest state in the region, it is the 2nd most populous state in the North East, the first being, Assam. According to the Census of 2001, Tripura has a total population of 3,191,168, with a density of 304 persons per sq km and ranks 22nd in India. It constitutes 0.31 per cent population of India and 8.18 per cent of the entire North East. Even though Tripura was a tribal majority state to begin with, it has lost its tribal nature largely due to large-scale migration from neighbouring Bangladesh. Tribals have been reduced to a minority status leading a social upheaval in the state. Bengali and Kakborak are the two principal languages in the state.

Agriculture is the mainstay of Tripura's economy. Agricultural sector provides employment to nearly 51 per cent of the total workers in the state. The per capita income at current prices of the state stands at Rs. 10,931 and at constant prices Rs. 6,813 in the financial year 2000-01. Tripura ranks 22nd in the human resource development index and 24th in the poverty index in India according to the sources of 1991.

The literacy rate of Tripura is 80.2 per cent, higher than the all India literacy rate of 67.6 per cent. Some quality timber like Sal, Garjan, Teak, Gamar are found abundantly in the forests of the state. The most important mineral resource of Tripura is oil and natural gas. However, the industrial sector in this State continues to be highly underdeveloped.

Tripura's gross state domestic product for 2004 is estimated at $2.1 billion in current prices. Agriculture is the mainstay of Tripura's economy. However, handicraft, particularly made of bamboo, also finds a special mention in the states' economy.

Tripura is surrounded by Bangladesh on three sides. Tripura, in the past, had excellent transportation links with the erstwhile East Bengal and through it, with West Bengal.

The straight-line distance between Agartala and Calcutta is only about 350 km (approximately the distance between Madras and Bangalore). Many large towns in Bangladesh are within 150 km of the towns in Tripura as can be seen from the following:

- Agartala-Dhaka: 150 km.
- Kailashahar-Sylhet: 90 km.
- Sabroom-Chittagong: 75 km.
- Sonamura-Comilla: 11 km.

The transportation links were through rail, road and waterways. The railway network of Bangladesh runs along the state's border. The economy of the state and the adjoining parts of Bangladesh has always been integral and any separation of trade, commerce and economy between the two is artificial and possibly, not maintainable.

The ties between Tripura and Bangladesh are further cemented by very strong social and cultural linkages. The people till date share kinship ties and relationships through marriages. The languages and dialects spoken in different parts of the state are common with those in the neighbouring districts of Bangladesh. Thus, the natural links of Tripura with Bangladesh are historical, deep-rooted and at several planes.

During recent years, a number of initiatives have been taken at the level of the government as well as the business community, aimed at re-establishing the historical links between Tripura and Bangladesh. The official trade between Tripura and Bangladesh was started during 1994-95.

As many as 8 Land Custom Stations have been notified for the purpose, out of which 3 are operational at present. The Bangladesh Government has also set up a Visa Office at Agartala. The present volume of trade in about Rs. 170 million per annum, but the same is expected to increase fast, with the bringing down of tariff and other barriers under SAARC initiative. The declared goal of SAARC nations to make South East Asia a "Free Trade Area" by 2001 has the potential of revolutionising the Tripura Economy, as it will put an end to the geographical isolation of Tripura.

Serious initiatives have also been taken in recent years for getting a transit route through Bangladesh, to connect Tripura with the rest of India as well as to the Chittagong Port of Bangladesh. Commencement of Border trade with Bangladesh is also under active consideration.

There are also suggestions to re-establish the old Rail/ Road/ Waterways links with Bangladesh. All this augurs well for Tripura. It will effectively integrate the Tripura Economy to the rest of India as well as to the other countries in the Region.

In fact, it will make Tripura the "Gateway to the Northeast" and will give a great boost to the state economy. It is expected that within next few years, the Tripura Economy will be effectively integrated with Eastern India as well as other countries in the Region. This would open up a vast market for the industrial units based in Tripura.

Tripura is a landlocked state endowed with vast green forests and abundant natural resources. It shares a long boundary with Bangladesh (856 km) and with neighbouring states of Assam and Mizoram. The state was merged with Indian Union on October 15, 1949.

The state is located in the Bio-geographic zone of 9B-Northeast Hills and possesses an extremely rich biodiversity. The local flora and faunal components of Indo-Malayan and Indo-Chinese subregions. There are 379 species of trees, 320 shrubs, 581 herbs, 165 climbers, 16 climbing shrubs, 35 fernsa and 45 epiphytes.

The state has 4 districts, 15 subdivisions, 38 development blocks and one autonomous council. The economy is predominantly agrarian. Tripura's geographical isolation and poor development in infrastructure have gone a long way to hinder the scope of its economic progress. In terms of infrastructure development, the CMIE index for the year 1992-93 is 63 compared to the All India average of 100.

The disparity in per capita income between Tripura and the nation has grown with time. The per capita income of the state has remained more or less stagnant during the last few years. The annual compound growth rate of NSDP from 1980-81 to 1996-97 has been worked out at 11.07 per cent at current prices and 5.31 per cent at constant prices.

In so far as the sectoral growth is concerned, it has been observed that between 1980-81 to 1996-97, agriculture, the major sector in the economy of the state demonstrated a growth rate of 9.92 per cent at current prices and 2.25 per cent at constant prices. Similarly, the manufacturing sector showed a growth of 5.48 per cent at current prices and 3.24 per cent at constant prices.

Tripura is one of the ten states enjoying the status of special category in India. The special category of states are those states which, due to their geo-economic disadvantages, deserve special preferential treatment from the Central Government for financing their annual plans.

According to the statutory provisions, the special category of states are entitled to receive central assistance of which comes 90 per cent as grants and 10 per cent as loans while the other so-called developed states get 30 per cent as grants and 70 per cent as loans. The plan and the non-plan expenditures are virtually financed by the Central Government for the special category of states.

In a sense, the responsibility of the Central Government is to ensure that the backward states are provided with adequate supports so that they also can develop at par with the other developed states. It is further envisioned that the status of special category ascribed to some of the states will cease once they become able to catch up with the rest of the country.

This text makes a modest attempt to scan the financial health of Tripura state—one of the beneficiaries under the special category of states. The period of scanning ranged particularly from the period of 1990-91 to 1998-99. In order to arrive at the logical conclusions through the scanning, the series of 'Budget At A Glance' and the various Reports of the Comptroller and Auditor General of India on the performances of the Govt. of Tripura were consulted for the specific period of time.

The annual budget is considered to be the mirror of the financial health status of a state. A close look into the trend of the budgets over the last decade is expected to provide the financial health situation of the state of Tripura. Being a small state in terms of population of 32 lakhs and geographic area of about 10 thousand square km, Tripura's budget is also small in size.

The total budgetary expenditures, for example, for the years of 1997-98, 1998-99, 2000-01 and 2001-02 are respectively Rs. 1,308.66 crores, Rs. 1,384.94 crores, Rs. 1,999.14 crores, Rs. 2,331.11 crores and Rs. 2,618.06 crores only.

It has been observed that every year the budget estimate increases at the rate of 10 per cent to 15 per cent only. Interestingly, with the usual increase of the size of the budget, there remains unchanged distributional pattern of the allocated resources amongst the various sectors.

The pattern of distribution of resources in the various departments, is more or less the same. The finance is at the top (19% to 24%), followed by School Education (15% to 16%) and then comes Power (8% to 11%). Agriculture with 2 per cent to 3 per cent of the total resource is given the least priority. It is an irony of fact that the Agriculture in the predominantly agrarian economy such as Tripura gets no priority at all.

The receipt side of the budgets provides interestingly revealing facts. The financing of the state's budget, as it has already been mentioned, is mainly done by the Central Government.

The contribution by the state itself towards the financing the budget forms 8 per cent to 9 per cent only and the rest comes form the Central Government in the form of plan assistance and non-plan assistance which comprises of the bulk of the total receipts for the budget.

The state Govt. depended heavily on the grants and loans from the Central Government for its annual plan. Since, the state's own resource generation from tax-revenue and non-tax revenue being only 8 per cent was negligible, there is no other option for the state but to rely on the Centre for meeting its budgetary expenditure. The Central Government provided to Tripura 90 per cent of the total revenue receipts (Rs. 1,139.39 crores) and 97 per cent of the revenue expenditures (Rs. 1,175.62 crores) only for the budget of 1998-99.

The Government expenditures are mainly of four types–plan, non-plan and revenue and capital, etc. As a matter of facts, the non-plan and revenue expenditure are meant for just maintenance of establishment and services while new assets are created by the plan and capital expenditures. The indicators such as:

- *plan expenditure as a percentage of*
  - revenue expenditure, and
  - capital expenditure.
- *capital expenditure to total expenditure and*
- *expenditure on general service on*
  - revenue, and
  - capital generally speak of the status of the quality of expenditures incurred under the budget provisions.

It is observed that the expenditure on general services on the capital side had been declining faster than the revenue side. The trend was downwardly secular since 1997-98. Again, over the span of five years starting from 1994-95, the capital expenditure to total expenditure exhibited a continuous fall since 1996-97.

Finally, the indicator of expenditure on general services on capital side showed a trend of drastic fall from 12 per cent in 1995-96 to 2 per cent only in 1998-99, whereas, the proportion of expenditure on general services on revenue side was on the rise from 30 per cent in 1994-95 to 35 per cent in 1998-99.

The indicators reflecting the quality of expenditures made by the Government of Tripura, unambiguously speak for the directionlessness of the state's exchequer. It becomes evident that the priority was accorded to the wrong agenda while the assets creation was although neglected.

It also points out that the budgetary allocations appeared to be guided by other criteria rather than economic consideration. Economic efficiency warrants that the scarce resource is to be put in that area where its return is the highest.

The expenditure on general services on revenue side was 35 per cent and the expenditure on general services on capital side was only 2 per cent. The Economic wisdom wanted the planners of the state to reschedule the budgetary allocations the other way so that the gap could have been made the least, if not possibly the reverse.

The performances of the Govt. of Tripura in regard to the debt management seem to be also disappointing. The total liability of the government had grown by 70 per cent during the period from 1994-95 to 1998-99. It has been observed that after the payment of principles and the interests on the earlier debt burdens, only less than one third of the new borrowings was made available for fresh investment.

While the outstanding debt burden was on the rise, the availability of net fund was, as a result, diminishing due to unproductive investment made in the past. The ratios of the debt to GSDP (Gross State Domestic Products) gives another revealing picture of the state's plunging into gradual debt-trap from where no return is apparently visible. The ever increasing debt ratio from 33 per cent in 1995-96 to 41 per cent in 1998-99 clearly keeps on sending alarming signal to the state planners to act before the economy slips further beyond recovery.

One of the main functions of any Government is to make expenditure under the provisions of budget to ensure that the assets are created for the welfare of the people of the state and at the same time to ensure that the liabilities are kept at the minimum level for the whole exercise to be meaningful. Unfortunately, the asset-liability scenario of the economy of Tripura is also shocking.

Business and Trade

Tripura being a poor and backward state, where industrial development is still at the lowest ebb, a section of the populace still clings to the practice of jhuming and a good chunk of the people are still tradition bound, the region is neither self sufficient in food products nor in the production of other utility goods. Resultantly the balance of trade is bound to be disfavourable to the state. The State imports large quantities of rice, wheat, maize, pulses sugar, edible oils, diesel, petroleum, liquid parafine gas, fabrics, drugs, chemicals, plastic goods, iron and steel, engineering goods, stationary, coal, kerosene, surgical equipment, scientific goods, office articles, milk products, electrical machinery, electronic goods, packing materials, power, fertilizers, transport equipment, cotton, metalware and brassware, etc. The exports from the state include plywood, pulp, articles manufactured out of bamboo, timber and canned fruit but the quantities exported are quite insignificant.

Natural Resources

The most important mineral potential possibility of Tripura is oil and natural gas. There were several gas seepages near Ampi Bazar, Saikhanbari headwaters of the Channel, Chara stream and about 2 km WNW of Kaphelapa village. The other minerals are:

Glass Sand: Deposits of white sand with an average silica content above 98 per cent and suitable for the manufacture at ordinary coloured glassware's occur along the bank of Bijainadi stream in Bisramganj with an estimated reserve of 1,60,000 tonnes, near old Agartala with an estimated reserve of 50,000 tonnes, and at Purba and Paschim Champamura. A glass factory was set up at Arundhutinagar near Agartala with a capacity of 2 tonnes of glassware per day. Sand deposits located at Agartala may meet the demand of raw material for the production of soda ash for use in the soap factory.

Clay: White plastic clay suitable for the manufacture of coloured ceramic products occurs at several places near Agartala, Dharmanagar and Bisramganj areas. Small deposits have been reported from the Teliamura — Ampi Bazar road cutting and near Khowai and Jogindernagar.

Grey plastic clay has been located on the hillsides near Paschim Champamura with a reserve of 914 tonnes, in Ranir Bazar with a reserve of 20,000 tonnes, at Sekerkot with an estimated reserve of 60,800 tonnes. Grey and white plastic clay occur at Tarkarjala village, Mohanpur and Latiachara areas.

Lignite: Small occurrences of pyritiferous non-cacing variety of lignite occur in the rocks on the western flank of Unkoti kolangshi hill, north of Kumarghat, at Betaga and Sabrum.

Limestone: Sporadic occurrences of occasionally fossiliferous siliceous limestone have been reported from the Sakhan and Jampui ranges.

Building Material: The shale deposits in the Atharamura range can be used for the manufacture of clay-cement-nodules to be used as road metal.

The lateritised conglomerate moorum with quartz pebble is being extensively quarried for road metal. Grey-coloured, tough calcareous sandstone found in Gagrachara can be used as road metal.

Natural Gas

Tripura has vast reserves of natural gas in non-associate form. The gas is of high quality, with high methane content of about 97 per cent and without any presence of H_2S of Sulphur and other impurities.

ONGC has been actively engaged in exploration activities in the state since 1972. Based on the exploration work of so far, ONGC has estimated the total Gas Reserves as under:

Prognosticated Reserves: 400 BCM

Established Gas Reserves: 30.65 BCM

Net Recoverable Reserves: 16.91 BCM

Present Production Potential: 2.03 MMSCMD

The Exploration activities are expected to be stepped up in near future. The Government of India is in the process of finalising a contract with M/S Oklands International of USA, for taking up exploration activities in Tripura, in addition to ONGC.

The target is to increase the Production Potential to 4.5 MMSCMD by the year 2001-02.

Presently, natural gas is being utilised mainly for the Power Projects of the State Government/NEEPCO (a Central Government Undertaking). The present utilisation of natural gas is about 0.80 MMSCMD, which is expected to increase to about 1.25 MMSCMD shortly.

A small quantity of gas is also being used for gas supply to domestic/ industrial consumers. The balance about 0.74 MMSCMD gas is presently available for setting up industrial projects, using natural gas as feedstock.

In a recent study conducted by the Engineers India Limited (a Government of India Undertaking), the following Projects have been identified:

Project	Product/Capacity	Gas requirement	Project Cost
Urea Complex	Urea- 1186 TPD	0.74 MMSCMD	Rs. 1145 crore (US $ 320 m)
Urea-PVC Complex	Urea- 741 TPD PVC- 261 TPD	0.74 MMSCMD	Rs. 1305 crore (US$ 364 m)
Urea-Methanol Complex	Urea- 866 TPD Methanol- 200 TPD	0.74 MMSCMD	Rs. 987 crore (US $ 275 m)
Liquid/Solid Hydro-carbons Complex	Diesel- 8000TPA Naphtha-4000TPA Soft Wax-12000TPA Hard Wax-24000TPA	0.40 MMSCMD	Rs. 376 crore (US $ 105 m)

One major advantage in setting up a gas-based project in Tripura is the concessional pricing of gas for Northeastern Region. The Government of India had announced the revised Pricing Policy, effective from October 1, 1997 and valid up to March 31, 2000.

The consumer price of gas at landfall points has been linked to the international price of a basket of LS/HS fuel oils. The concessional price for Northeastern Region vis-a-vis the General Price (expressed as percentage of the international price of a basket of internationally traded fuel oils) can be seen from the following table:

Year	General Price	Concessional Price for Northeastern States
1997-98	55%	30%
1998-99	65%	40%
1999-2000	75%	45%

As a result of the revision, the present price for gas has increased from Rs. 1,000/ MCM to about Rs. 1,250/MCM for Northeastern States, which is much lower than the

General Price of about Rs. 2,300/MCM. Not only that, a further discount of Rs. 300/MCM is available, on a case-to-case basis, for new consumers in the Northeastern Region for a period of 5 years. The availability of superior quality natural gas, at concessional price, offers a great opportunity to prospective investors, to set up gas-based industrial units, using natural gas as Feedstock.

Minerals

In Tripura, the other mineral resources are minor amounts of glass sands, limestone, plastic clay and hard rock; all of these materials are being used to a variable degree. Setting up of Ceramic tiles unit and other mineral based industries would be encouraged in the private sector. Efforts will also be made to set up Plastic Clay ad Glass Sand industries where natural gas has added advantage of being used as a fuel.

Other Opportunities - Service Sector:

- Tourism.
- Health.
- Education.

Tripura is an attractive tourist destination. The state has a rich cultural heritage. There are a number of historical Hindu, Buddhist sites. The State also has rich flora and fauna. There is also great potential for development of tourist circuits, involving all the NE states and if possible, Bangladesh as well. All this offers attractive opportunities for the Hospitality Industry. The Govt. of Tripura has always put a lot of emphasis on health care for all. Over the years, a reasonably good infrastructure of health institutions has been created in the state. However, providing good health care to all the citizens is a gigantic task and in this respect, private sector can play a very significant role. There are 2(two) Medical Colleges, one in Government sector and another one in Private sector. Also, there are some private Nursing Homes in the state and there is potential for more private investment in this important sector.

The Government of Tripura has similarly put a lot of emphasis on providing good education to all the people and the result is very high level of literacy in the state. The state has a university, an National Institute of Technology (NIT), and a Polytechnic Institute. However, there is a great potential for private investment in this field also, by way of setting up of educational institutions in fields like Information Technology, Telecommunication, Bio-Technology, etc.

Other Potential Sectors:

Organic Spices:

- The favourable agro-climatic condition, low use of chemicals and the availability of good varieties of spices offer good opportunities for development and procurement of spices.

- Major spices: Ginger (1,82,000 MT), Turmeric (2,67,000 MT), Chilli (75,000 MT), Black Pepper (10,000 MT)

- There is ample scope for area expansion under organic spices cultivation in Tripura. Major spices include Ginger, Turmeric, Chilli, Black Pepper, Cinnamon, Tezpatta.

Medicinal Plant Sector:

- Atleast 266 Medicinal plants with 68 species of trees, 71 herbs, 39 shrub and 88 climbers.

- The State Government has constituted the Medicinal Plant Board of Tripura.

- The Medicinal Plant Policy has been declared by the State Government.

Bio-Fuel Sector:

- Potential in Bio-Fuel sector by planting Jatropha curcas.

- Constitution of State Bio-Fuel Mission under Forest Department is in anvil.

- The State Government invites investment in this sector through PPP mode.

Eco-Tourism:

- One of the Global Bio diversity Hotspots with diverse kind of biological and cultural variance.

- Great potential for development of Eco Tourism in the designated protected areas of Trishna, Sepahijala and Roa.

Industry

Industries — small, medium and large — were conspicuous by their absence in Tripura till about 1950. The almost isolated geographical location of the state and lack of power and communication facilities have proved to be the major handicap for the development of industries in the state.

Tripura's handicrafts in structure, beauty and variety are of great demand outside. Tripura Handloom and Handicraft Development Corporation Ltd. has taken up marketing of the handicrafts in a big way and is exploring the possibilities of exporting its products.

For improving the design and quality of the products the All India Handicraft Board has set up a research unit at Agartala. About 5,000 craftsmen are now engaged in production of handicrafts (mainly cane and bamboo) products.

Handloom weaving is the single largest industry. It is essentially a tribal household industry. Another age-old industry of the state is silk. This industry is now confined to one small village in the suburb of Agartala town. The Sericulture industry is developing fast.

During the reign of Maharaja Birendrakishore Manikya (1909-23), a school was opened at Agartala for giving training in Sericultural weaving. The area under mulberry cultivation is about 500 hectares and production of cocoon is estimated to be 5,000 kg per year. Besides loin looms occupy the pride of place in the local industry of Tripura.

A jute mill set up in Agartala under public sector produces about 20 tones of jute products per day and employs about 2,000 persons. Tripura is abundant in natural gas and a number of gas-based industries have sprung up. Foundation has been laid for a Rs. 126 crore methanol project of the state owned Tripura petro-chemicals Ltd.

There are 809 small-scale industrial units in Tripura. In recent years the government has taken significant steps to educate the rural people in the technique of the industry so that the industry could be of real benefit to the rural people. The North-Eastern Council (NEC) has come forward for providing financial and other help for developing the industry.

In order to provide common facilities and services to the entrepreneurs, the State Government is running 5 industrial estates. One each at Arundhutinagar, Dhwajanagar, Dhukli, Kumarghat and Dharmanagar. Besides the state has three industrial centres, viz. Udaipur in south Tripura, Kailashahar in north and one at Agartala.

In order to coordinate the activities the state administration had also set up separate corporations/councils for handlooms, small industries, tea development and village and cottage industries.

The department of industries also runs 4 industrial centres — two at Indranagar, one each at Jatanbari and Kailashahar; three industrial development centres, viz. at Malaynagar and Takmacherra in West Tripura district and Uttakhali in North Tripura district.

The Government of India has recently taken a number of initiatives to develop infrastructural facilities in Tripura and other Northeastern States. A broad-gauge Railway line is being extended up to the state capital, Agartala. Roads and Airport facilities are also being developed. Telecommunication facilities are being upgraded. As regards Power, a number of Thermal/Hydel Power Projects in Tripura/ other Northeastern States are in an advance stage of implementation, as a result of which Tripura is expected to be Power-surplus by 1998.

The power tariff is also very low in Tripura, being less than Re. 1 per unit, as against about Re. 3 per unit in other parts on the country. Moreover, natural gas available in the state can also be used as fuel (as substitute for electric power), which provides an alternative to the industrial units coming up in the state.

As regards social infrastructure, it may be noted that the state has a vast pool of educated/ trained manpower. As mentioned earlier, the literacy rate in Tripura is quite high and the state has a good network of educational institutions, including technical institutions.

The unemployment rate of educated youth, including those who are technically qualified, is quite high. This can be turned into an advantage, by suitably deploying the available manpower, to meet the industrial needs.

Fruit Processing

The agro-climatic conditions in Tripura are ideally suited for production of a large variety of horticultural crops. The "Queen" and "Kew" varieties of pineapple, oranges, lichis and cashew of Tripura are well known in the rest of the country. These products are also free of any chemical residue. The present estimated annual production level of major horticultural crops is as under:

- Pineapple: 45000 MT.
- Lichi: 3000 MT.
- Orange: 24000 MT.
- Cashew: 1800 MT.
- Jackfruit: 22000 MT.
- Coconut: 1250 MT.

The production can be further increased, if demand is created by setting up Fruit Processing units. The Fruit Processing industry in Tripura is still at a nascent stage. As regards pineapple processing, NERAMAC (a Government of India undertaking), has set up a modern Pineapple Juice Concentrate Plant at Nalkata in North Tripura District, with a processing capacity of about 5,760 TPA.

The Plant at Nalkata is operating at a low level due to non-operation of aseptic filter. However, the same is being rectified and natural juice concentrate will be available from the pineapple season of this millennium year. TSIC (a State Government undertaking), is also operating a small Fruit Canning factory, producing fresh canned pineapple juice and other pineapple products.

The factory has processing capacity of 400 TPA. Cashew Processing has also been taken up by NERAMAC by setting up a small unit. As regards other fruit products, proper processing facilities are yet to be created. This offers a vast scope for setting up of Fruit Processing units in Tripura.

Rubber and Tea

Rubber has been identified as one of the thrust areas in Tripura, in view of its suitability to the terrain and the acceptability amongst the people. Studies have shown that about 100,000 hectares of area in the state can be brought under rubber plantation.

The area under rubber cultivation at present is estimated to be about 23,500 hectares, which is the second largest, after Kerala. The yield at the rate of 1,500 kg per hectare and the quality of rubber are also comparable to Kerala's plantations. In fact, Tripura has recently been declared the "Second Rubber Capital of India" by the Rubber Board.

The State Government has taken up an ambitious programme to increase the area under rubber plantations by another 20,000 MT by the end of Ninth Plan, i.e., by 2001-02, with assistance from the Central Government, the Rubber Board and the World Bank. As a result, it is expected that the rubber production, which is presently about 5,000 MT per annum, will increase to about 20,000 MT.

The State Government is very keen to promote processing of rubber and setting up of rubber-based industries in the state. TFDPC (a State Government undertaking) has already set up a Centrifugal Latex Processing factory, with installed capacity of 5.76 TPD, which is being increased to 13.44 TPD.

The State Government is also setting up a Process-cum-Product Development Centre at a cost of Rs. 12 million, with a view to create basic infrastructure for promotion of rubber-based industries. The availability of good quantity of high quality rubber offers ample scope for setting up of rubber-based industries in the state.

Tripura has been a traditional tea growing State. The agro-climatic conditions are suitable for tea plantation. There are as many as 57 tea gardens in the state, with total about 6,000 hectares of area under plantation.

The current production of made tea is about 6 million kg. Further, initiative has also been taken by some tea gardens in Tripura to produce "Bio-tea", which is free from any chemical residue. Some reputed exporters have shown interest in such tea. There is a vast scope to further develop the tea industry in Tripura.

Handicrafts

Excellent variety of handicrafts using bamboo and cane are made by different ethnic groups which have earned great name and fame throughout the country. The most famous handicraft products are Room Divider, Decorated wall panels, Attractive furniture of cane, Different decorative pieces using Bamboo roots, Bamboo Dining table mats, Floor mats and various other gift items. Tourist can watch the craft persons at work in different villages and buy handicraft and handloom products from Purbasha, a Govt. of Tripura undertaking Sales Emporium and other private Sales Emporium throughout the state.

Cane and Bamboo Handicrafts

From time immemorial Tripura has carved out a name for itself in the field of Handicrafts. The Gifted artisans produce wonderful objects of crafts from simple material like cane, bamboo and wood. There rare artistic skill has not been streamlined in the manufacture of exquisite household pieces. Tripura's unique topography and the gracious nature bestowed their choicest blessings on the hereditary artisans of Tripura. Here three distinct cultures, viz. Hinduism, Buddhism and Islam have converged together to give shape and content to a unique tradition that found eloquent expression through immemorable work of art and crafts made out of very simple materials like cane, bamboo, clay, wood, palm leaf, etc. With the passage of time, there has been changes in the demographic character of the state. But in each phase of her history, Tripura has shown remarkable inner strength of assimilation of synthesis, while retaining her own traditional heritage. With the original distinct tribal motifs were added the skills of Manipuri and Bengali artisans who came subsequently to settle in this land. Time has changed and so also the quick adaptability of our gifted artisans who never failed to respond to the demands of contemporary tastes.

Cane and Bamboo occupy a distinctive place in the life of Tripura. From cradle to grave, there is hardly any occasion, complete without the use of cane and bamboo.

Today the magnificent skill of artisans has been directed to produce of a wide range of more than 200 exquisite products. Presently, about 10,000 skilled artisans are engaged in production of various handicrafts in the state. However, the industry remains largely unorganised. There is a need to organise the industry in order to build up a proper production base capable of responding to the market requirements and to introduce the modern techniques. The State Government has already initiated steps in this direction, in view of the vast potential of the industry to grow, both in domestic as well as international markets. The state also welcomes private enterprise in this field.

Cane/Bamboo handicrafts of Tripura are acknowledged to be among the best in the country, due to their beauty, elegance and exquisite designs. A vast range of items are produced, including Furniture, Panels and Partitions, Table Mats and other Mat products, Lamp Shades, etc. Tripura handicrafts are also being exported to various countries.

For interior decoration Tripura Handicrafts offer a wide range of false ceilings, panelling, plaques, pot containers (Planters), etc. made of Gossamer thin bamboo mattress. Ornamated with wood inlay and cane and bamboo. The household items have blended utility with artistic beauty. Panels and partitions provide another wide range of utility items made out of solid but thinly splitted bamboo pasted on plywood.

The THHDC undertakes interior decoration works in hotels, conference rooms, show rooms interiors of different Govt. buildings with there beautiful bamboo and cane materials of Tripura on turnkey basis.

Lamp shades made of fine strips of cane and bamboo add distinct touch and glamour to the living room. Exhibiting a rare combination of tradition and talent, there products would brighten up the interiors demonstrating the taste and feeling of the connoisseurs. The supply capacity is much less for the exquisite item.

Furniture of Tripura once exclusive to royal palaces continue to have its excellence and exquisite workmanship. For the elegant Drawing Rooms there are Bamboo-Cane,

Sofa sets, Garden Chairs, Dinning Chairs, Baby Chairs, Centre and Side Tables, Morah, Apple Morah, etc.

Baskets knitted out of Cane and Bamboo Strips, offer a whole range of products. Exquisite tray Planters, Fruit Baskets of different shapes, sizes, pattern and designs as a rare combination of art and utility. A wide range of baskets and baskets with divisions are being used for making gift packages with some traditional artistic touches by the consumers.

Mat and mat articles, bamboo chatai, etc. have good demand in the market. There are different types of roll mats weaved in multicoloured designs which are familiar for making door and window screen, and also have various uses for room decoration.

Amongst the Mat articles ladies bag, Hand fans, Portfolio bag (for seminar), etc. are the most popular items.

On the consoetic table as well, there are quite a number of items to present. Some of those are small framed mirror, Hair Clips, Powder Case, Decorative Trays, etc.

Bamboo and cane Ornaments are also very intricate and exquisite in nature. Bamboo and cane ornaments are not available in any other part of the country as well as abroad.

Tripura Handloom — the Heritage

A slender strip of earth overgrown with trackless wood and thick foliage in the southwest extremity of Assam is TRIPURA- the tiny home of nearly three million people. Here there is nothing exotic or splendorous that may stir your eyes. But here in this ancient land, beneath the sylvan shadows, from time immemorial, there have been remarkable experiments in traditional art and the crafts that earned the lofty admiration of time-honoured connoisseurs like Hiuen Tsang, Travernier, Abul Fazal and even the great poet Rabindranath Tagore.

The art of weaving occupies a very sacred place in the traditional life of Tripura. In fact in our tribal society no right or ritual is sanctioned unless it is preceded by an worship of 'Riha' the hand-woven breast cover of the family elders. The ancient folk-lorries and fables of Tripura galore with innumerable examples of glorification of the art of weaving in the tribal society. We come across starting stories where a King marries an ordinary village damsel for her unique depiction of an intricate design in weaving, or another King pronouncing a royal decree of punishment upon a defiant community which prohibiting them from using any bright colour in their weaving apparels.

In the ups and downs of socio-political history, Tripura witnessed drastic changes in its demographic character, but the nimble fingers of our weavers continued with tradition and finesse. Nature has endowed the people of this land with a very high sense of aesthetic beauty which enabled their skilful hands to translate the vision in various forms of art in conformity with the unique aesthetic equilibrium of the nature, in all the details of sense, colour, perception forms and even rhythm.

Today, Tripura Handloom represents a unique harmonious blend of three traditions- Tribal, Bengalee and Manipuri weaving.

Tribal Fabrics

The Tribal fabrics of Tripura are well known for their elegant design, bold colour combination and lasting texture. The Tribal motifs skilfully depicted through stylised decorative designs are really in great demand. Modern made-up in tribal fabrics is very attractive indeed.

Manipuri Fabrics

The Manipuri community of Tripura specialises in certain traditional items of distinct heritage. Today, they represent a synthesised tradition quite distinct from the handloom of Manipur. They produce colourful bedspread Lysingphee and elegant furnishing fabrics with Typical Manipuri designs.

Bengalee Fabrics

With aforesaid two traditions of Handloom in Tripura, the third blending force is the one represented by Bengalee weavers who migrated erstwhile East Pakistan (Bangladesh). They have in many ways rejuvenated and supplemented handloom tradition of this land with greater Bengal weaving heritage. This has resulted into a wide variety of common use products like silk and cotton sharis, lungis, Shirting's, jute carpets, bedspreads and colourful furnishing fabrics.

In Tripura, weavers of all communities have shown a remarkable courage of conviction in freely adopting motifs and techniques from each others' tradition with a view to enriching their own.

Agriculture

Tripura is essentially an agriculture dominated state where 61.6 per cent of the total workers (main workers+marginal workers) are engaged in agriculture. Nearly 76 per cent of the people derive their sustenance directly from agriculture. About 70 per cent of the state revenue is also provided by agriculture.

The total area of the state is 10,43,696 hectares. Out of it only 2,55,000 hectares of land or 24.5 per cent is classed as net area sown. Nearly 56.4 per cent (5,69,000 hectares) of total land is under forests. Permanent pastures and grazing lands have claimed 90,400 hectares and 1,28,200 hectares of land (put to non-agricultural uses as well as barren and unculturable land) is not available for cultivation. A hectarage of 91,500 hectares falls in the category of other uncultivated land excluding fallow land while 4,000 hectares of land is fallow land.

Of the net area sown 1,77,000 hectares of land is cultivated more than once in a year. In the state two types-of farming practices are followed; settled cultivation and Jhuming or shifting cultivation.

Over 83 per cent of the total cropped land is given to food crops and paddy alone claims nearly 81 per cent of the hectarage devoted to food crops. Thus only one-sixth of the total cropped land is given to cash crops, among which jute (5.65%), cotton (3.61%), oil seeds (3.1%) and tea (2.10%) are the principal commercial crops.

In Jhuming cultivation, no attention is paid towards the identification and maintenance of soils but in the case of settled cultivation significant factor. Thus, it may not be out of place to assess and evaluate the soil resources of the state.

Farming

In Tripura two types of cultivation is carried on by people belonging to two different ethnic groups. Although, some of the tribal groups have given up the slash and burn based shifting cultivation, *i.e.* jhuming yet a large majority of such people still cling to this out dated and outmoded form of cultivation that has outlived its utility.

The plainsmen who constitute mostly immigrants from the areas of settled agriculture practice permanent cultivation an are always ready to make new and scientific experiments to raise the yield as well as total production of different crops.

Paddy as already stated is the principal crop of the region. Because of very suitable physical environment the state has out-paced even the average per acre yield of paddy at the national level. In some areas even three crops of paddy a year are raised. These are aush (aus in Bengali), poush (amari in Bengali) and boro.

The short staple cotton locally called Comilla cotton is raised in Tripura. It is very useful for being mixed with wool and Japan practically purchases the entire production. It is similar to the upland cotton, in heavy demand in the international market. The area currently given to Jhuming if properly reclaimed can raise bumper crops of cotton. Besides exporting, the state can earn revenue and offer employment opportunities by starting cotton ginning and cotton seed oil extraction plants.

Tripura, since centuries, has been producing ritesta for fibre. However, after partition the Bengali farmers with a know how of raising jute have done a commendable job of raising very good jute crops. Wheat, sweet potato, pulses, sugarcane, oilseeds, tobacco and chillies are other important crops.

Horticulture has fairly good potentialities in Tripura, although, at present its contribution to the state's economy is quite low. Tropical fruits and nuts like pineapples, papaya, guava, lichi, lemon, orange, mango, jackfruit, areca-nut, coconut cashew-nut hold good promise in the regions.

Some fruit plantations have been set up recently but all these fruit plants have been grown in the kitchen gardens of many families. Before partition when market existed in East Bengal, pineapple was produced and exported. Jampui oranges are also raised in Tripura.

Some low grade bananas was also grown. Cashew-nut can be profitably raised on jhum degraded slopes to rehabilitate the area. Boggy and marshy areas can be planted with coconuts. Rubber and coffee plantations can also be advantageously raised in Tripura.

The rubber plantation has already been laid out on area of 625 hectares in South Tripura. There are about 50 odd tea plantations in Tripura, developed indigenously by Indians. A tea plantation covering 400 to 500 hectares of land is thought to be economically viable but in Tripura no tea plantation is more than 300 hectares in it's a real coverage.

Moreover, the number of tea bushes is just half of the optimum number in a plantation. About 13,200 hectares of land is under tea gardens and the state annually produces 3,30,000 kg of tea every years.

Traditionally, potatoes and sweet potatoes are growing almost everywhere in the state. However, northern parts offer the ideal conditions for these vegetable crops. Sugarcane has also traditionally been grown in small quantities by each farmer since the people are very found of gin, *i.e.* jaggery. Gur making is an indigenous cottage industry.

Soils

In the state of Tripura two types of soils are found:

- On the hill slopes the soils are lateritic or sandy loans to lamy sands. Barring sandy loans, other types of soils become sticky even after light showers and thus are unworkable immediately after rains. Since these soils have developed from the weathered sedimentary rocks they are medium grained, coarse textured and brown to reddish brown in colour. Those soils which have developed from shales are medium to fine in texture. While the former are deeper soils the latter are shallow soils. Both these soils lying on the hill slopes are susceptible to erosion as a result of excessive and down pouring rains particularly during summers.

- On the valley bottoms and river basins and other plain pockets alluvial soils are met with. The alluvium largely consists of sand, silt and clay and keeps on getting renewed almost every year. Pure sandy soils are however, confined to river beds.

The soil resources in Tripura are unpromising and are light except where silt has accumulated in river valleys. By and large the soils of Tripura are not rich in humus although, it is a forest clothed region. On the slopes, as a result of excessive erosion, all the soil nutrients including humus get eroded. It is only in the valley bottoms that as a result of deposition the soils come to gather certain nutrients including humus.

On gentler slopes though, rate of soil erosion gets reduced yet the physical looseness of the soils does not permit them to hold water. As a result of heavy and torrential rains and tropical heat the soils get leached which leads to washing away of mineral nutrients. Small wonder the soils in Tripura are poor in humus, trace minerals, metrates, phosphates and potash.

The deficiency of these important ingredients affect adversely the health of grasses and plants and ultimately the health of men and animals who sustain themselves on the produce raised on these soils. Because of being grossly deficient in nitrates, potash and phosphates these soils cannot be turned productive even with the liberal dosages of acid fertilizers. Only hope is the ammonium phosphate, the production of which is very limited in India. CAN, *i.e.* calcium aluminium nitrate fertilizers are being used as second best alternative.

Irrigation

As the table shows only 39,200 hectares of land is under different means of irrigation. Looking at the sources, it can be said that they are not assured means of irrigation. This acreage has risen by about 29 per cent during one decade. On the whole only 15.33 per cent of the net own area receives irrigation facilities which other wise forms only 3.7 per cent of the total geographical area of the state.

However, it is estimated that on the whole only 8.75 per cent of the total cultivated area receives assured means of irrigation. Out of the total irrigated areas nearly 40.33 per cent gets irrigation facilities through seasonal bunds.

But the area irrigated by the seasonal bunds has fluctuated over the years. Nonetheless, minor irrigation works (including Kulials, *i.e.* zag contour water channels) are gradually becoming an assured means of irrigation.

Moreover, the area irrigated through this source is progressively on the increase. The area being irrigated by "over flows" of the streams during rains also fluctuates from year to year for obvious reasons. In the plain tract pumping sets by the government as well as individual entrepreneurs have been installed for irrigational purposes. The acreage so irrigated has also been fluctuating.

The table further reveals that about 85.5 per cent of the total irrigated area has been devoted to food crops and among these crops it is paddy which accounts for almost the entire so irrigated hectarage.

As a result of assured means of irrigation in some areas two crops of paddy a year are also raised. Sugarcane is the only cash crop in the state which receives some irrigation facilities but the area so irrigated has been highly fluctuating.

The state has drawn plans for 50 minor irrigation works in the region; 7 in Hawra basin, 8 in khowai basin, 8 in Dhalai Basin, 9 in Gumti basin and 5 in Muhari basin being important. Some have been completed while others are at different stages. No doubt there is still need for more schemes but there are serious constraints and limitations.

The indigenous device has been a simple diversion of the stream or rivulet by creating a temporary-semi-permanent bund locally called as *cherra bund*. The major irrigation schemes are not viable since the cultivable land exists in small, isolated and scattered pockets.

Moreover, the soil is porous and not fit for the construction of canals and heavy complexes. Well irrigation is not viable because loose and porous soil leads to caving in of inner walls. The inner walls may be made impermeable but unfortunately, the impermeable material for inner lining of walls is not available locally.

Tanks can be created as reservoirs of water but only on areas where gradient is not more than 30°. The other alternative is to install pumping sets for lifting water and in many cases such pumping sets have been installed. But lack of motive power is a serious bottleneck. To transport diesel in a mountainous region suffering from the want of rail routes and roads would be very expensive.

The development of hydroelectricity can go a long way in this regard and there exists potential for the generation of water power at many places because of many streams criss-crossing the region and their being numerous places fit for providing falls.

Shifting Cultivation or Jhuming

The oldest method of raising food crops on the hills of the mountains with crudest implements and most backward techniques, though, named differently in different parts of the world, is collectively called shifting cultivation or slash and burn cultivation. In many parts of India dominated by the tribal folks and aboriginals (aadivasees) this type of farming practices still continue. In Northeastern India, it is termed as Jhuming.

Jhuming as an economic activity besides being a means of providing succour to the most backward people also forms a factor that distinguishes a tribal society from a non-tribal society. In such a society, Jhuming is that pivot around which the entire sociocultures-economic life of the society revolves. The songs, dances, music, mirth, fairs, festivals, folk lore, socioreligious customs, work and leisure cycle, etc. are interwoven with Jhuming. It is in fact the emotional attachment of the Jhumias that stands in the way of its being replaced by settled and permanent cultivation.

Jhuming, *i.e.* slash and burn based shifting cultivation involves the tasks of selecting a suitable site, cutting and felling of trees, burning the slash, dibbling of seeds with available crude implements, raising the food crops, protecting same from insects, pests and wild animals and ultimately harvesting of the crop.

In Tripura before the beginning of monsoon rains the site for clearance is selected. Like all tribal societies, the Tripura Girijans many deities. Thus, the process of selecting a site is done quite mysteriously, which creates a sort of romance. These tribesmen splits a stalk of bamboo and throw it towards the sky to let it fall on the ground. Only if the converse portions turn up in two parts the proposed site is selected as a jhum field.

The whole process is accompanied with singing, dancing, fun-frolicking, feasting and merry making. The details of recreational-cum-deity-propitiating processes may vary from tribe to tribe and area to area one remarkable feature is that all member of the clan at such cultural functions are treated at par. It is only the clan chief who enjoys some discretion. After the gala day is over the selected site is accorded a distinguishing look by way of planting a bamboo or flag-post.

Again on a fixed day the entire community, to the tunes of drum beats and singing chores, clears the site of trees and other vegetal growth. It is a very happy and enviable feature of the tribal community life that the work of clearing the site is done not only by the jhum owner but by entire community. The strong feelings of mutual cooperation and brotherhood unite the community into one body and this feeling has been a proud possession of the simple and unsophisticated tribal folks.

Such feelings of fraternity if meaningfully exploited by the planners and statesman to the betterment of these people with no stings attached, may go a long way not only in socio-economically uplifting these hitherto neglected and utterly superstitious people but in also bringing about emotional integration of different tribes.

After the vegetal cover has been cut the Tripuri tribals wait for the wind to blow in a particular direction. Possibly, the origin of this superstition lay in the need of giving sufficient time for the removed slash to dry up. When the wind direction is favourable the community sets the dried slash on fire and takes all steps to check the spread of fire in the adjoining jungles.

This means the tribals extract only that part from nature which they need and do not permit the rest to be harmed in any way. After the slash is completely burnt the resultant ash is spread on the jhum field. With the first rain, the family members of the Jhumia dig holes either with pointed bamboo sticks or dao (a crude axe) and dibble the seeds of paddy, mesta, cotton, chillies and vegetables in them.

So as to save the standing crops from the attack of wild animals and birds the family constructs a *long-ghar* (a raised bamboo hut, like a machari) where some members of the family live for this purpose. When the crops mature these are harvested, threshed and stored in bamboo baskets. The first harvest from a jhum land is quite bumper. Virginity of soil and manuring by the ash help in the raising the fertility and growth of good crops.

The next crop if any is poor as now the crude methods of farming as well as the falling fertility of soil start giving their results. Ultimately, finding the field unproductive the family abandons the site and moves on to another field. Depending upon the population pressure the family has to retreat to this site after 7 to 12 years. In good old days when there was a very sparse population and limitless land resources, the jhian cycle had an interval of 30 years. Now it has shrunk to 7 to 12 years while in some areas it has still further limited a life.

It is known to the social scientist that till recently, the tribals had very limited wants and they solely lived on necessities. Probably, the words 'comforts' and 'luxuries' did not exist in their vocabularies.

In the name of recreations they had their occasional merry making and drinking bouts. Being least ambitious they had remained poor since the very dawn of their history. The low rate of jhum yield compared to that obtained under settled cultivation, coupled with the improvident habits of these people, had kept them in perpetual penury.

Of all the tribesmen, the jhumias are the most backward and their settlement is a major problem in the rehabilitation of Tripura economy. In fact, in view of total unawareness about economic prosperity and limited wants as well as low ambition the jhuming economy has served well these tribals. The economy has provided them complete protection against all vicissitudes and cross currents of history.

Apart from being socio-economically wedded to this system they are emotionally, psychologically and even biologically attached to this system which is besides being a menace to forest wealth is also 'primitive, wasterful and uneconomic' to the present-day economist, social scientist and the statesman.

On the other side the proud tribal has eulogised the system through his folklore evolved over the centuries while his religions beliefs as well as practices and daily routine conform to it.

Any propaganda decrying this cultural heritage closely related with jhuming makes them suspicious and hostiles as well. Once they become hostile, no inducement is going to bear fruitful results.

Thus it is Herculean task which requires the tactful resourcefulness and psychological treatment along with encouraging incentiveness to the tribals. No doubt with the discovery of shifting cultivation has turned wasteful, primitive, uneconomic and a nuisance to the floral wealth, yet one cannot expect a tradition bound and unenlightened community to altogether shun its ages old practices overnight.

One literesting feature of jhuming is that there is a tendency for the jhum yields to grow with the greater isolation and inaccessibility of the area, making it difficult to wean away the tribal people from the practice. People and more specifically, the peasants are mostly nostalgic about the herths and homes and more so are the tradition bound tribals who are least responsive to such a change. It is a difficult job to persuade the tribals to give up their ancestral moorings and move on to a colony. He is being asked to abandon the inherited and familiar practice for one which is not only unfamiliar but strange also to his traditional way of thinking.

Apart from it to bring the humia under settled system of cultivation does not merely bringing about certain psychological changes in the attitudes of the tribesmen towards living a life. There are physical limitations. In Tripura, in particular there is only limited arable area located in the plain tracts and valley basins.

The large influx of refugee farmers has further aggravated the problem. The influx of East Bengali refugees has already created problems related to social and economic integration, leaving apart emotional integration. So long as the tribal-villages and refugee-settlements are wide apart such problems are automatically at the lowest ebb.

The present turmoil in the state has resulted among other things by the relative closeness of tribal and non-tribal settlements. The jhumias do not reside in permanent houses and they make their *tong-ghar* with bamboo anywhere they like and bamboo grows in abundance in their surroundings.

For having settled colonies, besides land, concrete, timber and other building materials are required in plenty for which there is acute shortage in this land locked state surrounded on three sides by foreign territory and only tenuously linked with the mother country.

Last but by no means the least, the basic factor working against such colonies remains the same. Jhuming permits the tribal to have a gay and open life with vest space all round. He naturally feels suffocated and chained when he is surrounded by the four walls of a colony and the discipline that it requires. Not only in Tripura but everywhere such nomadic or semi-nomadic people have been least responsive to like changes.

The Gadia Lohars of Rajasthan deserted the colonies they were provided with and soon took to their ages old practice of leading the life of mobile caravan settlements. Psychologically, it is ingrained in them that their ancestors were asked by their leader Maharana Pratap to lead such a life till Mewar again came under the Rajputs.

Thus a sustained, phased and motivated approach of permanently settling these tribals possibly around their native surroundings is needed. The tribal should be persuaded by way of social amenities, incentives, services And marketing facilities to draw himself away gradually from his traditional mode of living not so much in principles as in practice. For this objective education can be a better tool and emphasis must be laid on properly educating such people.

Omesh Saigal in his title Tripura narrates an interesting incident. Once Mr. R. N. Chakravarty the Subdivisional Officer under whose jurisdiction fell the first such colony at Bishramganj, while trying to convince a tribal to lead a settled life politely asked 'why don't you come down and live a life that we live'? The hesitatingly adamant tribal very sweetly reacted, 'why don't you come up, Sir, and live the life that we live'? This explains the whole situation.

Now when as a result of growing population, shrinking land, curtailed jhum cycle and highly disturbed ecological balance 'the triple horror of malnutrition, hunger and famine' has very often started visiting even the *tong-ghar* and jhum settlements it is obligatory on the part of the welfare state to do away with the menace in a phased and tactful manner. In this respect the 'Agro Horticulture Taungya Scheme' practised in Burma as mentioned by Omesh Saigal merits serious consideration by the authorities.

The word Taungya refers to hill cultivation (*Taung* = hill, *ya* = cultivation) in Burmese language. It is a method of growing trees along with food crops. In order to cope with a growing pressure of human beings on land the Burmese replace the mono culture system by a sort of inter-culture. Besides growing some food crops fruit trees are also planted which apart from augmenting the income of farmers also help in the checking of soil erosion.

It has been observed in Tripura that although, a jhumia is reluctant to take to the plough and settled cultivation. Yet, he is very much enthused for trying his hand at horticulture. It is evidenced by the presence of small orchards covering about 2,000 hectares of land on the tillas and the thrill the jhumia owners feel at their efforts. Many of the others would like to go in for horticulture in a big way but are discouraged by the absence of requisite incentives and marketing facilities.

Under the Taungaya system the tribals would carry on jhuming and also develop their orchards. After they give up that plot for raising food crops the fruit plants would be 2 to 3 years old. While jhuming another plot and also planting fruit saplings there, they would continue to look after nurture and tender the fruit plants being raised on the earlier jhum field. A time shall positively come when the jhumia shall find that it was more lucrative to grow fruit and exchange the same for food crops grown by the plainsmen.

Nonetheless, the government as well as voluntary agencies shall have to come forward for providing them marketing and transport facilities. He shall have also to be educated that he is no longer an isolated individual who was required to fend himself.

Instead he was the member of a social order which had the patronage of the welfare state. Once all his suspensions, doubts and fears were removed through closer interaction with the caring organisation he shall be glad to abandon jhuming and opt for a more settled life.

Thus, the step based on the Burmese experiment would be the first step towards the settlement of the Jhumia tribal and that too in and around his homeland and ancestral moorings. Instead of thrusting and forcing a novel system on him, he is to be persuaded and convinced about its economic viability and social acceptability through successful demonstrations.

After having briefly reviewed both the agricultural practices followed in Tripura, it is worthwhile to sum up the agricultural scenario of the state. The agriculture in Tripura is basically subsistence farming dominated by paddy cultivation.

The lungal land (level, flat and plain area) is limited and is given to permanent and settled cultivation. Teh tilla land (land situated on hill slopes) is by and large under jhuming, *i.e.* shifting cultivation. It is estimated that every year about one-fifth of the cultivated hectarage if given to Jhiaming. An average Jhumia is emotionally attached to the system yet not prepared to abandon it, which has been found to be a harmful practice ecologically. Net area sown per cultivator is around 0.3 hectares only. The landholdings are small, scattered and isolated.

The size of holdings ranges between 1 to 1.25 hectares. The scope for further expansion of arable land is very small and that too at the cost of ecological balance. The uneven distribution of rainfall over space and time necessitates the application of artificial watering. However, steep gradient, loose and porous soils do not allow the planning and execution of major irrigation works. Crops intensity is very low. Farming techniques even on lunga land are backward, obsolete and unproductive.

Lack of transport and marketing facilities impede the development of horticulture while physical environment is conducive for fruit plantations. Once a self reliant region for its food crops, Tripura has now turned out to be a food deficit state particularly after the immigration of refugees from Bangladesh and still continuing influx of illegal intruders from the neighouring country.

Livestock and Poultry Farming: Cattle breeding and rearing of poultry birds in Tripura is an integral part of the subsistence agriculture and is neither pursued on commercial lines and nor managed on scientific lines. The animals and birds are reared for meat, milk, eggs, hides and skins, as also as beasts of burden. Because of inadequate and unbalanced fodder, forage, and poor upkeep, the productions of meat and milk from the animals are poor.

Moreover, the diseases of hoofs and mouth, rinderpest, septicamia, black quarter-haemorrhagic ailment and some poisonous flies heavily tell upon the health of birds and animals. The average per acre per cow annual milk production is 114 litres against 150 litres average production in the country as a whole. A pair of oxen can plough only about one hectare of cultivable land in a day while the national average is of 3.3 hectares a day. A look at the table gives a peep in the population of different animals and poultry birds in different districts of the state in the year 1985.

The climate of the region no doubt is highly conducive to the breeding of buffaloes yet their number is very low among the milk yielding bovino stock. The highly uneven, difficult and mountainous relief in most of Tripura discourages the breeding of buffaloes. Moreover, Jhumia cultivators who have to move from place to place as semi nomads don't find the buffalo as a convenient stock.

On the whole denser concentrations of animals are found in the plain region and valley basins in hilly and mountainous areas. All over the country the tribal culture appears to be inter related to pigs, goats, poultry fowls and chillies. Here also the same trend is observed. Goats are thought to be enemy number one of hilly areas. The goats browse the grass right from its roots and in no time clear the bush of its foliage moreover, its pointed hoofs loosen the soil and prepare it for soil erosion.

Unfortunately, the numbers of goat population have steeply been rising in Tripura. The goats need to be replaced with sheep if the environment and ecology in hilly areas, already degrading at a fast rate, need to be restored to their equilibrium.

Raising Fish

A majority of Tripura resident being Bengalis by origin relish fish eating. Earlier a major part of the demand for fish by Tripura was met by East Bengal but the partition in 1947, upset the trade. The riverine fishing is not significant because of the river courses being in hilly areas.

The major source of fish are bheels and Rudrasagar lake is the largest bheel of Tripura. Small quantity of fish is also obtained from reclaimed tanks and ponds. Many more tanks and ponds and natural depressions wait to be reclaimed and turned as fish grounds. The lakes and reservoirs impounding waters of irrigation projects have also become new sources of fisheries.

Under the North Eastern Council development programme the Regional Fish Farming and Breeding Farm has started functioning at Kumarghat in North Tripura. The farm which covers an area of twenty hectares is to ultimately produce 50 million fingerlings annually of distribution among the north eastern States of India.

Irrigated Area by Sources

(Area in hectares)

Year Bund Irrigation	Seasonal Private	Minor & Govt.	Over Flow Owner	Pumping Sources	Set by Pri- Irrigated	Other Total Area
1	2	3	4	5	6	7
1974-75	18,000	810	5,800	4,500	1,290	30,400
1975-76	8,000	1,800	5,770	4,940	7,090	21,600
1976-77	19,300	3,800	5,100	4,840	760	33,800
1977-78	17,100	7,760	5,100	3,990	850	28,800
1978-79	17,363	2,493	6,388	4,674	682	31,600
1979-80	16,375	4,389	6,435	4,126	2,975	34,300
1980-81	14,600	4,484	6,200	4,260	7,256	38,00
1981-82	15,800	5,595	5,140	4,075	7,490	38,100
1982-83	15,820	6,575	5,170	4,100	7,535	39,200

Irrigated Area under Different Crops

(Area in hactares)

Year Irrigated Area	Food crops	Pulses	Sugarcane	Cotton	Tobacco	Others	Total
1	2	3	4	5	6	7	8
1972-73	23,998	-	650	-	-	4,002	28,650
1973-74	21,000	-	1,200	-	-	7,450	29,750
1974-75	21,460	-	252	-	-	688	22,400
1975-76	24,090	-	300	-	-	8,310	32,700
1976-77	28,00	-	350	-	-	8,450	36,800
1977-78	19,700	-	400	-	-	8,700	28,800
1978-79	22,250	-	450	-	-	8,900	31,600
1979-80	24,625	-	475	-	-	9,200	34,300
1980-81	26,600	-	500	-	-	9,700	36,800
1981-82	33,145	-	235	-	-	4,610	38,100
1982-83	33,500	-	250	-	-	5,450	39,200

Area and Production of Principal Crops in Tripura

Crop	Area under it (Hectares)	Production (Tonnes)	Yield per hectare (Metric tonnes)
Rice	295,000	4,20,000	1.423
Wheat	3100	6,000	2.000
Pulses	5600	2,420	0.434
Potato	2600	34,500	13.349
Sweet Potato	1500	15,000	10.213
Sugarcane	2000	8,000	4.000
Cotton (Bale-170 kg)	1450	1,500	1.060
Jute (Bale-180 kg)	3800	30,500	8.130
Oil Seeds	6900	3,900	0.566
Tobacco	820	290	0.353
Mesta (Bale-180 kg)	9100	67,200	7.380
Chillies	1400	625	0.448

Distribution of Livestock Animals and Poultry Birds in Tripura

Animal/Birds	West Tripura	North Tripura	South Tripura	Total
Cattle	2,80,700	1,80,271	2,19,439	6,80,410
Buffaloes	3,006	7,327	5,571	15904
Mithun	12	82	-	94
Sheep	2,379	1,595	1,319	5,293
Goats	1,37,345	94,754	1,11,003	3,43,102
Horses and Ponies	1,119	293	234	1,726

Contd...

Animal/Birds	West Tripura	North Tripura	South Tripura	Total
Mules	6	8	-	14
Donkeys	2	3	-	5
Pigs	30,120	31,793	41,531	1,03,444
Dogs	39,854	29,877	42,663	1,11,394
Ducks	85,307	54,846	84,754	2,24,907
Fowls (Chicken)	2,84,279	2,21,933	2,79,728	7,95,938

Fisheries in Tripura

Items	Production in Tonnes		Average	Price per tonne	(Rs.)	Value Lukh Rupees	
	1987-88	1988-89	1987-88	1988-89	1988-89	1987-88	1988-89
1. Inland fish Product	8100	8500	19,000	20,000		1539.00	1700.00
2. Fish catch (non-professionals)	810	850	19000	20,000		153.90	170.00
3. Fish curing (Sued drying)	648	680	9000	10,000		58.32	68.00
Total:	9558	10,030	-	-		1751.22	1938.00

Transportation

The lack of adequate, efficient and cheap means of transport (roadways, railways, waterways and airways) have always stood as seriously insurmountable bottlenecks to the economic development, cultural integration and social diffusion in Tripura. About twelve decades ago Tripura (then Tipperah Hill region) did not have any rail route or road passing through it.

Only mule tracks and bridle paths were there. However, some time before the attainment of freedom by India the native ruler had started linking the capital town with the then patterns of interstate interaction Agartala had to be connected with other parts of India through East Bengal. Even in the case of Jammu and Kashmir, Jammu town was linked with the rest of the subcontinent through a rail route via Sialkot and Srinagar was well linked through Rawalpindi or the Mughal Road which directly linked the valley to Lahore.

In the case of Tripura even the mofussil areas of the state were connected with Agartala by fair weather roads which passed through the territory of East Bengal. Obviously when the subcontinent was partitioned and East Bengal became East Pakistan (now Bangla Desh) Tripura was completely isolated from other parts of India and in the name of transportational infrastructure it had a very precariously slender, unserviceable and insufficient roads.

Earlier the town of Agartala had rail links with Belonia and Khowai but these rotates passed through the East Pakistan and the stroke of India's partition threw the region out of the railway grid.

As observed by the National Council of Applied Economics and Research, "lack of transport, the largest single problem that Tripura faces has served to keep Tripura's economy backward and primitive and isolated from the rest of the country.

It has successfully blocked all efforts to industrialise the state, modernise agriculture, develop its mineral and forest resources and properly utilise its human resources by ensuring mobility and flexibility.

It has contributed its share towards keeping a fair proportion of the people on the verge of starvation and famine". Following have been the principal factors which have impeded the development of means of transport in Tripura:

- Mountainous terrain with six mountain rages which progressively rise higher and higher in elevation from west to east.

- Whereas, the hill surfaces are covered with dense bamboo thickets and canebrakes, the lowland surfaces in between carry vast and very thick covers of thatching grass.

- There are countless rivulets and streams which criss-cross the territory and would need bridges over them if roads and railway lines have to cross them.

- There is a great shortage of road building material in the state.

- Lack of inter communication between the tribals and non-tribals on the one hand and on the other hand among different tribal groups which carry hostile rivalaries among themselves.

- Economy continues to be primitive and subsistence in nature and does not inspire or promote the development of means of transportation.

Nevertheless, when the state became an integral part of the Indian Union, the authorities started paying attention towards building roads in the erstwhile hilly, mountainous, secluded and more particularly the strategically located and sensitive areas so that the hither to ignored and isolated people could be brought to the national mainstream.

The importance and significance, in this context, was properly realised and in 1949 steps were initiated to spread the net of roads out of the mere skeleton of road routes that the region inherited from the princely rule.

During the first Five Year plan period, the densely populated parts of the state were accorded top priority in the field of road construction. Many old wooden bridges were replaced by bridges built of concrete and some new bridges were also constructed.

The road building activity continued during the following plan periods. It was during the fourth and fifth Five Year plan periods that many of the hilly settlements were linked with the major towns and other economically active parts of the state by way of pucca and kachcha roads.

The kachcha road become unserviceable during rainy period while some pucca roads also got blocked due to landslides in times of heavy and incessant rains. Nonetheless, even after the completion of seven Five Year plans, there are still some settlements which no doubt function as service centres as well as administrative centres yet they remain to be effectively connected with the state capital or district headquarters.

Thus it would be apt to remark that the development of internal transport lines has not been commensurate with the requirements. That is why Omesh Saigal has rightfully observed that, "while internal transport communication facilities leave much to be desired, the external transport and communication facilities are still extremely limited."

Following are the two important and vital roads of Tripura:

- The Agartala-Assam road which connects through a 200 km length the state capital with Charibari in the Cachar district of Assam. And it is only through this road that the state of Tripura can be approached by road from any corner of the country. Four major Subdivisional headquarters are connected with link roads coming out of this road. Thus on it from Telimura, Amabasa, Kumarghat and Kurta that the link roads take out respectively for the towns of Khowai, Kamalpur, Kailashahar and Dharmanagar. The construction work on this road was started in 1948 and it took one decade to be completed. During the first Five Year plan period, the width of this road was kept 9 feet only. However, in the Second Plan period with the active support of the Central Public Works Department of the Union Government following improvements were effected on this road:

  — Its width was increased from 9 feet to 12 feet.

  — It was made black topped.

  — There concrete bridges were constructed to cross the Khowai, Manu and Deo streams.

- The Agartala-Sabroom road connects the important subdivisional headquarter towns located in southern Tripura. Hatiletha, Charilam, Udaipur, Karapan, Belonia and Sabroom towns are inter linked by this road. In recent years this road has been extended northward through Kalachara and terminates at Simna near the border. It is also a back topped all weather road.

By the end of the seventh plan 'the state had come to acquire the total road length of about 5,000 km out of which nearly 50 per cent of roads are fair weather Kachcha roads. Nonetheless, the achievement is remarkable in the sense that in the year 1948 when the state merged into the Indian Union it had a road length (Kachcha as well as Pucca roads) of only 300 km, much of which was in a highly depressing state. South Tripura District with nearly half of the total roads of the state leads other two districts where (North Tripura about 30 per cent and West Tripura about 20 per cent) half of the total road length of the state is found.

The road length in a way hints towards the levelling up of the inter-district economic imbalances. The District of South Tripura, otherwise at the lowest rung of the ladder of socio-economic development, is far ahead of the other two districts in the realm of road development.

One more factor which merits mention here is that the district of West Tripura is a plain tract where the straight running roads would ultimately make a shorter road length but in the mountainous and hilly tracts where roads run in zigzag and meandering courses and also take longer courses to negotiate elevated parts would obviously claims longer road lengths.

There is only one short stretch (12.35 km) of railway line in the state which links the town of Dharmenagar with Patharkandi in Assam. Steps are, however, being taken to link some other viable towns with a road route. Before partition some settlements had been connected even with Kolkata, the cultural Capital of the country, by means of waterways which passed through Bangladesh.

Now, only within the state, some of the river courses are used for internal navigation on which country made boats and steamers are plied. However, for obvious reasons the streams are navigable only for shorter distances.

During rainy periods, when the rivers are not in devastating spate the boats carrying load up to 4 tone each can be plied while throughout the remaining period boats carrying load up to 2 tons are only plies. Air transport is quite significant for Tripura. Whereas by rail and road, Agartala is at a distance of 2,400 km from Kolkata, by air it is only 315 km Mail is regularly sent by air via Kolkata to all parts of India excepting Northeastern India.

An infrastructural development plan for Tripura is being currently executed with the sole purpose of creating regular and effective transportational links between Tripura and other parts of the country. Kumarghat is being brought on the railway map of India.

This shall link the District of North Tripura with other parts of the country in a better way as compared to other districts of the state. Next in order falls West Tripura. The District of South Tripura has been accorded last priority. Not to bring this district on the railway map of India would certainly act as a serious handicap for the proper utilisation of its resources.

However, the observations made by Chib in this regard merit mention here. "Those who matter in authority should however, bear in mind that effective utilisation of resources (both human and material) and better administration principally depend upon the extension of roads, rail routes and other efficient means of transport as well as communications to the interior regions and more so in isolated, hilly, strategic, sensitive and tribal areas.

In view of the unparalleled instability, social, political and economic, created recently in North eastern India, there is an added reason to extend and multiply the lines of communication in all segments of this sensitive region of our country."

9

Polity

- -

System of Governance

Before October 15, 1949 when Tripura was integrated in the Union of India, it was directly administered by a native Prince with the help of a Dewan and other advisers. In 1950, Tripura was accorded the states of a part 'C' State and its administration was taken over by a Chief Commissioner (appointed by the Government of India) who was assisted by three advisers also, appointed by the President of India.

In pursuance with the advice of the States Reorganisation Commission, the state of Tripura was accorded the status of a Union Territory in 1956. The place of a Chief Commissioner was taken by an Administrator who functioned as Chief Executive. A Territorial Council consisting of 32 members (30 elected by the people and 2 nominated by the President of India) was provided.

The Council was headed by a chairman, elected from amongst the council members. In the year 1963, through a constitutional amendment, Tripura was provided with a Legislative Assembly and a Council of Ministers. The strength of the Legislature was kept at thirty three. Whereas, 30 members of the Legislative Assembly were elected directly by the electorate of Tripura, three were nominated by the President of India.

Out of these 30 assembly seats (constituencies) half, i.e. 15 were located in West Tripura, while North and South Tripura had 8 and 7 seats respectively. In West Tripura, 10 seats were in Sadar subdivision alone and Khowai and Sonamura had 3 and 2 seats respectively. Kailashahar, Dharmangar, Kamalpur subdivisions of North Tripura had 2,4 and 2 constituencies respectively while in South Tripura the subdivision of Udaipur, Amarpur, Belonia and Sabroom had 2,2,2 and 1 constituencies respectively.

The Council of Ministers was an advisory body to the Administrator. Nonetheless, the supreme authority was vested in the President of India who had a constitutional right to reject any decision or recommendation of the Union Territory Administration. Such a provision was made keeping in view of the strategic location and sensitive nature of Tripura.

In nearly 1971, the designation of the Administrator was changed into Lieutenant Governor. The Parliament of India, on December 30, 1971 passed Northeastern Areas Reorganisation Act vide this act the status of Tripura was elevated to statehood on January 21, 1972.

At present the state of Tripura has a unicameral Legislature consisting of 60 members elected through a popular vote. The leader of the majority party (or a front formed by a coalition) is designed as Chief Minister, who forms his Council of Minister.

The Governor is the head of the state. In the year 1972, there were 30 constituencies in West Tripura, 16 in North Tripura and 14 in South Tripura districts. In a way the numbers of legislative assembly seats were simply doubled. However, after five years making adjustments to population the numbers of these seats were fixed at 29, 16 and 15 each, Whereas, a seat was added to the South Tripura district, one seat was deducted from the West Tripura district.

At present subdivision-wise in the District of West Tripura the subdivisions of Sadar (18), Khowai (7), Sonarnura (4), in North Tripura the subdivisions of Kailashahar (5), Dharamanagar (7), Kamalpur (4) and in the District of South Tripura the subdivisions of Udaipur (5), Amarpur (3), Belonia (5) and Sabroom (2) had the number of constituencies as shown within parentheses, form the demarcation of constituencies the following inferences can be drawn:

- For obvious reasons the densely populated parts have more constituencies than the sparsely populated areas.

- The plain tracts have a higher number of legislative Assembly seats than the elevated, undulating and uneven sections.

- The areas dominated by immigrants have a larger share in the political lake of the state than enjoyed by the relatively older residents who are predominantly tribal.

- In view of the above, there are bound to be ethnic tensions, political conflicts, ideolgical differences and regional disparities as well as social imbalances.

The entire state consists of one seat in the Indian Parliament, *i.e.* Lok Sabha. Nonetheless, the elections to Lok Sabha as well as those to the Vidhan Sabha during the last two decades have shown that there is a fairly high degree of political consciousness in the state as evidenced by the votes polled and the percentage of valid votes. For instance, in the 1980

Lok Sabha elections out of an electorate of 10,22,506 as many as 8,45,729 voters exercised their franchise.

Out of these votes 82.71 per cent of the polled votes were valid votes. Similarly in the Vidhan Sabha Elections of 1983 out of the total votes of 11,34,257 as many as 9,41,786 votes were polled out of which 81.73 per cent were valid votes. In none of the subdivisions the percentage of polled votes to the number of total votes was less than 74 per cent.

Instead in subdivisions like sonamura (87.27%) Belonia (85.28%), sabroom (84.15%), Udaipur (83.89), Kamalpur (83.19), Khowai (82.66%), Kailashar (81.42%) and Sadar (81.19 per cent) the degree of polled votes was higher than fourth fifth of the total votes.

From the study of the different demographic characteristics and historical events it has been found that the region has always been under the impact of Bengal, a region inhabited by socially awakened, politically enlightened and culturally rich people. And an overwhelming majority of the immigrants to Tripura have come from Bengal.

On the other hand, Bengal has been known for its radical views, socialistic overtones, communistic leanings and revolutionary ideals. Such triats the outcome of industrial belt of Calcutta. No wonder, the Kolkata ideology spread in all parts of Bengal and with them to other regions also wherever they want in sufficient numbers.

Thus as a result of the arrival of a large number of Bengalis in Tripura particularly after partition the political atmosphere in Tripura started getting discharged. On the other side when Bengalis made all out efforts to popularise their language, literature and culture, there was bound to be a sharp reaction from the natives and particularly the tribals who brook no interference in their sociocultural *milieu*. Resultantly they too started becoming politically conscious and socially awakened.

The other effect of such a complex situation was that the Communist Party (Marxist) came to dominate the political scenario of Tripura, a strange happening in a state where industrial activity is at the lowest ebb and where given all other things, the ground was otherwise fir for the activities of the Communist Party of India, a political party having roots in the country side.

The Communist Party of India (Marxist), Indian National Congress, Tripura Upajati Juba Samita (TUJS) a regional party supporting the cause of the natives, particularly the scheduled tribes and scheduled castes), Janta, (now Janata Dal), Republican Socialist Party, Forward Block (a party formed by Subhash Chandra Bose), Communist Party of India, Bharatiya Janata Party, etc. have been those parties which have a net of their political activities.

Nonetheless, all the elections so far held (both the Lok Sabha polls) have shown that only CPI(M), INC, TUOS and RSP have and Vidhan Sabha some following. It is the Communist Party of India (Marxist) which has an upper hand and secures 45 to 60 per cent of the votes. The TUOS a regional party manages to secure only 10 to 12 per cent of the votes while the Indian National Congress obtains about 30 per cent votes. In the state, it is either the CPM or the CPM led left Front which rules. Even the CPM Janata combine could not function here properly.

However, this strategic as well as sensitive State needs a stable government and it shall be in the interest of all political parties and the people that a majority government once constituted in the state is given a fair chance and tendencies of horse-trading are put to art end.

The State of Tripura is divided into 4 districts which are further subdivided into 10 subdivisions. There are 17 development blocks in all these 10 subdivisions. On the Civil judicial administration side there are 4 district judges and 16 Stipendary Judges. The criminal judiciary is administered by 6 Session Judges and 25 District Magistrates, Chief Judicial Magistrate and other Judicial Magistrates.

The judiciary is helped by the Police which have 35 Police Stations and 56 Police Out Posts in the state. The State has a strong Police contingent which currently costs Rupees 2500 lakh by way of their salaries and other allowances. The Inspector General of Police heads the force. He is assisted by one Deputy Inspector General and four Assistant Inspector Generals of Police. Each district has a police chief of the rank of Superintendent of Police.

The total number of SPs, ASPs and DSPs is 80 in the state. Some of them working with the armed wing of the police have been designated as Commandants and Assistant Commandants. The numbers of the Inspectors and Sub-Inspectors is 720 in the state. The constabulary consists of 6,000 constables while other ranks (Lance Naik, Naik, Head Constables and Sergeants) run into 1,500. Here it may not be out of place to mention that the incidence of unemployment is driving many and educated young women and men to crimes and cognisable offences.

In the year 1989, the total number of persons convicted was 337 (280 males + 57 females) out of which 236 (70%) were educated consisting of 185 males and 51 females. A fair majority of convicts, *i.e.* 171 (159 males and 12 females) were aged between 22 to 40 years. The position is alarming in relation to other States and better the authorities rise equal to the situation.

Government of the State

The government and administration in Tripura is controlled on the same lines as in other states of the country.

The state follows a unicameral system of government, i.e. it has only one house – the Tripura Legislative Assembly (Vidhan Sabha) consists of 60 members.

Tripura has 2 seats in the Lok Sabha – the lower house of Parliament. Like all other states of India, the head of the state is the Governor, appointed by the President of India. His or her post is largely ceremonial.

The Chief Minister is headed by a group of ministers with independent power. The Chief Minister is the head of government and is vested with most of the executive powers.

Tripura is governed through a parliamentary system of representative democracy, a feature the state shares with other Indian states. Universal suffrage is granted to residents. There are three branches of government. The legislature, the Tripura Legislative Assembly, consists of elected members and special office bearers such as the Speaker and Deputy Speaker, that are elected by the members. Assembly meetings are presided over by the Speaker or the Deputy Speaker in the Speaker's absence.

The judiciary is composed of the Guwahati High Court (Agartala Bench) and a system of lower courts. Executive authority is vested in the Council of Ministers headed by the Chief Minister, although the titular head of government is the Governor. The Governor is the head of state appointed by the President of India.

The leader of the party or coalition with a majority in the Legislative Assembly is appointed as the Chief Minister by the Governor, and the Council of Ministers are appointed by the Governor on the advice of the Chief Minister. The Council of Ministers reports to the Legislative Assembly. The Assembly is unicameral with 60 Members of the Legislative Assembly, or MLAs.

Terms of office run for 5 years, unless the Assembly is dissolved prior to the completion of the term. Tripura sends 2 representatives to the Lok Sabha and 1 representative to the Rajya Sabha. Auxiliary authorities known as panchayats, for which local body elections are regularly held, govern local affairs. Tripura also has an autonomous tribal council, the Tripura Tribal Areas Autonomous District Council which has it headquarters in Khumulwng.

The main political parties are the Left Front and the National Socialist Party of Tripura. Tripura is currently governed by Left Front, with Manik Sarkar as Chief Minister. Until 1977 the state was governed by the Indian National Congress. The left front governed from 1978 to 1988, and then returned in power in 1993. During 1988-93 the state was governed by a coalition of the Congress and Tripura Upajati Juba Samiti.

The Tripura government is a well-organised government, which provides almost all the services that are expected from a good State Government.

The Tripura has a couple of policies, which have helped and are still helping the state to progress in various spheres of life. State Government is also taking a lot of initiative to spread mass awareness of the various policies meant for the development of the region.

The National Liberation Front of Tripura is a significant part of the history of government. It was established in the year 1989 with an aim to establish a separate identity of Tripura as a full-fledged state.

Divisions

For administrative purposes, the state has been divided into 4 districts, 17 subdivisions, 40 development blocks.

Major towns of the state are Agartala, Badharghat, Jogendranagar, Dharmanagar, Pratapgarh, Udaipur, Kailashahar, Teliamura, Indranagar, Khowai, and Belonia. Badharghat, Jogendranagar, and Indranagar are now parts of the Agartala municipality.

Legislative Assembly

The Tripura Legislative Assembly is a very important part of the administrative system of the state. This assembly is an integral part of the government after the declaration of the region as a state, though it came into existence before that time.

Till October 1949, Tripura was considered a princely state. The regency council was established for a brief time period prior to its freedom. This council was continued till October 1949. After the state was declared a union territory in November 1956, a Territorial Council was established in 1957.

In the Territorial Council, two were chosen by the central government of India and 30 others were voted for by the common people. On 1st July 1963, this Territorial Council was replaced by the Legislative Council and the Council of Ministers. The members of the territorial Council were made the members of the Council of Ministers and the legislative council of Tripura.

Since Tripura has been declared a state in January 1972, the legislative assembly comprises 60 members. The span of a particular assembly is 5 years. If necessary, an assembly can span for less than 5 years. Generally, four sessions of the legislative council are held in a year. The legislative assembly consists of 14 committees.

The Ujjayanta Palace is the place that is generally used for holding the meetings of the Legislative Council.

Judiciary

The Judiciary of Tripura comprises a department of Law that takes note of all the legal cases of the state. The State Judiciary deals with civil as well as criminal cases.

The Law Department has introduced several measures to effectively deal with the judicial cases of the state. The Nodal Officers of the Law Department hold responsibility for quick dispatch of cases related to a particular department and keep a record of the development of a particular case and accordingly inform the Law Department.

The Law Department further takes important decisions in regard to the expansion of infrastructure of the state judiciary, construction of new buildings for courts, formation of new posts in the field of judiciary and maintenance of budget for the state judiciary.

The judiciary is under the strict jurisdiction of the High Court of Guwahati. Tripura has several lower courts that effectively deal with civil and criminal cases. The native population is allowed to appeal in the High Court of Guwahati, in case they are not satisfied with the decision of the lower courts.

The Law Department has devised several policies for efficient working of the Judiciary. The Department of Law orders establishment of several Tribunals and Commissions for investigation of particular cases of special significance.

Judiciary has organised numerous camps in the recent years to enlighten the local inhabitants of the state regarding the various legal steps one might take in case of any problems related to the civil or criminal cases.

Political Parties

There are several Tripura Political Parties that are vying to attain a stronghold in the political scenario of the northeast Indian state. Apart from the dominant national parties like the Congress and the CPI (M), several prominent state parties have mushroomed in the state. Although these parties are local state based political groups, they are by no means insignificant and are doing phenomenal work to make their presence felt.

Amongst the notable political parties of Tripura, the Indigenous Peoples Front of Tripura is one of the noteworthy parties that was formed on 9th June 1997 by the coalition of the Tripura Tribal National Conference with the Tripura Hill People's Party. The Tripura Tribal Areas Autonomous District Council elections in the year 2000 earned the party its first ever political breakthrough. The insurgence operations and the guerrilla attacks of the National Liberation Front of Tripura indirectly paved the way for the Indigenous Peoples Front of Tripura (IPFT) to win the elections. The addition of another significant political group, the Tripura Upajati Juba Samiti to the existing party enabled the party to spread its wings further in the state.

Another leading political party that spearheads the governance of Tripura is the Janganotantrik Morcha (People's Democratic Front). Popularly known by the acronym PDF, the party was formed by Ajoy Biswas, a disgruntled member of the CPI(M) who had failed to secure a Lok Sabha ticket for the upcoming elections. The formation of this party, however resulted in a lot of political unrest in the state that was caused by a divide in the teacher's movement of the CPI (M).

Tripura Indigenous People's Front

The Tripura Indigenous People's Front or the Indigenous Peoples Front of Tripura is one of the predominant political parties that spearheads the political scenario in the northeast Indian state. The coalition of two notable state parties namely, the Tripura Tribal National Conference and the Tripura Hill People's Party resulted in the creation of the Indigenous Peoples Front of Tripura on 9th June 1997.

It had been presumed that besides the Tripura Tribal National Conference and the Tripura Hill People's Party, the National Volunteers Party formed by Bijoy Hrangkwal would also coalesce to form the Tripura Indigenous People's Front (IPTF). However, this merger did not occur and the party was formed by the active participation of the two parties.

Shri. Debabrata Koloi, a candidate from the erstwhile Tripura Hill People's Party (THPP) was elected the first ever general secretary of the IPFT. The year 2000 marked the first milestone in the party's political career. The Tripura Tribal Areas Autonomous District Council elections in the year 2000 earned the party its first ever political breakthrough. The insurgence operations and the guerrilla attacks of the National Liberation Front of Tripura (NLFT) had resulted in tremendous political turmoil in the state. The extremist organisation had also demanded that only IPFT be allowed to contest the elections. While majority of the parties cowered under the threat, the Left Front stood up and went ahead with the elections despite numerous threats, kidnappings and assassinations of the key party members. However, the active support of the NLFT resulted in a landslide victory for the IPFT.

The inclusion of the Tripura Upajati Juba Samiti under the wing of the IPFT in the year 2001 enabled the party to spread its wings further in the state.

Tripura Janganotantrik Morcha

The Tripura Janganotantrik Morcha or the Janganotantrik Morcha (People's Democratic Front) is one of the prominent political parties that is rapidly making its presence felt in the Northeastern State of Tripura. The party was formed by Shri. Ajoy Biswas, a disgruntled member of the Lok Sabha of the Communist Party of India (Marxist) or the CPI (M). Popularly known as the PDF, Shri. Biswas who had broken out of the party after being refused a Lok Sabha ticket, formed the party based on his political ideologies. However, the party's official emblem still remains the same as that of its parent organisation, the CPI (M) with its trademark the red banner with a hammer and a sickle.

The formation of the Tripura Janganotantrik Morcha, however had its own setbacks. The emergence of the party resulted in a political divide between the teacher's association of the CPI (M) in the state and caused tremendous political upheaval. The members of the CPI (M) led Tripura Government Teachers Association (TGTA) that was responsible for all the government schools in the state and the Tripura Teachers Association (TTA) that accounted for the private institutions were flung into a dilemma creating by the unbridgeable divide. The extent of the split was so extreme and deep rooted that the stalwarts of the CPI (M) came to be recognised as the TGTA (HGB Road) and TTA (HGB Road) and those who swore their allegiance to the policies of Ajoy Biswas were known as allies of the TGTA (Ajoy Biswas) or the TTA (Ajoy Biswas).

Tripura National Volunteers

Tripura National Volunteers was formed as a political party by Shri Bijoy Harankhwal in the month of December of 1978. The primary aim of the Tripura National Volunteers was to separate Tripura from the Indian Union. Comprised of several veteran leaders, the Tripura National Volunteers is one of the prominent Tripura political parties.

The members of the Tripura National Volunteers wanted complete expulsion of Bengali immigrants from the state. The Tripura National Volunteers wanted a separate state for the local indigenous inhabitants of the state so that there is adequate social, economic and political security in the region.

The State Government of Tripura had tried out several methods to curb the regional sentiments of the native population of the state. However, the members of the Tripura National Volunteers continued with their agitation to free the state from the inhabitants of other states of India. The State Government of Tripura was compelled to ban the activities of the political group of the Tripura National Volunteers. The well known leader of the political party, Shri Bijoy Harankhwal was arrested by the police to bring the volatile situation of the state under control of the state machinery. However, after the release of the political leader, Shri Bijoy Harankhwal had disbanded the political party of Tripura National Volunteers.

The agitation of the local indigenous inhabitants did not stop with the suspension of the Tripura National Volunteers. The Tripura National Volunteers party was reformed in the year of 1982 under the able leadership of Shri Bijoy Harankhwal to revive their demand of removal of foreigners from their land.

Indigenous Nationalist Party of Tripura

Indigenous Nationalist Party of Tripura is a political organisation that comprises of members from the aboriginal tribal communities of the state. The chief aim of the Indigenous Nationalist Party of Tripura is to promote a feeling of togetherness and brotherhood among the local inhabitants of the state.

The members of Indigenous Nationalist Party reflect the regional allegiance of the native population to their state of Tripura. One of the prominent Tripura political parties,

Indigenous Nationalist Party has a considerable influence on local citizens of the state. A strong opposition of the State Government of Tripura, the members of the Indigenous Nationalist Party took several landmark decisions for the development of the state.

The brains behind the formation of the tribal political organisation of Indigenous Nationalist Party were that of Shri Bijoy Kumar Hrangkhawl, who was the head of Tripura National Volunteers and Shri Harinath Debnath who was the head of IPFT. The establishment of the new political party of the tribal communities of Tripura gave a boast to the development of the state.

Indigenous Nationalist Party looks after the urgent needs of the various tribal groups of the state of Tripura. The party has witnessed several bouts of success and failures. However, all the members of the Indigenous Nationalist Party of Tripura firmly believe in the unity of the various tribal groups.

Under the able guidance of the veteran members of the political party, the Indigenous Nationalist Party will contribute to the development of social, economic and political stability of Tripura.

National Socialist Party of Tripura

National Socialist Party of Tripura is one of the major parties of the state of Tripura in India. This party is one of the parties of the country of India that follow leftist principles. Tripura National Socialist Party came into existence due to a political split among the members of the party called the Indigenous Nationalist Party of Tripura. This split took place in the summer of the year 2003.

The Indigenous Nationalist Party of Tripura is one of the most well known political parties of Tripura. The well known political figure Hirendra Tripura, along with many other people, separated themselves from the Indigenous Nationalist Party of Tripura. Shyamcharan Tripura, who was one of the most important leaders of the Indigenous Nationalist Party of Tripura, also joined the National Socialist Party of Tripura. This party took assistance from those members of the Tripura Tribal Areas Autonomous District Council who were CPI(M) followers.

In the elections of the year 2005, the National Socialist Party of Tripura contested as many as four seats with the support of the Left Front. All these four people won the election. One very important fact about this political party of Tripura is that it has no connection with Nazism, contrary to what he name 'national socialism' suggests.

National Socialist Party at Tripura, being one of the main Tripura political parties, is an integral part of the political life of the state of Tripura.

National Conference of Tripura

National Conference of Tripura (NCT) is a new regional party of the state of Tripura, India formed in December 2006 at Darjeelingpara in Teliamura. It has been formed by

Rabindra Kishore Deb Barma (formerly of the GMP of the CPIM party in Tripura) and Amlesh Deb Barma (of INPT). NCT comprises many dissidents of the TSU, TYF and GMP of the CPIM party in Tripura and also many disgrunted leaders from INPT.

Tripura Rajya Muslim Praja Majlish

Tripura Rajya Muslim Praja Majlish was Muslim political party in Tripura, India, formed sometime around 1946. The party competed with Anjuman Islamia over the political influence over the Muslim community, but failed to make any lasting impact.

Tripura Ganatantrik Manch

Tripura Ganatantrik Manch is a splinter group of Janganotantrik Morcha, which itself is a splinter group of Communist Party of India (Marxist) in Tripura.

TGM participates in the Confederation of Indian Communists and Democratic Socialists.

10

Tourism

Tripura is one of the eight states in the north eastern part of India. Within its small geographical area, Tripura offers plenty of attractions for the tourists in the form of magnificent palaces (Ujjayanta Palace and Kunjaban Palace at Agartala and Neermahal — Lake Palace at Melaghar), splendid rock-cut carvings and stone images (Unakoti near Kailashahar, Debtamura near Amarpur and Pilak in Belonia Subdivisions), important temples of Hindus and Buddhists including the famous Mata Tripureswari temple (one of the 51 Pithasthans as per Hindu mythology) at Udaipur, vast natural as well as artificial lakes namely Dumboor lake in Gandacherra subdivision, Rudrasagar at Melaghar, Amarsagar, Jagannath Dighi, Kalyan Sagar, etc. at Udaipur, the beautiful hill station of Jampui hill bordering Mizoram, wildlife sanctuaries at Sepahijala, Gumti, Rowa and Trishna and rich cultural heritage of Tribals, Bengalis and Manipuri communities residing in the state.

About 2/3rd area of the state is under forest cover where different species of trees, orchids, birds and wildlife are found. Tripura offers excellent opportunities for eco-friendly tourism and different wildlife sanctuaries in the state offer various attractions to the tourists. There are huge lakes at Udaipur namely Amarsagar, Kalyansagar, Jagannath Dighi, Mahadev Dighi and Sukh Sagar which were excavated by the then Maharajas. These lakes add beauty to the Udaipur town which is also known as City of temples and lakes.

Enhancing Tourism

Tucked away in a corner of the North-East, surrounded by Bangladesh on three sides, the lush green mountains and valleys of Tripura have attracted many different peoples over the centuries. Since 1949 its fate has been entwined with that of Bengal. Tripura is more like India proper than the other North-East hill states and its connections with the Bangladeshi plains are strong. It has always been associated closely with the poet laureate, Rabindranath Tagore. Such cultural exchanges have helped to enrich the culture of Tripura itself. Referred to as one of the seven Northeastern States of India it is situated in the remotest part of India. As a tourist destination, hence, it is quite popular. After all every individual craves for serenity and tranquillity while on a holiday.

Tourist Attractions

Tripura has a picturesque surrounding covered with hills and dales, sprawling green valleys and hilly brooks. The popular Tripura attractions are Kamalasagar Lake, Dumboor Lake, Ujjayanta Palace, Neermahal, Kunjaban Palace, Tripura Government Museum, Jampui Hill, Dumboor Lake, etc. The state is surrounded on the north, south and west by Bangladesh, on the North-East by the state of Assam and by Mizoram on the east.

Nature Tourism

Tripura is marked by low ranges running in a northwest to southeast direction. Tehse ranges reach up to 3,000 feet.

On the road to Udaipur, 35 km south of Agartala, the nature reserve at Sepahijala extends over 18 square kilometres, with a lake, zoo and botanical gardens, and is home to primates including the Hoolock gibbon and golden langur and around 150 species of birds.

Trishna Wildlife Sanctuary is located 100 kilometres away from Agartala in South Tripura District. Besides these the travellers can also explore Dumboor Lake, near Agartala and Rudrasagar Lake, near Melaghar.

Leisure Tourism

The history of the Kingdom of Tripura and its Manikya rulers, who claimed descent from far-off Rajput Kshatriyas, is told in a curious Bengali poem, the Rajmah. You will also see lots of quite graphic clay sculptures of Kali, Bengal's favourite goddess, made by households for their monthly pujas. English is not widely spoken here.

The State Museum at Agartala displays interesting ethnographic and archaeological exhibits. One of its gallery is completely devoted to the excavations at Unakoti in the forests of northern Tripura. It is open for visitors from Monday to Saturday from 10 am till 5 pm. The entry into the museum is free.

The Tribal Cultural Research Institute and Museum at Supari Bagan lies well hidden in the backstreets of Krishna Nagar district, near the Jagannath temple. It is open on all working days from 11 am to 1 pm. The entry into the tribal museum is without fare.

The romantic water palace of Neermahal, in the middle of Rudrasagar Lake is located at 55 km south of Agartala. It was built in 1930 as a summer residence for Maharaja Bir Bikram Kishore Manikya. Inspired by Mughal architecture, the palace is rather derelict inside but the exterior and gardens nave been restored and the sight of the domes and pavilions reflected in the lake, especially under the early evening floodlights, is impressive. The travellers can rent boats to cross the lake to the palace from just opposite the tourist lodge, a very pleasant journey among lily pads, dragonflies, ducks and cormorants.

The lake is l km from the town of Melaghar, which has bus connections with Agartala and Udaipur. Neermahal can be visited together with Udaipur as a day-trip from Agartala.

Ujjayanta Palace in Agartala was built by Maharaja Radha Kishore Manikya during 1899-1901. It is an important historical building.

Kunjaban Palace is famous for the Rabindra Kanan. Is was built as a place to retreat by Maharaja Birendra Kishore Manikya.

Wildlife Tourism

About 2/3rd area of the state is under forest cover where different species of trees, orchids, birds and wildlife are found. Tripura offers excellent opportunities for eco-friendly tourism and different wildlife sanctuaries in the state offer various attractions to the tourists.

Tripura, the tiny land-locked state, has a wide variety of forests and wildlife, which can prove attractive enough for the tourists and the inquisitive. Rowa, Sepahijala, Trishna and Gumti are the four sanctuaries in this state. There is a vast water reservoir covering approximately 300 sq km in Gumti. This reservoir attracts many resident and migratory birds. Rowa presents ample scope for a Botanist's study. In Trishna, there are patches of virgin forests, which are rich in rare vegetation. The crab eating Mongoose, which were last sighted about 72 years ago in India, has been rediscovered in Sepahijala.

Sepahijala Wildlife Sanctuary

Sepahijala Wildlife Sanctuary was constituted on 2nd February 1987. The sanctuary has 456 plant species of monocotyledon and dicotyledon. Trees of Sal, Chamal, Garjan and Kanak exist predominantly. The secondary species consist of Pichla, Kurcha, Awla, Bahera, Hargaja, Amlaki, Bamboos and grasses. Sanctuary has the 4489 cum per ha of timber biomass. Sanctuary has abundant Rauwalfia serpentina and home to other endangered and endemic species. Agar (aggreria agglocha) (the state tree), Nageshwar (Mesua ferrea — state flower), Dukul (the green Imperial pegion — state bird) and groups of Spectacled langur (Phary's leaf monkey-State animal) Spectacle monkeycan easily be sighted inside the sanctuary area.

Tropical moist deciduous Forest of Sepahijala harbours five different species of primates like Rhesus macaque, pigtailed macaque, Capped langur, spectacled langur, slow Lories and a lot of many other wild animals. More than 100 species of birds are found here. Wonderful habitat of Sepahijala attracts lot of migratory birds of which lesser whistling teal, white ibis, open billed stork is of prime importance.

Trishna Wildlife Sanctuary

Trishna wildlife Sanctuary was notified in the year November 1988. Total area of the Sanctuary is 194.704 sq km. Trishna Sanctuary has diversity in its floral and faunal contents. The Sanctuary is famous for Bison locally known as "Gaba" and home to several species of "Primates". Sanctuary has a numbers of perennial water rivulets, water bodies, and grass land. One species of Bamboo (Oxtenanthera Nigrocilliate) locally known as Kaillai is plenty here, leaves of which are liked by Bison.

Gumti Wildlife Sanctuary

Gumti Wildlife Sanctuary is the second sanctuary of the South Tripura district located in the southeast corner of the state. Its area is 389.54 km. Close to the sanctuary, there is a vast water reservoir covering almost 300 sq km of an area. This water reservoir attracts several resident and migratory water birds. Gumti Wildlife Sanctuary in Tripura has Elephants, Bison, Sambar, Barking deer, Wild goat or Sarow apart from many other animals and reptiles. This is a very ideal destination for the tourists interested in eco-tourism. The sanctuary boasts of a rich flora and fauna. One can find numerous medical and therapeutical botanical species in abundance in the surroundings of the sanctuary.

Rowa Wildlife Sanctuary

Rowa Wildlife Sanctuary, situated in the north of the district, can be approached from Panisagar and is adjacent to the National Highway. Rowa Wildlife Sanctuary in Tripura is a small wildlife sanctuary covering an area of 85 hectares and it is one of the few remains of the natural forests left. This sanctuary is easily accessible to the tourists from all around. Rowa Wildlife Sanctuary provides plenty of scope for study by the botanists, ecologists, environmentalist and students of wildlife system.

Rowa Wildlife sanctuary provides shelter to numerous species of birds, wild animals as well as primates and reptiles. Ornithologists, etymologists, botanists as well as wildlife enthusiasts have a merry time exploring the sanctuary and its offerings.

Pilgrimage Tourism

No state is bereft of religious places. Religion is integrally associated with the traditions and society in India. The entire origin of the land is steeped in religion. The temple of Tripura Sundari in Udaipur, Tripura is one of the foremost religious shrines in Tripura. The state itself derives its name from the mother goddess.

Most of the temples are located at hilltops. Religion believes that the divinity is not easily achieved. That is why most of the important Hindu temples are a little difficult to access.

Besides the Hindu shrines Tripura is also the abode of Buddhist pilgrimages.

Places of Interest

Tripura has been a secludedly isolated region and thus attached no tourists for a pretty long period of its existence. The tribal and aboriginese dominated areas even elsewhere not often visited parts. The intra and inter tribal warfares and other disturbances always kept the visitors at bay.

Moreover, till the region was merged in the Indian Union it had 110 system of trails port and this factor made it remote too. Nevertheless, with the initiation of economic planning and particularly the road development activity some visitors have started pouring in the region and resultantly some places have been identified as places of travel.

Before it that these couple of places are described it shall be meaningfully worthwhile to narrate the evolution and development of means of transportation in the state, which directly as well as indirectly promote tourism and allied socio-economic activities.

Significant Places

It may be a hard nut to crack for a common tourist to reach Tripura, particularly the places on the eastern side of Kolkata. The foreign tourists who can afford to travel by air may not like to go to Tripura because of the disturbances which very often rock different parts of India.

The home tourists who normally travel by road or rail route shall find it very inconvenient to reach Tripura, beyond Kolkata. Moreover, the system of internal transport in Tripura, so far, is not only inadequate but highly irregular and erratic also. There are not very many satisfactory lodging facilities in different parts of the state. Nevertheless, it is a paradise for the hikkers, trekkers and mountaineers as also for other adventurous visitors. Those who can manage to reach Agartala and are prepared to bear with the existing facilities have certain places to visit.

As already described Tripura has been a princely state for quite long a period. Our princely rulers notwithstanding the general poverty of their subjects and underdevelopment regional all around were fond of building palatial palaces, temples, tanks and other such places for satisfying their egoistic fondness.

In the heart of the Agartala town the Ujjayanta places spread over an area of one square kilometre is an instance of the extravagance of the rulers although its architecture, woodwork, lawns gardens and out houses do speak about their artistic taste and a very high aesthetic sense.

Two large tanks to work as source of water in the past, were also got built in its vicinity. A Mughal style of garden is the link between the place and the tanks. There is a museum in the city which besides being a haven for many of the old royal belongings has also now come to have many artistic pieces acquired from other parts of the country. Some of the temples in the city also hold charm for the visitors in their architecture and wall paintings. At a distance of about 8 km from the present town of Agartala is located the town of Old Agartala which once housed the capital of Tripura.

These too one finds a royal palace, though not properly maintained but holds good prospects for students of art, architecture and archaeology. However, it is the Chaturdesh Devatabari Hindu shrine in Old Agartala which attracts thousands of pilgrims and devotees. The Bengali Hindus from West Bengal, Assam and other parts of the country who happen to visit Agartala make it a point to pay their respects at this temple.

This temple was once a place of royal worship and its location in the near vicinity of the palace is a testimony. The idols now placed in this temple were once placed in a royal shrine attached to the palace in Udaipur, the town which was the capital of the native princely rulers for a long time.

On the lines of the "Lake palace" of Udaipur in Rajasthan, which has its own beauty, charm and majestic appearance, the princely rulers of Tripura also dream of having a place erected in the centre of a water body. Though they did not get constructed as large a palace as has been built in Udaipur (Rajasthan) but the one got built at a distance of 56 km from Agartala in the Rudrasagar lake can be called a mini portrait of the Lake palace of Rajasthan.

It has been named as Neer Mahal. The word neer in many Indian languages, including Bangla, refers to water and is justified the name of the palace. Visitors go to the place to enjoy the grandeur of this palace, which was once used as a pleasure resort by the royal families.

On the bank of the Guniti stream, at a distance of one hundred kilometres from Agartala, are found the Dumber waterfalls. The roaring waters of these waterfalls had been attracting visitors since time immemorial. Now these waterfalls have become a place for the harnessing of water power and the visitors miss the veil that used to decorate the slopes along which the water flows.

In the neighbourhood of these waterfalls is a place named Tirathmukh where thousands of pilgrims take a holy dip on the sacred occasion of Uttarayaria Sariskrartti. On way to the Dumber falls and the Tirathmukh Agartala one passes through some rare, bewithchingly panoromic spots.

The lush forested patches and pastures simply throw a magic of their charm on the passers by. Some places have been developed as picnic spots where people on Sundays and other holidays spend their leisure amidst natural beauty.

Udaipur, now renamed as Radhakishorepur after the name an illustrious native ruler of the same name, as already stated had been the seat of princely administration for quite long a time. From the present site at a distance of three kilometres, are located the ruins of some very imposing structure.

It is called *Piiraru Rajbari*, an old dwelling complex of a ruling house. It was a royal palace got built by King Govinda Manikya about three hundred years ago. It is known for its lonely splendour located on the mond of a hill. The ruins testify that in its construction a very high sense of art and architecture had been employed.

It also appears that the native rulers of Tripura had ever been deeply religious. The Bhubaneswari temple located very close to the Purani Rajbari stands as a witness. Although the palace is in ruins, the shrine still attracts visitors and till recently the royal house had been paying annual visits to the shrine of their ancestors. In his poetic compositions Rajshri and Bisarjari, the first Nobel laureate of India, Rabindra Nath Tagore has immortalised the shrine.

At a distance of about 200 kilometres from Agartala is located the settlement of Unakheti. At this place a section of the settlement is called *Uriakoti tiratha* which affords a rare sight of colossol figures artistically carved out of monoliths. These carvings have been found to be dating back to the early Buddhist and Hindu periods by archaelogists as well as historians. Countless figures of Hindu dailies find adorned in these carvings but those depicting Lord Rama Lord Shiva, Lakshmana, Ganapati and Hunaman, are noteworthy.

The Rudrarup image of Lord Shiva obtains awful reverence. The Bhadraghat blackstone images in the close neighbourhood of Agartala are also visited by many people. There are many Buddhist Monasteries found dotted over western and Southern Tripura and often visited by scholars of Buddhist studies and archaeologists.

Bibliography

Adhikari, O. S.: *Four Immigrants Tribes of Tripura,* Directorate of Research, Government of Tripura, Tripura, 1988.

Aiyar, S.P. and Mehta, Usha : *Essays on Indian States,* Popular Prakashan, Bombay, 1965.

Ali, B. : *North-East India : A Bioanthropological Overview,* APH, New Delhi, 2000.

Archer, W.G.: *The Hill of Flutes: Life, Love and Poetry in Tribal India: A Portrait of the Santals,* University of Pittsburgh Press, Pittsburgh, 1974.

Barman, Debapriya Deb: *Treatise on Traditional Social Institutions of the Tripuri Community,* Directorate of Research, Government of Tripura, Tripura, 1983.

Basu, Pradip Kumar: *The Communist Movement in Tripura,* Progressive Publishers, Calcutta, 1996.

Bhan, Susheela: *Impact of Ethnic Violence on Youth: A Study of Tribal-Nontribal Violence in Kokrajhar, Assam,* Shipra Publications, New Delhi, 1999.

Bhattacharjee, J.B.: *North East Indian Perspectives in History,* Vikas Publishing House, New Delhi, 1995.

Bhattacharjee, Pravas Ranjan: *Economic Transition in Tripura,* Vikas Publishing House Pvt. Ltd., New Delhi, 1993.

Bhattacharjee, Prodip Nath: *The Garos of Tripura,* Directorate of Research Tribal Welfare Department, Government of Tripura, Agartala, 1987.

—————: *The Jamatiyas of Tripura,* Directorate of Research, Agartala, 1983.

Bhattacharya, Suchintya: *From Jhuming to Tapping,* Directorate of Research, Tripura, 1992.

Bhattacherjee, P. A. and Singh, R. S.: *Tea Plantation and the Tribes of Tripura,* Tripura State Tribal Cultural Research Institute and Museum, Tripura, 1995.

Bhaumik, Subir: *Insurgent Cross Fire: North-East India,* Lancer Publishers, New Delhi, 1996.

Bhola Nath Ghosh: *Women in Governance in Tripura,* Concept, 2008.

Bhuyan, S.K.: *Tripura Buranji,* Concept Pub., Calcutta, 1962.

Bodding, P.O.: *Materials for a Santali Grammar I*, Dumka, 1922.

——————: *Santal Folk Tales*, Harvard University Press, Cambridge, 1925.

——————: *Santal Riddles and Witchcraft among the Santals*, A.W. Brøggers, Oslo, 1940.

——————: *Studies in Santal Medicine and Connected Folklore*, 1940.

Bompas, Cecil Henry and Bodding, P.O.: *Folklore of the Santal Parganas*, D. Nutt, London, 1909.

Chakrabarti, Dr. Byomkes: *A Comparative Study of Santali and Bengali*, KP Bagchi, Calcutta, 1994.

Chakravarti, Mahadev: *The Tribal Areas Autonomous Dictrict Council and the Tribal Problems: A perspective*, Information, Cultural Affairs and Tourism Department, Government of Tripura, Agartala, 2001.

Chakravarti, Tapati: *Economic Participation of Rural Tribal Women of Tripura: A Case Study*, Tripura State Tribal Cultural Research Institute & Museum, Agartala, 1998.

Chandrika Basu Majumder and Paramita Saha: *Ageing in North East India*, Tripura Perspective, Akansha, 2008.

Chaudhuri, A.B.: *State Formation among Tribals: A Quest for Santal Identity*, Gyan Pub. House, New Delhi, 1993.

Chaudhuri, Dipak Kumar: *Administration Report of the Political Agency, Hill Tipperah 1872-1878*, Tripura State Cultural Research Institute & Museum, Agartala, 1995.

Chaudhuri, Jagadis Gan: *The Riangs of Tripura*, Directorate of Research, Agartala, 1983.

Chauley, G.C.: *Art Treasures of Unakoti*, Agam Kala Prakashan, Tripura, 2007.

Culshaw, W.J.: *Tribal Heritage: a Study of the Santals*, Lutterworth Press, London, 1949.

Darlong, Letthuama: *The Darlongs of Tripura*, Directorate of Tribal Research Institute, Government of Tripura, Agartala, 1995.

Das, N.C.: *Ferns and Fern-Allies of Tripura: North East India*, International Book Distributors, 2007.

Das, Ratna: *Art & Architecture of Tripura*, Tribal Research Institute, Government of Tripura, Agartala, 1997.

Datta, A. M.: *A Study on the Lushais of Jampui Hills in Tripura*, Directorate of Research, Government of Tripura, Tripura, 1987.

Deb, Dasarath: *Mukti Parishader Itikatha*, National Book Agency, Kolkata, 1999.

Debendra Bijoy Deb: *The Flora of Tripura State: 1981-1983*, 1990.

Deepa, D. Nair, Gupta, A.K. Himangshu Bikash Das and Atanu Chakraborti: *Medicinal Plants of Tripura*, A Photo Descriptive Field Manual, Concept, 2009.

Devashish Kar: *Fundamentals of Limnology and Aquaculture Biotechnology: A Treatise on the Limnology and Fisheries of the Water Bodies in Southern Assam,* Mizoram and Tripura, Daya, 2007.

Devender Kumar Sikri: *Census of India 2001: Tripura Administrative Atlas,* Controller of Publication, 2006.

Dipannita Chakraborty: *Land Question in Tripura,* Akansha Pub, 2004.

Dutta, P.S. : *History of the North-East,* Omsons Publications, Gauhati, 1986.

Edward Duyker Tribal Guerrillas: *The Santals of West Bengal and the Naxalite Movement,* Oxford University Press, New Delhi, 1987.

Esqr, Asok Bose: *Geological Survey of Hill Tippera 1909-10,* Tripura State Tribal Cultural Research Institute & Museum, Tripura, 1995.

Forest, G.N.: *A History of Indian Mutiny,* MacMillan, London, 1904.

Forster, George: *Journey from Bengal to England Through the Northern Parts of India, Kashmir, Afghanistan and Persia and into Russia by the Caspian Sea,* Crown Publishing House, London, 1798.

Gana-Chaudhury, Jagadis : *Tripura: The Land and its People,* Rima Publishing House, Delhi, 1979.

Gangopadahyay, Niladri Sekhar: *Insurgency and Media: A Study on Tripura,* Nabankur, Agartala, 2002.

Gautam Kumar Bera, Birinchi K. Medhi, Athparia, R.P. and Jose K. SVD: *Tribal Development in Tripura,* EBH Pub an imprint of Eastern Book House, 2009.

Goswami, Debabrata: *Military History of Tripura: 1490 to 1947,* Tripura State Tribal Cultural Research Institute & Museum, Agartala, 1996.

Hembrom, T.: *The Santals: Anthropological-Theological Reflections on Santali and Biblical Creation Traditions,* Punthi Pustak, Calcutta, 1996.

Jagadis Ganchaudhuri: *A Cultural History of Tripura,* Basudeb Pal, 2006.

Jagadish Ganchaudhuri, S. Sailo and Datta, M.S.: *People of India,* Tripura, Seagull Books, 1996.

Joshi, L.D.: *Tribal People of the Himalayas,* Himalaya Pub., Delhi, 1984.

Joshi, L.M. Printworld, D.K.: *Lalita-Sahasranama: Roman Transliteration,* Critical Explanation of Each Name, Reprint, 2006.

Khanna, S.K.: *Encyclopaedia of North-East India: Arunachal Pradesh, Assam, Manipur, Meghalaya, Tripura, Sikkim, Mizoram and Nagaland Tripura Sikkim,* Indian Pub, India, 1999.

Kilikdar, Bibhas Kanti: *Customary Laws and Practices: Reangs of Tripura,* Tribal Research Institute, Tripura, 1998.

Kiran Sankar Chakraborty: *Empowerment and Status of Women in Tripura*, Akansha, 2008.

—————: *Entrepreneurship and Small Business Development: With Special Reference to Tripura*, Mittal, 2006.

Krishna Nath: *Status and Empowerment of Tribal Women in Tripura*, Kalpaz, 2005.

Maitra, S.R.: *Ethnographic Study of the Chakma of Tripura*, Anthropological Survey of India, India, 2002.

Majumder, Benimadhab: *The Legislative Opposition in Tripura*, Tripura State Tribal Cultural Research Institute & Museum, Agartala, 1997.

Malabika Das Gupta: *Economic Impact of Raids on the Shifting Cultivators of Tripura*, The Asiatic Society, 2008.

Manas Paul: *The Eyewitness: Tales From Tripura's Ethnic Conflict*, Lancer, 2009.

Orans, Martin: *The Santal a Tribe in Search of a Great Tradition*, Wayne State University Press, Chicago, 1965.

Prasad, Onkar: *Santal Music: A Study in Pattern and Process of Cultural Persistence*, Tribal Studies of India Series, New Delhi, 1985.

Projit Kumar Palit: *History of Religion in Tripura*, Kaveri, 2004.

Puri, Balraj : *Jammu and Kashmir—Triumph and Tragedy of India*, Academic Pub., New Delhi, 2001.

Rahman, S.A.: *The Beautiful India*, Reference Press, Tripura, 2006.

Ramnika Jalali and Rajni Mankotia: *A Glimpse of Kalachuris of Tripurari*, Vinod Pub, New York, 2003.

Ranjit Kumar De: *Socio-Political Movements in India*, A Historical Study of Tripura, Mittal, 1998.

Roy Chaudhury: *Indu: Folk Tales of the Santals*, Sterling Publishers, New Delhi, 1973.

Saha, S. B.: *Socio-Economic Survey of the Noatia Tribes*, Tribal Welfare Department, Government of Tripura, Agartala, 1986.

Saigal Omesh: *Tripura*, Concept Publishing Company, New Delhi, 1978.

Sen, S.N. : *Rulers of Tripura, Chunta of India: Northeastern India*, Crown Pub., New Delhi, 1986.

Shri Tripura-Rahasyam: *Jnana-Khanda: Discourse on Wisdom*, Eastern Book Linkers, Tripura, 2003.

Singh, K. S.: *People of Tripura*, Seagull Books, Calcutta, 1996.

Singh, R. G. Barma and Arun Deb: *History of Tripura*, Tripura State Tribal Cultural Research Institute & Museum, Tripura, 1915.

Sipra Sen: *Tribes of Tripura: Description,* Ethnology and Bibliography, 1993.

State Fauna Series: Fauna of Tripura, Part II. Insects, Zoological Survey of India, 2000.

Sukhendu Debbarma: *Origin and Growth of Christianity in Tripura: With Special Reference to the New Zealand Baptist Missionary Society 1938-1988,* Indus, 1996.

Suren Deb Barman: *Rabindranath Tagore and Tripura,* Minerva, 2006.

Syamal Kumar Ray: *India's North-East and the Travails of Tripura,* Minerva, 2003.

Thakurta, S. N. Guha: *India-The Land of the People: Tripura,* National Book Trust, New Delhi, 1986.

Trivady, A.N.: *A Note on the Finding of Vertebrate Fauna in the Surma Series of Tripura and its Bearing on the Stratigraphy of the Area,* 1966.

Troisi, J.: *The Santals: A Classified and Annotated Bibliography,* Manohar Book Service, New Delhi, 1976.

Troisi, J.: *Tribal Religion: Religious Beliefs and Practices among the Santals,* Manohar, New Delhi, 2000.

Unakoh : *Tripura Directorate of Education,* Crown Pub., Aggartala, 1972.

Varman, S. B. K. Dev: *A Study Over the Jhum and Jhumia Rehabilitation in the Union Territory of Tripura,* Directorate of Research, Agartala, 1999.

——————: *The Tribes of Tripura: A dissertation,* Directorate of Research, Government of Tripura, Agartala, 1986.

Index

❏❏❏

www.ingramcontent.com/pod-product-compliance
Lightning Source LLC
Chambersburg PA
CBHW061830260326
41914CB00005B/942